Rural Society and Cotton in Colonial Zaire

Rural Society and Cotton in Colonial Zaire

OSUMAKA LIKAKA

THE UNIVERSITY OF WISCONSIN PRESS

The University of Wisconsin Press
114 North Murray Street
Madison, Wisconsin 53715

3 Henrietta Street
London WC2E 8LU, England

5   4   3   2   1

Printed in the United States of America

Library of Congress Cataloging-in-Publication Data
Likaka, Osumaka, 1953–
    Rural society and cotton in colonial Zaire / Osumaka Likaka.
    206 p.   cm.
    Includes bibliographical references and index.
    ISBN 0-299-15330-4 (hardcover: alk. paper).
    ISBN 0-299-15334-7 (pbk.: alk. paper).
    1. Cotton farmers—Zaire—History. 2. Cotton trade—Zaire—
History. 3. Peasantry—Zaire—History. 4. Zaire—Rural
conditions. I. Title.
HD8039.C662Z285   1997
338.1'7351'0967510941—dc20   96–36690

To Pierrette Aoka

Fate is unkind,
but my love for you is stronger than time

The Belgian Congo is in fact like one vast plantation in which the natives toil from dusk to dawn [*sic*] to enrich their Belgian task masters.

—*West Africa Pilot*, January 12, 1953

Contents

Illustrations and Map

Illustrations

Map

Tables

Acknowledgments

Many institutions and individuals have helped to bring this book to completion. I am indebted to the Social Science Research Council and the American Council of Learned Societies for a fellowship which allowed me to collect data in Belgium and Zaire. The Graduate School of the University of Minnesota provided support during the writing of the dissertation which led to this book. The Frederick Douglass Institute of the University of Rochester provided financial support for revising the dissertation and also structured opportunities for discussion. A PSC-CUNY award funded research to complete data collection, and the Graduate School of Wayne State University granted funds for making maps and developing films.

I express my appreciation to Allen Isaacman, my advisor and friend. For more than ten years now, he has been more than a great teacher and scholar whose ideas have had a profound impact on my own. He provided financial aid and moral support when they were most needed. I am deeply thankful to Professor Jan Vansina, who read the entire manuscript. He made available not only his unparalleled scholarship, but he took pains to point out incongruities and gallicisms. I am indebted to Ellen and Jeff Hoover, teachers and friends who for years have encouraged my intellectual growth. I thank Delinda for her patience as I constantly changed the text and tables.

Death affects each of us differently. When it knocked many times at my door, nothing seemed to have meaning. Many people helped soften the loss of my daughter. I heartily thank Eulalie and F. Kumeso, Brigitte and A. Ngoyi, Ngoyi Bukonda, Luise White, T. Sunseri, Nkasa Yelengi, E. Mandala, G. Corbin, Obotela Lingule, Silika Litofe, S. Mbaki, R. Ngandali, Gilbertine, Souza, Masengo, Kashinde, and Umba. I was moved by the generosity of my colleagues and friends in the History

Departments at Wayne State University and the University of Minnesota, the Frederick Douglass Institute at the University of Rochester, and many others—the list is too long to mention them by name. I am indebted to my good friends Nancy Hunt and Pier Larson who raised the Memorial Fund for Pierrette Aoka.

Rural Society and Cotton in Colonial Zaire

Introduction

In the past two decades, researchers have increasingly focused on the poverty and distorted rural economics of African nations. The recognition that African nations are unable to feed themselves has led social scientists to examine the historical roots of this crippled peasant social existence. Some scholars attribute the contemporary African food crises to the destruction of "natural economies," which undermined the peasants' reproductive capacity as well as their ability to cope with ecological disasters.[1] Others contend that African inability to develop stemmed from a systematic transfer of surplus value through unequal exchange.[2] Researchers have recognized that peasant production, the most pervasive form of labor organization, brought the colonial state and different fractions of capital closer to remote Central and South Central African communities.[3] The wide adoption of this form of production resulted from the assumption that Africans, clinging to their outmoded natural economies, underused their productive forces. In its scholarly form, the tenet was elaborated as the vent-for-surplus theory, which, simply put, maintains that prior to their integration into the international market, African societies were subject to substantial underemployment of both land and labor. International trade was assumed to provide an outlet for these idle resources. This acknowledgement notwithstanding, these researchers have paid little attention to the ways peasants produced commodities. Vent-for-surplus theorists, underdevelopmentalists, and Marxists have emphasized transnational factors in gauging the rate of surplus extraction, while neglecting the conditions under which peasants produced. To increase our understanding of what happened to peasants, we need to explore not only the conditions under which they traded and what they received in return, but also the conditions under which they worked. In short, any study of a peasant community is incomplete without an analysis of how peasants organized work to produce commodities.[4]

This is particularly relevant for cotton-producing peasantries for two reasons. First, some crops, such as coffee, tea, and cocoa, despite the relative demand for labor, permitted the continued production of food crops. Cotton, by contrast, because of its great labor intensity, interfered with the production of food crops, caused food shortages and out-migrations in many places, and compensated the African peasant with low prices. Second, a comparative approach demonstrates that to fully understand these peasantries, they must be examined in relation to the global economy in which cotton was produced. In fact, the encounter of capitalism with African communities and the consequent restructuring of the latter to fit the requirements of the former were not uniform processes. Different ecological and demographic conditions as well as varied labor requirements produced different results. In Mozambique, for example, Portugal's lack of capital and its dependency upon the exportation of African labor to South Africa and Zimbabwe partly molded the organization of cotton production, which severely exploited women's labor and determined the social outcome of the peasantry.[5] The lack of minerals and the need to shift an economy based on French trade in West Equatorial Africa accounts for a "system of forced labor supervised by local chiefs [that] accomplished cotton cultivation by the local population" in Chad, the Ivory Coast, and the Central African Republic, where *coton du commandant* became the metaphorical expression for cotton-generated exploitation and oppression. In contrast, in Malawi and Uganda favorable ecological and market factors encouraged peasants to grow the crop voluntarily.[6]

Moving away from the previous economism, I examine in chapter 1 the social organization of cotton production, emphasizing the roles played by labor, land, and ecology. I highlight the ways that labor scarcity, competition among different sectors of the colonial economy, and the low level of development in agricultural technology shaped the social organization of production so that the Africans became periodic workers and eternal peasants. To ensure food security, peasants had to cultivate cotton and food crops simultaneously, a situation which heightened labor conflicts, especially during peak labor periods. In this chapter I also examine a variety of intrahousehold, local, and macro-level strategies that peasants and the state created to cope with and overcome labor bottlenecks.

As stated earlier, recent scholarship has focused on the labor process to explain the historical roots of the crippled economies of postcolonial African nations. This scholarship has pointed out the existence of a variety of peasantries, including petty commodity producers, forced commodity producers, labor tenants or squatters, sharecroppers, independent household producers, and oscillating peasant workers.[7] Whatever form of work organization and labor control these scholars have found, they have emphasized the role of structural constraints and coercion by the use and threat of force that made peasants ready to give up a portion of the product of their labor. Even though legal constraints and force certainly produced exploitative relations, they still had limits. Whatever the role of the African police, state-appointed chiefs, and colonial armies, peasants resisted, and rural radicalism was produced in addition to the intended result of obedience.[8] I shall argue that in order to carry out cotton cropping successfully, the colonial state and cotton companies imposed a system of social control involving not only the threat and use of force, but also structural reforms, material incentives, and colonial propaganda using African popular culture. As allies, the colonial state and cotton companies sought to "manufacture" docile peasants who would divert labor from the food economy and bow to a variety of overseers entrusted with the mission of enforcing agricultural instructions.

The salient feature of the cotton economy in colonial Zaire was state control of production and exchange relations. While control over production shifted the costs of production from cotton companies to peasant households, control over local markets channeled wealth to the cotton companies, with pauperization as a social outcome. In fact, the forced cotton cultivation established networks and structures which have determined much of the destiny of cotton-producing peasantries since 1917. Total social wealth was perhaps the legitimation put forward by the colonial legislation and propaganda, but in fact it never occurred. Indeed, the increase of production by peasants was a paradox because, in contrast to the erroneous view that increased cash crop production was beneficial to Africans, it brought exploitation and repression that peasants had to struggle against even to survive. The wealth of Africa, as B. Rau puts it, "was, and remains, at the service of others."[9] The core of chapter 3 examines the mechanisms of economic exploitation that the state and cotton companies used to extract surpluses. I explore two distinct phases during which the state and cotton companies modified the ways they pumped wealth out of peasants: the free market and the monopsony phases. During the period of the free market, dating from 1917 to 1920, though the agents of companies periodically handed some cash to peasants, exchange relations were based on barter that generated robbery. The monopsony phase began in 1921 and continued throughout the cotton economy. During this phase, monopsony protected the interests of the cotton companies, but changes in the market after 1936 forced the state and its allies to rationalize the strategies of exploitation through the *barême de prix* (scale of prices) and the *avance provisionnellee* (advance), which yielded high dividends, swelling shares and capital gains, while remitting reduced income to the producers.

Overemphasis on economic mechanisms of exploitation tends to neglect the social relationships that developed in the encounters between peasants and cotton buyers at the trading posts. As a result, studies often fail to encapsulate a great portion of peasant experience and a number of the mechanisms whereby cotton company agents attempted to maximize the profit beyond approved means, including cheating on weights by misreading and rigging scales, and the manipulation of cotton grades. Examining these mechanisms is a strategic entry point to examining exploitation beyond the calculation of prices, and expands our understanding of what happened to peasants.

Emphasis on differentiation is becoming a major issue in the literature on peasants. Researchers have moved away from the conception of the peasantry as a homogeneous and undifferentiated group, and most agree that peasants included both exploiters and exploited.[10] This scholarship stands as a corrective to the center-periphery dichotomy which, while appropriately emphasizing the exploitation of the productive unit, ignores unequal relations within the community and household. For all its contribution, overemphasis on social differentiation, when extracted from international factors, shares the ideological parti pris of the former underdevelopment theory. I argue in chapter 4 that emphasis on internal social differentiation has real meaning only when the transfer of wealth from the household to the cotton companies and colonial state has been made explicit as well. In spite of their entrepreneurship and ability to take the advantage of the economic opportunities opened by cash crop production, the affluent peasants, Zunde land owners, and cocoa planters, ended up experiencing the collapse of their economic ventures, and poverty quickly replaced their prosperity. This is even more true for chiefs whose economic prosperity was premised on their loyalty to the colonial regime and services to different fractions of capital. Evidence from Zaire shows that despite the privileged position occupied by these African subordinates in the colonial social aggregate and the substantial material wealth this yielded, they remained both a fragile and exploited class. Despite their seemingly important revenues, chiefs remained relatively impoverished when compared to their colonial overlords.[11]

Inequality developed within the cotton-producing regions, especially between chiefs and cotton producers. I argue that social differentiation emerging between chiefs and peasants was a conscious and controlled process that primarily benefited the state, although it channeled a substantial amount of wealth to chiefs who did not necessarily transform it into capital. In chapter 4, I demonstrate that the sources of inequities between chiefs and peasants were the appropriation of unpaid labor for commodity production, the pricing system that withheld peasant income to pay chiefs' bonuses, chiefs' exemption from taxes, and the power of the judiciary. I also explore inequities within the household, pointing out unequal allocation of agricultural tasks and scarce resources. To analyze household inequality, I examine the process of decision making and the sites of investment and priorities. Central to this section is the view that the male head of the household reproduced historical and unequal division of labor and allotted most of the household's poor earnings to his priorities by controlling the levers of power. I argue that because of the overwhelming poverty, inequities within the household are better described as the unequal distribution of poverty rather than exploitation of women by men, since exploitation implies the accumulation of wealth by the household.

Structurally, cotton agriculture in colonial Zaire established a three way sociocommercial relationship among cultivators, the colonial state, and cotton companies. This linkage resulted in a systematic transfer of resources from the household, thereby reducing peasant economic security and autonomy. In response, peasants engaged in several forms of resistance to protect their autonomy, both as social and cultural space. Colonial reports devoted to ascertaining the state of mind of rural communities erroneously concluded that "there is nothing to complain about; people are busy and silent," when there were no open acts of defiance. They failed to discern that the completion of assigned work covered hostility and hatred, and that the peasants' silence was active and their conformity calculated. For peasants, being silent did not mean the absence of thoughts and acts of defiance. In fact, peasants were engaged in many forms of struggle that were often perceived by colonial administrators as expressions of "African laziness" and "African incapacity to foresee the future." African laziness was ultimately a constant struggle against cotton production.

In chapter 5, I examine several ways that peasants coped with and struggled against cotton production. Cotton growers rarely engaged in collective, open rebellions and only occasionally, in a fit of anger, attacked *moniteurs-coton* (cotton-monitors) rude chiefs, crop supervisors, territorial administrators, and state agronomists. The dangers of reprisal were great. Instead they protested individually and clandestinely. Opposition to cotton production included a set of actions to undermine the reproductive cycle of the crop and to control the work schedule in order to prevent cotton cultivation from diverting all the labor from food production: refusal to weed and cut off old stalks, late seeding and harvesting, roasting and boiling seeds before planting, planting cotton on infertile soils, and the reduction of plot sizes. Peasants also opted for internal migrations, flights to neighboring countries and cities, and a number fled into the deep forests where they created "camouflaged villages" comparable to maroon communities in the Americas, the Caribbean Islands, and Quilombo in Brazil. Though each type of action bore a particular political intent, overall such actions reflect the struggle of men and women to control their work schedule. The market also became an arena of struggle. Here, peasants created three major tactics. Some mixed their cotton with heavy materials, hoping to compensate for prices forced below the value of labor. Others did what they rightly called "taking back one's own cotton" from the companies' warehouses to sell it in the second or third sale session. Furthermore, others left their cotton to rot on the stalks when they received bad prices during the first sale session. Finally, peasants engaged in calculated silence to disguise their hostility and impede colonial planners from impinging further into their intimate life. I argue that resistance to cotton production is better explained in terms of cultural autonomy, which highlights understanding the conditions of production and exploitation of peasants, and the ways peasants articulated their grievances. Indeed, to define and protect their cultural autonomy, peasants appropriated the religion of the oppressors and restructured traditional secret societies. This autonomy served as a resource for the elaboration of a language, ideologies, and strategies to circumvent work obligations and confront at minimal cost the most visible territorial officials and African subordinates, namely the *moniteurs-coton*, chiefs, and headmen. This provides evidence that history and society are created by constant and purposeful individual actions that, notwithstanding their intentions, are in turn affected by history and society.[12]

One of the most salient features of peasant studies has been the failure to recognize peasants as complex people, capable of producing culture as well as agricultural commodities. Whatever paradigms scholars have used, they have compartmentalized peasants. For example, some scholars have viewed them as "rational peasants" who make individual choices and decisions, and take risks.[13] Others have stressed their avoidance of risk.[14] The periphery/center dichotomy has rendered them passive historical actors who had no control over their lives. If peasant experiences have been fragmented for analytical convenience, the result has been that vast parts of their daily lives, their social outlook and understanding of the universe, fall outside the scope of scholarly investigation. The complexity of peasant experience cannot be understood by simple descriptive terms such as *rational peasant* and *peasant moral economy,* which fail to account for human agency. Such one-dimensional approaches fail to capture the interplay between structure and agency. To take into account the dialectical relationship between structure and agency, this study addresses the labor process; the identification of techniques of pumping out surpluses from the household to larger economic and political structures; the effects of cotton production on gender relations and social differentiation; and social protest. These issues help us to move from a very specific issue of economic and political history—the imposition of cotton cultivation in the Congo under Belgian rule—to much broader social and cultural concerns.

There are few scholarly works on cotton cultivation in colonial Zaire. Lumpungu's unpublished work, "Difficultés du paysannat cotonnier dans le Tanganyika," and master's thesis, "Culture cotonnière et société rurale dans le nord du Katanga," and Ruelle's "Introduction du coton au Congo belge: Motivations économique et financière" are the principal studies dealing with the subject. Lumpungu's work highlights the contribution of cotton to the development of peasant agriculture in northern Katanga as well as the major causes of its collapse. For all its strength, Lumpungu's work fails to address the crucial question of how the state and cotton companies shifted their costs of production to the households, while transferring resources to the companies. The result is a rather dry calculation of prices without any reference to the daily life of the producers. Ruelle's study is an excessively economistic view of the differing motives which enticed Belgian interests into cotton cultivation in 1921. Like Mulambu's "Cultures obligatoires et colonisation dans l'ex-Congo belge," Ruelle's synchronic analysis ignores other factors which affected the cotton scheme: ecology, the quality of the soil, and the availability of labor all influenced the decision of Belgian companies to invest in cotton production. Neither examined how the imposition of cotton production transformed the economy and the social universe of rural Zairian society. My study fills this gap in the social history of Zairian peasants.

This study is drawn from a mix of oral, archival, and published sources. I collected oral data during the summer of 1986 and in 1988 and 1989. During this period I interviewed more than fifty former male and female cotton producers—from Kasai, Tanganyika, Maniema, Uele, and Ubangi districts—and their descendants, as well as African policemen, state agricultural agents, and chiefs. I also collected peasant songs, proverbs, nicknames of colonial officials, and data about religious movements and closed associations. These interviews provide an inside view of the cotton scheme as well as the ways peasants coped with and struggled against the scheme. They also provide insights into peasant consciousness and ideology, issues neglected in colonial records. They show that beyond the barriers of languages and geography, peasants shared a common ideology and conscience. Drawing from the Ngbandi *parave* (watch out), the Azande "scraper of heaps," the broken Ciluba *buloba kutamba kapia* (The sun is burning cotton), to the widely used, cross-cultural *matala-tala* (wearing glasses), this data illustrates that peasants were aware of close supervision and were able to cope with the scheme in a subtle way. Like any kind of historical record, interviews have their weaknesses. First, they are active reconstructions of the past from the present, and from this perspective, they are subject to manipulations and misrepresentations. Zaire is a country where peasants still suffer from political repression, hunger, and rampant inflation that reduces their income to nothing. The degradation of health care facilities and the destruction of roads prevent producers from selling their products. This predicament has a bearing on peasants' perception of the past. On many occasions, informants praised the colonial era and easily forgot that roads were constructed with their money and that those who failed to cooperate were flogged, fined, and jailed. Often oral testimonies were vague about the areas under cultivation, prices, income, and changes over time. Second, the distortion of specific issues was frequent among the respondents who benefited from the cotton economy. Chiefs and policemen, for example, tried to justify their roles. The third complication is that life expectancy is short in Africa, and it is becoming difficult to find those who might recall the early period of the cotton economy.

To overcome these weaknesses, I supplemented interviews with archival and published data. In recent years, historians writing history from below have been shying away from using colonial archives and have relied excessively on oral data. They have claimed that archives fail to reveal an inside view of African societies and are therefore unreliable, for example, for such critical issues as gender. While these concerns are legitimate, the use of either interviews or archives alone is no solution. The most fruitful approach appears to be to mix oral, archival, and published materials, with careful analysis and cross-reference of all available sources. This study, in an effort to employ such a fruitful mixing of sources, has teased information from plays, films, court records, comic books, and pamphlets to provide reliable information to supplement the oral data. African peasants were complex people who struggled in complex circumstances, the scholarship that focuses on them must reflect this complexity. This study endeavors to improve on existing scholarship by more fully addressing these complex and interacting issues. Archives are the single most important source for the reconstruction of the political economy of cotton. Of utmost importance are the *Agri, dossiers coton,* housed in the Archives Africaines at Brussels. In addition to these files, there are published documents such as *rapports annuels sur l'administration du Congo aux chambres législatives belges, rapports annuels AIMO, comités régionaux, conseils de province, conseil de gouvernement,* as well as unpublished correspondence, located in the Archives Nationales in Zaire, especially the regional archives in Kisangani. These materials provide information about agricultural policies that defined the political and economic organization of the cotton economy. They include extremely important documents such as plays, films, pamphlets, comic books, and a rich collection of photographs that make this study a major contribution to the field.

To analyze the household dimension, I collected the following primarily from archival sources and published materials: prices of cotton and other crops used in plant rotation to cope with food shortage, erosion, and land exhaustion; the prices of consumer goods such as shirts, slacks, fabrics, and household items; the amount of taxes for each area; and the household budgets calculated by colonial officers. In addition, I consulted native court registers, annual reports of Territories, the *rapports annuels d'inspection of Territoires,* which recorded statistics of divorces, adulteries, repayments of brideprice, and elopements. These documents yield information that provides a strategic point of entry into the nature of gender relations and internal household conflicts and inequality. Despite all their strength and value, archival sources are not to be accepted without caution and assessment. First, all territorial administrators were not "pro-cotton." Hence, one finds a good deal of critique of the system in the reports of these officials, including Pierre Ryckmans's post-1935 correspondence. The problem is complicated by the existence of twisted categories and semantic distortion and manipulation that hide the fact that women and children were used extensively for cotton production. Second, archives provide scanty and incomplete information on how peasants viewed the cotton economy. Apart from native court documents that provide an African voice, the voices of peasants are almost always mediated by a missionary or a territorial administrator whose class position, personality, and belief inevitably filtered the message. Therefore, a mix of archival, oral, and published data is the most fruitful approach for the reconstruction of the social history of cotton.

1

The Organization of Production: The Cotton Labor Process

Introduction

Cotton cultivation in colonial Zaire depended on control over producers and regulation of their access to land and technology, particularly at the household level. Land was abundant in colonial Zaire but producers were not. Although between 1891 and 1908 the state and different capitalist sectors had appropriated much of the native land through the grant of concessions and a ban on productive activity by Africans outside subsistence production, the state rescinded the rights of concessionary companies thereafter; at the time of the cotton imposition in 1917, peasants had the land necessary for food production. In 1910, for example, the administration estimated that peasants used just about one-thirtieth of the total of 235 million hectares of arable land. What was critically important remained reaching producers in low-density African communities scattered over a large area. Indeed, labor scarcity was a recurring theme throughout the colonial period. During the discussion of the 1914 budget, E. Leplae, the director-general of the Department of Agriculture, pointed out that "hands were lacking," emphasizing that the growth of agriculture would intensify this labor scarcity.[1] An economic planner of the Uele District stated in 1924, "It is not the land, but the labor which shapes the economic development of the Congo."[2] Furthermore, the use of machetes, axes, and hoes not only limited the amount of land under cultivation, but also contributed to labor scarcity.

In this chapter, I examine the social organization of cotton production to which labor, land, and ecology were integrally linked. I emphasize how labor scarcity, competition among various sectors of the colonial economy, and the low level of development in agricultural technology shaped the organization of production, affecting the implementation of labor policies, so that Africans became periodic workers and eternal peasants. To ensure food security, peasants had to simultaneously cultivate cotton and food crops, a situation which heightened labor conflicts, especially during peak labor periods. In this chapter, I also examine a variety of intrahousehold, local, and macro-level strategies that peasants and the state created to cope with and overcome labor bottlenecks.

Efforts by the colonial state to organize cotton production can be divided into three distinct phases. During an experimental phase dating from 1917 to 1920, the colonial administration endeavored to create a cotton-producing peasantry, requiring cotton producers to work collectively under chiefs and elders. After 1920, the administration passed legislation that established cotton concessions, and defined how and when peasants had to clear the land, hoe, weed, and harvest the crop. After World War II, the state added the *paysannats* (agricultural development scheme) to the concession system as part of its policy to modernize peasant agriculture and halt migrations.

Creating a Cotton-Producing Peasantry, 1917–1920

After numerous unsuccessful attempts by the colonial state to develop cotton production, the colonial administration decided in 1917 on forced cultivation of two days per week, not especially of cotton.[3] Creating a cotton-producing peasantry remained, however, a difficult task. At that time, the state still had only incomplete information about rainfall patterns, climate variations, and soil types in the areas that were to become the main centers of cotton production. Lack of transportation, low population density, and people's opposition to a rigid labor regime posed additional obstacles. Moreover, gold and copper mining increasingly competed with agriculture for labor and for the dominant position in the colonial economy, as evidenced by the increasing percentage of mineral exports over agricultural exports. In 1915, mineral exports reached 60 percent of the value of total exports.[4] As a result, the central administration was concerned with the mining industry, and priority was given to recruiting mineworkers. Meanwhile, since European farmers had failed to meet the food need, the production of foodstuffs sufficient to feed mineworkers remained in African hands. The Brussels officials responsible for colonial agriculture favored compulsory growing, while other interests preferred a free market with both African peasant agriculture and European plantation sectors.[5] Finally, many colonial officials were convinced that gold, copper, tin mining, coffee, palm oil, palm kernels, copal, maize (among others), and cotton cultivation involved mutually exclusive economic activities. These factors made it difficult to divide African labor among household requirements, a rigid system of cotton cultivation, and competing colonial impositions. Thus cotton zones would be determined by suitable natural environment and competition among labor requirements for migrant labor (mines) and other crops. The existence of competition gave some latitude to African producers (especially in marginal areas) in deciding which of these exploitations they saw as a lesser evil.

These obstacles complicated the shift from production in experimental stations to production in African households. The administration first targeted those peasants living in the environs of stations. At the same time, because cotton cultivation remained entirely a state venture during this phase, the territorial administrators and state agricultural officers sought to persuade the Belgian textile industry that cotton could be grown in the colony at minimal costs, and to persuade the Africans that cotton cultivation was in their interest since it would stave off poverty. Success in expanding cotton production depended partly on fitting it into the existing systems of production.[6] The absence of preestablished patterns for working cotton among the local people led to the importation of a cultivation system designed in the government's agricultural experimental stations for some African communities, which was supervised by the African chiefs. Beginning in 1915, these leaders tried to convince their people to grow cotton on collective cotton fields, which were established for demonstration purposes. The number of people in the village and the amount of cotton seeds available in experimental stations determined the size of these collective plots.[7] The following year, three agronomists succeeded in convincing 177 people at Nyangwe and Kasongo in the Maniema district to work in cotton fields that together covered about 50 hectares by exempting peasants from heavy porterage during the First World War. Since women were entrusted with the task of producing food, their participation in working these cotton fields remained minimal.[8] In 1917, these producers worked about two hundred cotton plots which covered over 60 hectares. Simultaneously, E. Fisher and U. Blommaert, two cotton experts, expanded cotton cultivation to the Sankuru district, where E. Fisher experimented with Triumph, Simkins, Nyassaland, and Allen long staple varieties. Because the surrounding people lived on sandy, clay, and light soil that ranged from average to high fertility, the experiments were successful; this led to Sankuru's incorporation into the scheme.

These early efforts fueled the enthusiasm of the colonial state. The First World War justified the reintroduction of forced labor, abolished in

Fig. 1.1. Peasants clearing the land before 1920

1910 (see figures 1.1 and 1.2). In addition to the war effort, the rationalization for the imposition of cotton was the need to create a reliable source of cotton in the colony that would reduce the Belgian dependency on American and Indian cotton imports. In 1913, for example, Belgium imported 66 and 32 percent of its cotton from the United States and India, respectively.[9] A look at the supply side of the world market indicates that cotton imposition in African colonies by colonial governments was the best option for supplying cotton to their textile industries and reducing their dependency on American imports. In 1917, just one year before the imposition of cotton in colonial Zaire, the world production of cotton was about twenty-four million bales of 500 pounds each. Of this quantity of cotton, the United States alone provided fourteen million bales, representing more than one half of the total world output. And, most important, this supply was rarely over demand. The European textile industries in general and the Belgian textile industry in particular faced a serious threat. A bad harvest in the United States would raise prices. Speculation on the American stock exchange could cause price fluctuations that would severely affect other countries. Furthermore, the fear that construction and expansion of the American spinning industry would lead to increasing local consumption and decrease exports to foreign spinners worried the owners of European textile industries. The

Fig. 1.2. Peasants hoeing the land before 1920

propaganda of the Brussels administration, already influenced by the Société Générale de Belgique just before they handed out the large concessions, claimed then that cotton growing in colonial Zaire offered Belgium the hope of producing large quantities of cotton at minimal cost and creating a cotton market at Antwerp that would supply a great portion of the raw material required by the Belgian spinning and weaving industries, which had hitherto spent about forty-two million francs to purchase American, Egyptian, and Indian cotton. Also, Belgian propaganda claimed that cotton represented "for many Belgian nationals, a source of revenues,"[10] because it created job opportunities. Though territorial officials were aware that it would take time, capital, and energy to produce cotton on a scale that would adequately supply the Belgian textile industries, "there was, nevertheless, much at stake for Belgium to have in the colony, an independent source of raw materials."[11]

Initially, the colonial administration introduced a set of incentives to stimulate cotton cultivation. In 1918, it established "free markets," where trading-house agents bought cotton and bartered for it with cheap European goods. Although the *impôt de cueillette* (taxes in goods) had been totally illegal since 1910, and although the state had opted for the monetization of the economy by imposing a money tax, state agents in charge of cotton often accepted in the earlier years (1917–1920) *impôt de cueillette,* whereby peasants hostile to cotton discharged tax obligations in seed cotton. While the state at first confined the installation of large-capacity ginning machines to sites near communication lines and waterways, it later reversed this policy by installing small hand-gins in remote areas to stimulate cotton production. Because carrying cotton to the trading stations infuriated peasants, the state again confined cotton cultivation to areas that were particularly accessible. The markets at Nyangwe and Lusambo, and small trading posts in the Uele region were located at communication points. Nyangwe was crossed by the Zaire River and by the Compagnie du Chemin de Fer du Congo Supérieur aux Grands Lacs Africains (Great Lakes Railways Company; C. F. L.) railroad, built in 1906. Lusambo was located at the terminus of the navigable part of the Sankuru River and was exploited by the Société Nationale des Transports Fluviaux. Cotton cultivation in the Uele region was first organized along the "Route Royale Congo-Nile."[12] More often than not, this preoccupation with markets made colonial officers overlook all other factors, such as the quality of the soils, population density, and even climate variations and rainfall patterns.[13]

As indicated earlier, limited success from 1917 to 1920 raised high hopes among colonial officials. Output rose from 26 to 640 tons of seed cotton. The area under cultivation increased from 44 hectares in 1916 to 1,000 hectares in 1918 and 2,300 in 1920. Despite this success, several factors hampered the ability of the peasants to meet the needs of the Belgian textile industry during this phase, including the cost and scarcity of transportation, and the failure of the colonial state to control labor and manage it according to the needs of the different sectors of the colonial economy. The embryonic organization of production discouraged the peasants and left territorial administrators and state agronomists with mixed feelings. In the meantime, the yields per hectare decreased drastically from 595 kilograms in 1916 to 324 kilograms in 1919, and 278 kilograms in 1920. Furthermore, robbery, peculiar to the barter system, and the artificially depressed producer prices made cotton less profitable and discouraged peasants from production.[14] The involvement of banks and industries controlled by the Société Générale in the cotton scheme, through the establishment of the Compagnie Cotonnière Congolaise (Cotonco) in 1920, reduced opposition to cotton cultivation in Brussels, and resulted in the concession system that changed the labor regime and gave a new impetus to the cotton venture.

The Concession System and Cotton Cultivation, 1920–1946

The involvement of financial capital in the cotton scheme through the creation of Cotonco in 1920 expanded the cotton economy.

The idea probably arose in discussions between the Société Générale and the Brussels government in a context of depression. One year later, the colonial administration enacted new legislation that granted concessions to cotton companies, thereby transforming the division of rural labor. Under this new legislation, the state's highest priorities were to establish a rigorous labor regime, expand the cotton scheme to areas that offered any prospect for cotton cultivation, and improve the conditions of production. As I will demonstrate, this legislation reinforced the role of the state in the development of agriculture in general and of the cotton economy in particular.

The State, Labor, and Cotton Production

The most significant innovation in the organization of production was the creation of the cotton concession system. This was a labor-management system that allowed the state to grant, from 1921 on, concessions to each of the twelve cotton companies operating in the northern and southern regions of Zaire that were divided into numerous cotton zones (see map). According to A. Bertrand, a consistent critic in Province Orientale of labor and cotton policies, these cotton zones were "a wonderful device to obtain labor from the indigenous people for the benefit of private individuals."[15] Cotton concessions were both a result of and response to the colonial economic planners' dependence on a depleted labor force and competition among different sectors of the colonial economy for the same scarce labor.[16] These cotton concessions differed from charter companies and land grants previously awarded by the "Congo Free State." Whereas the former system granted land rights to the charter companies, the new system awarded, in theory, cotton concession holders only the exclusive rights to purchase specific cash crops from the peasant households within their concessions. In practice, however, they gave a labor monopoly to cotton companies because they operated much like the *repartimiento* in colonial Latin America. The state in fact guaranteed a number of potential crop producers to the holder of a cotton concession by encapsulating Africans living in a certain geographical area into a concession and by coercing them to perform labor obligations. Households in cotton concessions were at the mercy of the company; they could not choose to withhold sales, shift to another cash crop, or benefit from competition by other companies. The system also enabled the colonial state to exercise some control at the point of production and in the market as well, and to introduce to some extent a working monetary economy into the remote African villages.

State-controlled cotton-growing areas in colonial Zaire

The concession system, therefore, served to reach depleted and scattered labor and provided a legal means to arbitrate labor competition.

Between 1921 and 1933, the administration granted numerous ten-year cotton zones of 800 square kilometers to twelve cotton companies (see table 1.1), each (ideally) with a saw-gin or several hand-operated gins at its center.[17] During this first decade, approximately 200 cotton zones of 1,250 square kilometers each formed the total cotton-growing area. After the Great Depression, the state grouped several cotton zones together, suppressed others, and redefined their dimensions. A cotton zone became a twenty-year concession whose size varied from 1,000 to

19

Table 1.1. Cotton companies and capitalization

Companies	Year of founding	Capitalization (F)	Shareholders
Cotonco	1920	51,420,000	Société Générale, government
Cotonepo	1925	12,680,000	Société Générale, Cotonco
Bomokandi	1925		Cotonco
Cotanga	1933		Cotonco
Colocoton	1925	2,219,000	N. Masson, wool trader, and J. Couturier and G. Mignot, two spinners, owned 51%
Combelga		14,133,000	
Congolaise Bunge			S. A. Bunge
Compagnie du Lubilashi			
Compagnie du Luisa			
NAHV	1921	4,000,000	
Texaf	1925	38,100,000	Groupe Lagashe held 92% of shares
Sabbe et Puppa	1927	11,430,000	Cotonco, Puppa et Sabbe

Sources: L. Banneux, "Quelques données économiques sur le coton au Congo belge," *Bulletin de l'information de l'INEAC'*, *séie technique*, no. 22 (1938): 4; A. Landeghem, "La compagnie cotonnière congolaise," *Bulletin agricole du Congo belge*, 21, no. 1 (1930): 820.

8,000 square kilometers, depending on population density and the development of rural infrastructure—mainly roads.[18] Started in 1933, this reorganization resulted in consolidating the hold of the largest companies over the whole sector. In 1934 for example, Texaf was thrown out of the Maniema area by Cotonco.[19]

The population density and infrastructure notwithstanding, there could be no cotton on any appreciable scale without gins. Hand-operated gins were sufficient as long as the total output and yield remained low. But because the objective of the cotton scheme was the increase of output, hand-operated gins quickly became obsolete, and there was an increase of saw-gins, a vital factor in expanding the cotton economy. In 1920, there were only 2 state-owned saw-gins; in 1936, the number jumped to 119; and in 1946 it reached 124.[20] The increase in the number of gins along with technical modernization also helped expand the cotton-growing areas and stimulated production. Technical changes in the factories affected production outputs because cotton companies had no use for cotton beyond the capacity of their milling machines. When outputs were small at the beginning, they used hand-gins, which were able to mill between 200 and 250 kilograms of seed cotton in a ten-hour day. Later, cotton concession holders bought saw-gins, which were capable of ginning 3,000 kilograms of seed cotton in an eight-hour day. By 1923, the first factories, operating with technically advanced saw-gins capable of milling 6,000 kilograms of cotton in an eight-hour day, were completed. In the 1930s, there were 175 gins equipped with 80 saws and costing from 339,000 to 950,000 Belgian francs operating in colonial Zaire. From 1947 to 1957, some eighteen automated factories were installed.[21] Table 1.2 shows a concomitant increase in gins, outputs, and trading posts over twenty-five years, which reflects the importance of gins in expanding cotton cultivation.

Cotton concessions were granted where geographical conditions, such as climate, rainfall, and soil type, seemed to be appropriate and where no other concessions (e.g., for palm products) existed. Because the excessive temperature variations at high altitudes are unfit for cotton, its cultivation was inappropriate in the high plateaus of eastern Zaire. Cotton's water requirements—from 800 to 1,100 mm in a five- or six-month period—prevented it from being grown along the equator, where the rainfalls do not alternate with a long dry season. These facts confined the growing of cotton to two geographical areas. The northern cotton-growing area lay approximately between 2.5 and 5 degrees north of the equator and covered the Ubangi and Uele districts and a portion of the Kibali-Ituri districts. By 1927, the cotton scheme had incorporated 80 percent of the Uele population.[22] The southern cotton-growing area spread between 2.5 and 12 degrees south of the equator and encompassed the Sankuru, Kasai, Lomami, Tanganyika, and Lulua districts and parts of the Maniema districts. The administration partitioned these two cotton-growing areas among the following companies. The Compagnie Cotonnière Congolaise, the most important company by area and capitalization, owned concessions in portions of the Upper and Lower Uele, Ubangi, Maniema, Kivu, Sankuru, Kasai, and Lomami districts. Since 1938, it had also participated in buying cotton in Dilolo, the so-called free market area. The Société de Nepoko was first confined to a part of the Uele district, but in 1948 it began to operate in the Stanleyville district when peasants in Basoko, Banalia, and Bafwasende were forced to cultivate the crop. The Société Cotonnière de Bomokandi concentrated its activities in the Upper Uele district in

Table 1.2. Number of saw-gins, trading posts, and outputs, 1920–1946

Year	Gins	Outputs (tons of seed cotton)	Trading posts
1920	2	800	—
1921	—	1,770	—
1930	—	30,600	254
1931	—	44,822	288
1932	95	26,700	301
1934	108	59,160	508
1936	119	92,105	—
1937	126	110,454	963
1938	—	127,488	1,050
1939	120	127,000	1,130
1940	126	135,689	1,200
1941	126	141,566	—
1946	124	122,734	—

Sources: A. Landenghem, "1921–1936, Quinze années de culture cotonnière au Congo belge," 4 (1936), 3; "Monographie du coton congolais," *Bulletin du Comité Cotonnier Congolais*, 6 (1937): 57; A. De Bauw, ed., *Trente années de culture cotonnière au Congo belge* (Brussels: Cotonco, 1948), 43; A. Brixhe, *Le Coton au Congo belge* (Brussels: Ministère des Colonies, 1958), 17; L. Banneux, "Quelques données économiques sur le coton au Congo belge," *Bulletin d'information de l'INEAC*, série technique, 22 (1938): 25; "Documentation sur le Coton au Congo belge," 24, A.R.H.Z., Kisangani.

the Bomokandi River Valley. The Comptoir Colonial Belgika owned concessions in the Uele district and later in the Stanleyville district. Created in the "Congo Free State" years, the Nieuwe Afrikaansche-Handels-Vennootschap (N.A.H.V.) got a concession in 1921, but never expended its monopsony beyond the Yakoma, Libo, Amadi, and Tapili Territories. The Société Textile Africaine (Texaf), altough it was only a textile and trading firm, bought cotton from peasants in the Ubangi and Uele districts, and later the south became its most important sphere of operation. Sabbe and Puppa, two Greek settlers, marketed cotton in the Mahagi Territory.[23]

Cotton interests divided the southern cotton-growing area among the Compagnie Cotonnière du Tanganyika (Cotanga), which purchased cotton from the Tanganyika district, mainly in the Kongolo, Kabalo, Manono, Mwanza, and Kabongo Territories; the Compagnie Cotonnière Coloniale (Colocoton), which bought cotton from peasants in Lodja, Kabinda, and Kole; the Compagnie Commerciale Belgo-Africaine, (Combelga), which enjoyed monopsony over Dimbelenge, Lodja, and Tshofa Territories; and Compagnie Cotonnière Congolaise (Cotonco), which dominated the market in Sankuru, Kasai, and Lomami. This subdivision transformed villages into "vast work camps rationally managed to meet exterior needs."[24]

In addition to these concessionary areas, there were also free zones to the south. After a study conducted in Uganda and Tanzania and published in 1934, the state very reluctantly allowed the sale of cotton within the free markets in the Dilolo and Luisa areas. Here, any cotton company helping to introduce cotton in the area enjoyed a five-year monopsony. After this period, peasants supplied cotton not to a single cotton company but to any cotton company holding a buying license.[25] Why the state allowed free markets in Dilolo and Luisa is not clear. The reason may have been the influence of Union Minière du Haut Katanga and Forminière recruiters who were cut off from labor previously recruited from the copper belt when the British began mining copper in Zambia in the early 1930s. By 1946, for example, the cotton buying in Dilolo was done by the Société Congolaise Bunge, which also operated in Kamina, Bukama, and part of Sandoa and Kabongo Territories, and the Compagnie du Lubilashi, which concentrated its activities in Mutombo-Mukulu Territory. The Société Cotonnière de Luisa bought cotton in Luisa Territory.

As stated at the beginning of this chapter, the labor shortage was the crucial issue in developing the colonial economy. The objective of the colonial government was to maintain healthy villages which would supply adequate workers to the mines, plantations, and other sectors of the colonial economy. In 1925, a labor commission recommended that companies could recruit from any chiefdom only 25 percent of its healthy adult males. This recommendation was very often ignored, as can be seen in the ratio of workers to peasants, which increased from 19 percent in 1940 to 33 percent in 1950 and 39 percent in 1956 (see table 1.3). In the Katanga, Leopoldville, and Kivu provinces, the ratio reached 50 percent in 1956.[26]

Concessions were designed to arbitrate competition over labor and drive producers into production. In practice, however, they did not entirely eliminate competition between cotton and other economic sectors. This failure was linked to the nature of regional economies which shaped the implementation of agricultural and labor policies. In the north, cotton cultivation competed with peasant food production, state-owned gold mines, a weak settler agriculture, and public projects. These competing demands squeezed cotton producers, but competition often offered peasants some flexibility. Evidence shows that when the administrative pressure became excessive, cotton cultivators worked in mines and settler agriculture as laborers. Excessive administrative

Table 1.3. Ratio of workers to healthy adult males

Year	Total population	Healthy adult males	Workforce size	Ratio of workers to healthy adult males
1940	10,353,909	2,697,201	518,263	19
1945	10,508,449	2,746,679	701,101	25
1950	11,331,793	2,886,831	929,009	33
1955	12,562,631	3,042,048	1,182,871	35
1956	12,843,574	3,075,803	1,197,896	39
1957	13,174,884	3,088,925	1,477,712	37

Source: *Bulletin de la Banque du Congo belge* 9 (1958): 249.

pressure, therefore, shifted labor from cotton cultivation to the mines and settler agriculture, which harmed cotton expansion.[27] Conversely, bad working conditions in gold mines and the terms of labor contracts, ranging from three years for regular workers to two months for migrant workers, sent workers back to their villages, making it difficult for the territorial administrators to use African labor efficiently in cotton agriculture.[28] As part of additional efforts to split labor functionally among the various sectors of the economy and reduce labor competition to a minimum, the administration applied a series of economic policies. In 1928, it subdivided the countryside into economic zones and assigned each zone a specified economic role. In this system the state arbitrated competition for labor and conflicts among territorial administrations, companies, and missions which did not want migrant labor to deplete their areas. Although this geographic division of labor did not eliminate the movement of population, it did reduce antagonistic relations between competing users of African labor, as Dufour noted ten years later:

> The concentration of food production in specified areas facilitates the organization of the propaganda and eliminates the causes of conflicts between the companies interested in getting different indigenous products. It is advisable not to forget that the organization of economic zones proposed by the 1928 commission must adapt to economic needs and evolve along with the economy of the region. It was not foreseen in 1928 that the mining companies working in Wamba would use in 1938 over 6,000 workers, in addition to 2,000 in Bondo, and more in Bafwasende.[29]

Simultaneously, the administration regulated labor drafts and casual labor for coffee picking in settler coffee plantations, diminished the use of migrants, and made the return of these temporary workers to their communities at the expiration of their contracts mandatory. This set of policies virtually reduced the Africans to periodic workers and permanent peasants. The administration forbade labor exports where population density tended to be lower. For example, labor recruitment for the Kilo and Moto gold mines was forbidden, even though mining companies and settlers still conscripted a group of peasants whom the agricultural officers conducting production surveys labeled "bad cultivators," whose behavior would have a negative affect on good cultivators.[30] The draft of these unpliant peasants further reduced opposition to cotton cultivation. In the meantime, the state enacted a wide range of policies which diverted labor from the production of other cash crops. It enforced the rigid policy which increasingly allotted more land to cotton than to any other crops; and it increased producer prices for cotton while lowering the prices for any other agricultural commodity, a policy aimed at showing peasants that cotton was the ideal money-earning crop.[31] This policy was given wide publicity by territorial administrators and missionaries, as I shall show in chapter 2.

As in the north, cotton cultivation in the south suffered competition from palm products, food production, coffee plantations, and the expanding copper, diamond, and tin mining in Katanga, Kasai, and Maniema. Bad working and living conditions in the early labor camps sent workers back to their villages, which paralleled the situation peasants faced in the north, making them eternal peasants. Bwana Lumpungu Saidi recalled,

> Life at the camp was pleasant; only the food did not suit us . . . The people from Maniema died in large numbers, because they were not accustomed to the maize flour. Yes, we lost many of our people at Ruashi, some died from work accidents, other, the majority, from diarrhea. The man who had diarrhea one day died in two or three days. All of us wanted only one thing: to terminate our contract and return to our country. We were so frightened by the number of people who died each day.[32]

In contrast to the northern cotton-growing area, the population in Katanga was relatively scarce and scattered. There were two plausible explanations for the incorporation of population-scarce areas of Katanga into the cotton scheme in 1933, in addition to Kasai, Maniema, Sankuru, and Lomami, all pioneering cotton-producing districts. First, the great depression (1928–1933) led to the layoff of workers and temporarily reduced the demand for food by mining companies in the Tanganyika district, the main site of cotton production in Katanga. Second, the rotation of seasons between the north and south, a unique climatic advantage found nowhere else in cotton-producing colonial Africa, enabled the colonial state and cotton companies to have peasants supply raw cotton to the Belgian textile industries all year long. The population scarcity led mine management to seek labor beyond the mine hinterland. The situation became critical when the British, opening mining ventures in Zambia, halted international labor migrations in the copper belt in the 1930s. Then, cut off from labor previously recruited from as far as Malawi, the colonial administration began not only to impinge on the labor of cotton-producing Kasai and Maniema districts, but to require cotton producers in the former district to produce food for the copper mines.[33] These conditions explain the existence of free cotton zones in Dilolo and Luisa. Until 1937, this competition determined the way territorial administrators in the south organized households to produce cotton in Kabinda. In this area, which was simultaneously a cotton-producing area, a labor reservoir for the Union Minière du Haut-Katanga and Société Forestière et Minière de Bakwanga, and a food-producing area, the colonial administration subdivided local people into small crews of fifteen households placed under the supervision of a village headman who was responsible for production targets. When peasants who were left behind, especially women, failed to reach production targets, kinsmen and husbands working for European companies were called upon. These temporary workers returned for the safety of their wives and children, who were very often taken as hostages. When they were not taken as hostages, a network of supervisors from diverse social backgrounds watched over them. The practice was widespread in the sphere of operation of Colocoton, where Catholic catechists for whom the company paid head tax supplemented the endeavor of chiefs and village headmen who were enticed to cotton by production premiums in cash. Colocoton itself had numerous itinerant cotton-monitors whose main task was to denounce unmanageable producers.[34] These policies increased the state's ability to enforce work obligations by restricting people's autonomy.

Cotton Producers at Work

Granting cotton concessions and making additional labor policies were only first steps. State intervention to organize work and mobilize men and women at the household level remained the key to the success of the cotton scheme. From the governor-general down to the territorial administrators, everyone believed, at least until 1933, that unlike the plantation system, peasant production was the ideal labor form to shift the costs of production to the households. The territorial administrators expected a possible influx of cash for taxes, and many believed this would increase the standards of living, especially in 1922–29 and after 1945. Among them, a good proportion were quick to protest by the 1930s and later when they saw that the living standards of cotton producers did not increase. This led to protest by the governor-general and a speech by the Prince of Brabant in Parliament.

In practice, the system did shift the costs to households. First, by a decree of July 1914, the notion of *homme adulte valide*, meaning "healthy adult male," became a unit of labor for all industry, labor, and taxation. This constructed administrative category and semantic distortion hid the central role of women and children in cotton cultivation. In fact, Belgian economic planners, seeking to avoid condemnation by critics who opposed the use of child labor and the exploitation of rural women in forced commodity production in general and the cotton cultivation in particular, used the notion of healthy adult male to make their opponents think that the male head of the household was the only person in the household to grow the crop. This manipulation, as I shall show in chapter 4, established the liaison between a male head of the household and the local administration, heightened his power, determined the distribution of cotton money, and kept women behind the scene. Second, because the global colonial economy relied on an estimated nine million people who were difficult to reach, the administration applied a wide range of labor policies which turned most Africans into migrant laborers or peasants, without allowing them to pursue other ways of making a living. Third, as customary law was created between local chiefs or elders and agents of the territorial and judicial administration after 1912 and mostly from 1920 onward, local African leaders succeeded in creating customs which led to the appropriation of unpaid labor for collective public work on the chiefs' cotton plots. Moreover, the polygyny of these same leaders increased at first, making them more affluent. In the south, brideservice had been confined to food crops but now extended to cotton growing as well. Finally, territorial administrators and company managers opposed the mechanization of production on the ground that its costs were prohibitive. They became convinced of this when a technical study carried out in 1926 concluded that a 1-hectare plot could cost over 120 francs, an expense they deemed too high to shoulder.[35]

Despite differences in pace and in methods for incorporating the local population into the cotton scheme, and despite the removal of women from official statistics of production, cotton cultivation was based on the use of household labor that was organized into three units: unmarried cultivators, and monogynous and polygynous conjugal households. To each productive unit, government agronomists allotted a plot of a specified size and imposed a rigid work calendar that set planting, seeding, weeding, and harvesting dates and showed the care to be given to the crop. Usually, territorial administrators stressed that the plot should be small when an area was newly incorporated into the scheme, and that the size be gradually extended as peasants became more involved in production. In 1919, for example, peasants cultivated only 3 ares; this rose to 50 ares in 1931, and it reached over 1 hectare during the Second World War in such areas as Buta and Bambesa.[36]

The unmarried cultivators relied on their own labor to produce cotton. However, evidence indicates that during peak labor periods, they sought supplementary labor. Until 1945, state agronomists allotted plots of equal size to unmarried peasants, and monogynous and polygynous conjugal households. This apparently egalitarian allocation based on the healthy adult male made unmarried peasants the most burdened group of cotton producers. They were, in the words of P. Tschoffen, "wretched men who cultivated cotton and traveled themselves in order to sell their cotton."[37] Because statistics based on healthy adult males omitted women, cotton fields maintained by single women were not listed. Yet a careful reading of the colonial records reveals that single females and widows labored in cotton fields. A production survey conducted by Lesage in 1943 in Kabinda shows that there were single women who intercropped cotton with manioc and maize, and that their plots were as large as those of single males.[38] This situation was not the result of war efforts. In the Sankuru district, records indicate that at the beginning of cotton cultivation both Tetela women and men cultivated separate cotton fields, the former growing a 3-are plot, the latter a 6-are plot.[39] In the polygynous conjugal household, each wife worked her corner with or without her older children. The husband alternately worked the plot of each wife. Within the monogynous household, wife and husband worked the plot together. However, "working together" was far from meaning that each did an equal share of agricultural work, as I explain in chapter 4.

The actual workdays required to cultivate these plots varied considerably, depending on the nature of the ecology. In the forest, a 1-hectare plot required between 154 and 210 workdays. In the savanna the time increased, fluctuating between 172 and 241. There were variations in agronomists' reports about the workdays spent on producing cotton. The annual agricultural report of the Uele-Nepoko district for 1930 provides the workdays required to cultivate a 1-hectare plot, which varied between 590 and 640 workdays in the primary forest and between 405 and 445 in the secondary forest. However, the report provides estimates ranging from 120 to 210 in matete savanna, 100 to 130 in prairie, and 190 to 225 in bush savanna. Averages derived from figures provided by the Department of Agriculture accommodate these regional variations and stand at 237, 209, and 184 workdays for forest, fallow land, and savanna, respectively. Official records remain silent about how many hours peasants worked per day on their plots. G. Malengreau has estimated that these were five-hour workdays, although they were unevenly spread over the cotton cycle, as the following section shows.[40]

Work and Daily Life

The colonial hidden agenda identified work in the fields with control of the fabric of daily life. Most former cotton cultivators agreed that although they did not work twenty-four hours a day and though the actual workdays they spent on cotton cultivation were uneven, the nine months of the cotton cycle structured the rhythm of their activities and daily lives. These peasants were tied to their work, from clearing the land to marketing, including hoeing, seeding, thinning out, seeding, harvesting, cutting off, gathering and burning bush, and carrying cotton to the trading posts. Analytically, I have kept these work phases separate, but in reality they very often overlapped, causing labor bottlenecks. In the northern cotton-growing area, clearing the land was the first stage in the cotton cycle. It stretched from January to April and involved clearing the bushwood, felling trees, and burning slashes. Estimates of workdays required to clear a 1-hectare plot varied from 105 to 130 in the primary forest, 100 to 120 in the secondary forest, 80 to 90 in eight-year fallow lands, and 60 in bush savanna.[41] In most cotton-growing societies, clearing land was considered men's work. Two interrelated factors help explain the absence of women in this work. First, clearing land coincided with cotton harvesting, which started in mid-December, intensified in January–February, and ended in April. Second, because clearing land was a difficult and dangerous activity and because an enduring cultural belief associated strength and hardness with men and "soft work" with women, harvesting cotton became a woman's task, while clearing land became a man's. This belief was validated by poor technology, which convinced territorial administrators that women should be excluded from clearing the land. Felling heavy trees with axes was such harsh and dangerous work that a government agronomist, who observed cotton cultivators clearing the land in Maniema

Fig. 1.3. Peasants clearing the land after 1920

said, "it makes one's heart bleed to see those poor Blacks chopping giant primary forest trees with blunt axes, spending hours to fell one tree, a work which can be done by a single machine."[42] Thus, the overlapping of two types of work and the continued use of rudimentary tools perpetuated the gender division of labor (see Figures 1.3 and 1.4).

Hoeing began in April, continued in June, and ended by August 20. It included the preparation and breaking up of the soil and grassland, and the making of furrows. Hoeing also involved stalking, which indicated the spacing of the plants in the rows. Peasants hoed much of their fields in June and August, and a 1-hectare plot of cotton required up to ten days of labor, which made hoeing relatively light work, though it was intertwined with seeding, thinning, and weeding. Women started seeding in June and ended by August 20. This involved making seed holes and putting seeds into them. "When the plants grew, they uprooted some because there must be one plant in each hole."[43] Generally, cotton producers needed twenty workdays to seed a one-hectare plot. The maintenance of these fields stretched from August to November, and included the first weeding after nine weeks, the second one after fourteen or fifteen weeks, and additional thinning out, transplanting,

Fig. 1.4. Peasants sorting their cotton

and earthing up. Weeding was so important that a colonial rule stressed that "a cotton field must be like a [flower] garden" and that "if there were a couple of weeds on the field, you were jailed. You must weed so the plants get fresh air, otherwise you are in trouble."[44] Whenever pests and boll-worms attacked the plants, peasants spent a great deal of time picking and killing them. After 1945 fertilizer (trisupersphosphates) was used in the area of the Babua people, which required another three workdays. To maintain the fields, the household worked between forty and sixty-five days.[45]

When they were not busy clearing the land, male cultivators harvested cotton, but this task remained primarily the work of women and children. It included picking, drying, and sorting cotton, and most important, transporting it to the trading posts. Agricultural officers established sixty workdays as necessary for this work, but these figures were underestimated because officials discounted the participation of women and children in cotton agriculture. E. Dejong, a noted cotton agronomist who worked mostly in experimental stations where women were not involved, recorded that "the harvest, the longest operation in growing cotton, must be done without respite between three and four months."[46] In addition to the fact that it spread over long months, the cotton harvest could not be postponed and followed a schedule of three sale sessions that regulated peasant activities and the rhythms of their lives more than other tasks (see Figures 1.5 and 1.6):

Fig. 1.5. Peasants carrying cotton to the market

The frequency of the cotton market, set in such a way as to facili-
tate the sales in specified dates and stations . . . forms an obligation
for the native to travel at fixed dates in order to sell his cotton and
this regularity does not meet his sympathy. In fact, the native who,
every three or four weeks has to go to a cotton marketplace to sell
his cotton remains tied to his village between three and four months
of dry season, the most favorable time for hunting, fishing, and
long trips.[47]

In contrast to a twisted notion that "to pick cotton one needed only
to have a basket, to hold it and begin to harvest; and once the basket is
full, to go to pile it somewhere," harvesting cotton was an intensive
and painful activity due to the hot climate and the army of flies flitting
around the ears.[48] It needed to be sorted, dried, and put in baskets,
which had to be ready. All this required sixteen workdays per hectare.
Furthermore, harvesting cotton did not fall outside the typical tyranny
of forced cotton cultivation. Cotonco's letter to Ngbandi peasants is
telling; it asserted that peasants must never pick cotton before nine in
the morning, that they must remove lint without pulling up capsules,
because this would mix debris with lint, that they must put good lint in
one basket and the yellow lint in another, and that they must dry the
lint for three to five days.[49]

Sorting cotton was an important task because it determined the
quality of the produce and its competitiveness on the world market. For
African cotton growers, this meant long hours of painful care. The most
valid evidence of this is that the colonial cotton was always highly

Fig. 1.6. Peasants waiting to sell their cotton

classified and graded. Between 1946 and 1949, for example, 54 to 77 percent of the colonial cotton was classified middling fair, strict good middling, and good middling. In 1952, when 1, 50, and 49 percent of the American cotton was graded strict good middling, middling, and low middling, respectively, 80 and 10 percent of colonial output was graded strict good middling and middling, respectively, while the remaining 10 percent was classified low middling. As late as 1957, 75 to 85 percent of colonial cotton was classified as middling fair.[50] The grades the colonial cotton received on the world market expand our understanding of the hard treatment that cotton cultivators received when they brought badly sorted cotton to the market.[51]

Transporting cotton was the most hated of the phases of agricultural work because it dislocated domestic obligations, especially for peasants located far from communication lines and the markets. General Governor P. Ryckmans, addressing the members of the Orientale Province Council in 1936, said that, "from twenty kilometers [to the market] cotton cultivators needed almost as many days to carry their cotton to the trading posts as to produce it."[52] A. Bertrand observed that "for carrying cotton, no average labor days can be proposed."[53] Though these considerations may seem exaggerated, they strongly suggest that each season forced peasants to undergo harsh and long journeys.[54]

Apparently, December was the only month when northern peasants were not in the fields. Yet there was no leisure time, because they spent the month preparing for the harvest by making the mats and baskets needed to dry and transport cotton. An extra week was needed to uproot the plants and burn them after the harvest.

Peasants in the south performed the same work routines. From January to March, peasants seeded, weeded, uprooted the unneeded plants, and propped up the plants. In April and May, they performed additional weeding, collected leaf-eating insects, and made baskets and mats for drying cotton. Harvesting and marketing sessions stretched from June to September, and this phase coincided with the clearing of the land, which included either felling trees on forested land or burning grasses in the savanna. It also involved burning woods and hoeing, cutting and burning bush—work which extended to October.[55] The number of the days women and men worked varied greatly, depending on the ecology and vegetation.[56] As in the north, cotton production in the south displaced domestic obligations: there were long walks, and at times there were food shortages. As an extreme example, at the beginning of cotton cultivation in Malonga, Cokwe peasants traveled over 100 kilometers to sell some 20 kilograms of cotton; later, however they traveled only half that distance to get to a marketplace. A single trip in 1928 kept Cokwe cotton cultivators away for ten days to sell the remainder of the cotton. In 1939, these cotton cultivators still needed three days to reach the markets.[57] These walks had negative effects on people's daily lives. The harvest and carrying of cotton, as indicated earlier, were women's tasks and coincided with the dry season, the most favorable time for hunting, fishing, and collecting edible caterpillars. Fragmentary evidence suggests that these journeys not only reduced meat and fish supplies, but also affected child care as mothers stayed away to sell cotton. An agent observed that "preparing a cotton plot, seeding, weeding, harvesting, and transporting cotton to a marketplace tie the native to the village for a long period—ten to eleven months— and do not allow him to be absent for fishing, hunting, attending palaver, and visiting parents or friends for a long time anymore."[58]

In addition to working their fields, cotton producers worked chiefs' plots. Wherever group work on chiefs' fields was maintained, it was organized in basically the same way. "A date was set when everybody in the village was to go and do the work. Men cleared the land and prepared the soil. Women made holes, seeded, weeded, and harvested the crop. Usually one work-week produced a huge field."[59] Collective work on chiefs' cotton fields burdened peasants and was part of the "colonial negotiation." In order to involve the chiefs, they had to be motivated by the premiums and by having the corvée work for them (by the invention of the customary law). The cotton companies and their allies in government did not dream of transforming local chiefs into plantation owners; they merely wanted them to combine their moral authority with the new administrative power to tap the labor of their subjects. Hence, the chiefs appropriated a portion of the colletive labor for the cotton economy.

Outside the circle of African chiefs, no other group of the African population drew upon unpaid or hired labor for growing cotton. In fact, since every healthy adult male had to plant cotton, hired labor was not available. Catholic catechists seemed to be the only known African collaborators who drew on unpaid labor by illegally using the labor of school children, as well as that of men and women who received religious instruction under them. In 1936, the Dungu report, for example, raised suspicions that parents withdrew their children from schools because they were abused by these missionary collaborators in their chapel farm.[60] Because peasants were split between competing labor demands, they faced labor conflicts, to which I shall now turn.

Overcoming the Labor Bottlenecks

Cotton cultivation generated labor bottlenecks. We have seen before that single women at Kabinda in 1943 intercropped cotton with food crops. Such intercropping was normally forbidden. The *Encyclopédie du Congo belge* stipulated : "Until now [1951] cotton propaganda does not tolerate intercropping as in Uganda. However, experiments are being conducted."[61] In addition to their cotton fields, peasants cultivated food crops. Cotton fields were often located far from the food fields because the land chosen for cotton was to be cultivated in blocks—if possible near a road, and not necessarily close to food farms.[62] This meant additional work. Peasants also provided labor for "public works." These conflicting work demands interfered with cotton production; every household's labor pool shrank, and all peasants faced seasonal labor bottlenecks. One territorial administrator observed that "peasants were short of time for enjoyable activities like dances."[63] Another said that "peasants no longer had time for visiting and attending palaver, which were previously important aspects of their community life."[64] A former Abarambo cotton producer from Poko recalled, "We had little control over our lives; we belonged to them [the state, cotton companies]. We had no rest. We were very often called upon by the physician and the nurses for physical examination. Then, there was the agricultural monitor. This man asked us to show him the crops. There was also the administrator who took the censuses and collected taxes. You cannot be free if the agronomist has not passed yet through the village to show the new ways of cultivating cotton. By the time we wanted to rest a bit, the chief called upon us to work either on his fields or on public projects without pay."[65]

Households faced two peak labor periods: the time of clearing and harvesting, and the time of weeding. Labor bottlenecks occurred in both periods, but they were particularly acute during clearing and harvesting, as the two tasks occurred simultaneously. Coping strategies to alleviate these labor constraints varied according to gender, household composition, and economic differentiation, and these strategies unevenly affected the work loads of household members. In resource-poor monogynous conjugal households and widow-headed households, women circumvented monocropping by interspersing cotton with vegetables or food crops to avoid food insecurity. Well-off households used limited festive labor, while chiefs and elders resorted to unpaid collective labor. Unmarried cotton cultivators driven into cotton cultivation coped with labor bottlenecks in two ways. At the beginning of the cotton scheme, unmarried peasants called upon the collective labor of kinfolk. In reality, single cultivators did not have much more trouble than monogynous and polygynous conjugal households in clearing land. However, because clearing and harvesting overlapped, this bottleneck hit them severely. To be sure, the system offered them a few options. Everywhere, not just in cotton-growing areas, every *homme adulte valide*, an able-bodied person between the ages of fifteen and fifty, was registered; the ages were guessed, and hence bribery was possible to exclude men as too young, too old, or the contrary. The structure of repression hid behind the system and left little room for acts of defiance which could lead to a complete escape from the system of forced cotton cultivation.[66] The system, therefore, restricted the choices of unmarried producers because it precluded the hiring of workers and whoever failed to cultivate cotton was jailed, flogged and fined.

The most feasible alternative for single cultivators was to call upon kinship networks for help. A vast body of evidence I collected among the Hemba of the Tanganyika district in Katanga, where the Compagnie Cotonnière du Tanganyika was granted concessions from 1933 onward, shows that elders helped kinsmen avoid punishment by calling upon their kins to work the plot of a kinsman which would not otherwise be ready when an agronomist, a crop supervisor, or a cotton-monitor would pass through the village.[67] This ad hoc cooperative labor did not initially require equal and reciprocal compensation. Cooperative workers were volunteers, drawn to work by kinship ties, who only expected some food and drink as compensation. The changing economic context transformed the meaning of this family-based collective labor, and attendance at group work increasingly required additional compensation. Kinship ties still entitled anybody to call upon traditional communal work, but the remuneration expected for it—cash, chicken, goats, and calabashes of beer—was lacking in most families.[68] Therefore, to cope with labor bottlenecks, unmarried cotton cultivators, especially new ones, sought wives who would share the workload, but such marriages of young men to women who would share agricultural work in order to cope with labor shortages remained a limited option.

The expansion of cotton required macro-level strategies, including the use of crop rotations and high-yielding varieties of cotton. Devising these macro-level solutions to cope with labor constraints and avoid food shortages became a priority in 1933, when the state created the Institut National pour l'Etude Agronomique au Congo (INEAC). Among other things, this agricultural research institute focused on cotton selection and breeding, intercropping, crop rotation, and high-yielding cotton varieties. To carry out these tasks, which had been done by the state laboratories before INEAC was founded, the institute took over existing central agricultural research stations. The Bambesa station, located in the forests of the northern cotton-growing area, and the Ngandajika station, located in the savanna to the south, provided new varieties of cotton and plans for crop rotation that saved a great deal of labor and made the scheme attractive to peasants. By 1943, the Triumph Big Boll variety, whose output per hectare had continuously declined in the north, was replaced by Stonville, a high-yielding variety. Research in Ngandajika produced similar results; here, high-yielding Gar and C2 replaced Allen Long Staple and Triumph in the Tanganyika and Lomami districts.[69] These higher-yielding varieties helped reduce the size of household plots without decreasing the output. In addition to developing higher-yielding varieties of cotton, INEAC research stations provided typical crop rotation plans that served purposes. Some of these rotations reduced food insecurity by deflecting the competition of cotton with food without undermining the dominance of cotton over other crops. The Doruma crop rotation plan designed in 1927 is a case in point. Trying to preserve the Azande diet based on labor-intensive millet and eleusine, agricultural officers imposed a crop rotation based on a three-year cycle. Obviously, the objective was to free the household from annually clearing the land for these labor-intensive food crops that competed with cotton.[70] Crop rotation plans were not successful everywhere. The state agronomists established the crucial rule that "cotton always comes first" because it is very demanding and it greatly impoverishes the soil. Any food crops, such as maize and groundnuts, that follow cotton will not give a good yield, and it was about this that the people of Ubangi seem to have rebelled the most. Often, the administration either encouraged peasants to grow only a few day and labor-saving crops or phased out labor-intensive crops. The Azande producers, for example, abandoned eleusine and millet, even though missionaries and territorial administrators acknowledged that these crops were important for infants' nutrition.

The conclusion emerging from this discussion is that macro-level coping mechanisms to overcome labor bottlenecks created a rigid gender inequality, as we will see in chapter 4. Collective labor used for clearing the land, a man's task, reduced male loads; weeding and harvesting, which were female tasks, did not benefit from collective labor. Although Alur women organized transport in rotation to carry cotton to the markets, they gained only moral support and pleasurable companionship in enduring the harshness of the journey, since the amount of work remained the same. Similarly, crop rotations freed men from clearing land yearly because the plans stressed multi-year use of plots; however, the plans tied women to the cotton and food fields, since prolonged use of the same plot encouraged the proliferation of weeds, whose cutting remained a woman's task.

Cotton Cultivation and Food

The season calendars explained earlier showed an overlap of work for women in the weeding, harvest, and postharvest operations. This had an effect on food and nutrition. First, overburdened women could no longer maintain or gather small crops, nor could men hunt, fish, and gather. This meant a loss of protein, vitamins, and minerals in the diet, which came close to causing malnutrition in some areas.[71] Thus both food and nutritional quality declined. Women at least tried to produce the bulk of the food needed. They concentrated on a few staples, but soon grew only manioc, which is primarily carbohydrates. Even the use of manioc leaves as vegetables added only a few vitamins and minerals. Thus, although there was food in bulk, it could not meet the nutritional needs of cotton producers, as confirmed by studies of physical anthropology.

Kanda-Kanda was one area where cotton cultivation severely affected food and nutrition. In October 1936 the colonial administration, overwhelmed by numerous reports about malnutrition among cotton producers, asked the state agronomist Corbion to investigate the food crisis there, especially in the Bakwa-Kalondji chiefdom. After a careful investigation, Corbion concluded, "The natives of the territory have but absolutely insufficient quantities of food, and notably cereals are entirely lacking." On October 12, 1936, Dr. Muller was asked to examine the food supply in the same region. His findings supported Corbion's conclusion, showing that "among the Bakwa-Kalondji, . . . food supplies are becoming less and less abundant as mandatory cotton cultivation expands. We have the impression that the situation will worsen and that famine in the area will set in permanently. The natives are realizing this but they cannot convince those who benefit from stabilization and the quick enrichment brought by cotton cultivation."[72]

As late as 1944 the members of the Conseil de Province d'Elisabethville acknowledged that "peasants no longer had time for hunting."[73] Although game was not previously a sufficient source of protein, its elimination from the domestic food supply made the lack of meat acute. Dupont, the district assistant of the Uele district, inspected the Dungu area in 1953 and concluded that "most Azande people have the same living standards as the one they had twenty years ago. . . . They are undernourished and continue to vegetate. . . . The only and hardly visible progress one can see is some affluence due to the high prices of crops, notably cotton."[74] Further evidence is provided by the *Rapport d'inspection* for the same period, which pointed to the malnutrition of the same Azande cotton producers.[75]

Paysannats and Cotton Production, 1947–1959

The paysannats started in 1933 after the Prince de Brabant speech, and the scheme was linked to the foundation of the INEAC. The goals of this new "development" scheme were on the one hand to create a prosperous African farming middle-class involving individual farms and land ownership, and on the other hand to raise exports while keeping production costs as low as possible. The system began slowly. Blocks of land were discussed, and rotations had to be studied by the INEAC. The idea was to use mechanized cultivation of fields in blocks of several hectares where peasants were to apply a variety of crop rotations and to use fertilizers and insecticides on whatever crops were planted.

Until World War II, concessions remained the agricultural model for involving peasants in cotton cultivation. Although in 1943 a paysannat operated in the Sankuru district, it was only after the war that the system expanded, and paysannats and cotton cooperatives operated in Uele, Kasai, Lomami, and Tanganyika.[76] These paysannats were predominantly located within cotton-producing regions, where the research stations were, and they were intended to raise living standards in order to halt outmigrations from cotton zones.[77]

Central to the scheme were crop rotations. These rotations were not new, but there was a shift in emphasis. Generally, earlier crop rotations integrated food crops into the production cycle to avoid food shortages. In the Ubangi district, most Ngbaka, but mainly Ngbandi peasants and all others were encouraged to grow maize alone or in association with squash at the beginning of the rotation; after they had harvested cotton, peasants were allowed to grow staples. Actually, they were obliged to plant manioc and plantain.[78] From 1947 to 1959, the paysannat introduced new crop rotations whose objective was not only to increase food production for household needs but to increase cash crop production that would supplement peasants' earnings from cotton. The crop rotation applied in the Kanda-Kanda area indicates that cotton still benefited from most soil nutrients during the first two years in the cycle and was followed by a few day staples. At the end of the cycle, women grew manioc. Peasants in the Kabinda paysannat rotated cotton with corn, beans, manioc, and other crops; cotton contributed 12 percent to the household income.[79]

Conclusion: Cotton, Work, and Peasant Autonomy

Table 1.4 throws a great deal of light on the dynamics of the cotton scheme. From 1917 to 1930, the objectives were to incorporate new districts and more people into the scheme and increase the land under cultivation, which yielded a corresponding increased output. In 1931, the number of producers increased by seven times but not the acreage, which did not increase by that much until 1939. The decline of production in 1932 was caused by (1) the suppression of cotton zones located far from the communication lines; (2) a drop in prices; (3) plant diseases; (4) and the closing of a great number of trading posts, forcing the cotton cultivators to travel long distances, specially for those in Orientale Province. The smaller increase in output by 1937 shows increasing inefficiencies. The highest labor input ever was in 1940 with no change in acreage from that of 1935 and a rise in output of almost twice the increase from 1917 to 1935. After that, there was a loss of labor (to 600,000) until 1947, no doubt because the war effort "used" people elsewhere for mandatory rubber collection and food production, and there was conscription of peasants to serve as carriers in the *Force Publique*, in addition to peasant migration. Furthermore, the state preyed on the remaining agricultural population by recruiting labor for mines and strategic work as part of the war effort. The reduction of European personnel loosened social control at the point of production. Acreage peaked in 1943 because of mechanization in the major paysannats, such as Buta and Ngandajika. Output reached a peak in 1941 and then began to oscillate because of a fall in prices, the severity of the buyers regarding the quality of cotton, and an unfavorable climate. After 1946, normality returned: labor jumped in 1951, then increased slowly until 1955, the plateau, and jumped again in 1959; acreage advanced more or less in line with jumps in 1952 and 1959. After World War II output did not increase any longer with acreage but oscillated, climbing to a 1952 peak, falling in 1953, and climbing again to a peak in 1956. There was a loss in 1957–1958 and an absolute peak in 1959 in line with a jump in households and a peak in acreage. Oscillations in output may be related to weather, but also certainly to an increase in yield per acre and to mechanization. From 1951 to 1959, the number of households, the area under cultivation, and the total output did not decrease significantly as the paysannats raised living standards when coercion was no longer possible, especially in disturbed Kasai, which attracted more farmers.

In the preceding discussion of the labor process, I have focused on the total workdays that African peasants spent in their fields in an attempt to determine the degree of their autonomy. The most important conclusion emerging from the analysis is that colonial economic planners succeeded organizing work in ways that structured and shaped the rhythm of the activities and daily lives of peasants: "People do not have the freedom to act on their own anymore, they find themselves more and more obliged to eliminate from their economic, social, and familial life, pleasure, negligence and lack of foresight. And they increasingly stick to orders . . . and work."[80] The combination of low agricultural technology and the competition of cotton with other crops and employment determined the outcome. Contemporary observations and peasants' voices reflect this. At the end of the war a number of administative officials who had seen an all-out exploitation of the population during the war effort now spoke out against it. Some among them blamed cotton as the root of all evil. Thus the district commissioner of Tanganyika noted:

> Villages are not merely empty because of mine recruitment but because the Black wants to flee. Finding a job among whites is an escape from the birthplace which has become odious. The reason is *cotton* [my emphasis] which the Blacks hate. . . . It tied them so they cannot attend palavers, collect debts, mourn old aunt. . . . When a private employer complains of bad faith, laziness, low yields or desertion, administrators reply "Treat them better, pay more, avoid these difficulties." Yet, government itself employs classic methods of cotton cultivation contrary to this advice: a few weeds in the plot—the whip; a couple of square yards unplanted—a fine . . .

Table 1.4. Cotton growers, outputs, and acreage, 1917–1959

Year	Households	Acreage (hectares)	Outputs (tons of seed cotton)
1917	(few)	112	532
1918	15,000	277	524
1919	—	595	650
1920	—	874	800
1921	15,000	2,241	1,770
1922	—	4,930	3,105
1923	—	5,509	2,610
1924	—	4,603	5,130
1925	—	6,309	9,166
1926	—	10,897	14,938
1927	—	26,006	17,639
1928	—	37,683	20,207
1929	—	48,123	21,755
1930	105,556	49,883	30,600
1931	714,000	67,063	44,822
1932	—	65,166	27,700
1933	714,000	—	46,264
1934	—	—	59,160
1935	—	—	77,781
1936	700,000	342,360	96,105
1937	664,270	342,360	110,454
1938	—	342,360	127,488
1939	800,000	345,585	117,633
1940	905,578	342,360	135,689
1941	700,000	—	141,566
1942	—	345,735	120,442
1943	—	380,553	132,469
1944	775,210	328,559	93,664
1945	—	308,273	113,549
1946	600,000	306,513	122,734
1947	—	—	121,600
1948	317,852	131,100	—
1949	314,402	150,900	—
1950	330,331	147,000	—
1951	784,000	344,987	137,100
1952	826,000	363,421	162,600
1953	847,000	363,491	142,200
1954	833,000	343,618	150,000
1955	835,000	349,208	152,000
1956	820,000	336,977	159,000
1957	823,719	331,472	137,000
1958	828,410	339,409	150,000
1959	874,000	368,000	177,000

Sources: Van Geem, *Etude comparative des législations cotonnières en Afrique équatoriale* (Brussels: Comité Cotonnier Congolais, 1934), 11; "Agri (128)," "(374) 13," "Dossier coton C 25," A. A., Brussels; *Bulletin de la banque du Congo* belge et du Ruanda-Urundi (June

Cotton pulverizes native custom. . . . In compulsory planting all risks are borne by the Blacks: drought, ravages, caterpillars, locusts, flood, barren soils, world price fluctuations, everything is against our savage. . . . Yet the Black must subsist . . . millet, sweet potatoes, oil palms, beans, tobacco all require further labor. . . . And what about fishing and hunting, for our man cannot live on cassava and peanuts alone?[81]

The chairman of the Katanga Province Council for 1944 struck a similar chord. At the annual meeting for that year, he explained the effect of cotton cultivation on peasants' autonomy while pointing out that

Cotton's first place at the head of the agricultural cycle is not sufficient to explain why cotton is in disfavor. . . . Because cultivating cotton is particularly demanding, it gives to the native the impression that he is prevented free movement during long months every year. We must avoid any exaggeration while imposing cotton. At this point, we must pay much attention to the qualitative progress of the crop and to the imposition of optimal acreage which assures substantial revenues for a normal effort. Everywhere, cotton is out of people's favor, because during 10 to 11 months of the year, it is a hindrance to them.[82]

Thus, poor technology, the total colonial demands, and household obligations determined the capacity of peasants to work.[83] The quantification of workdays is important because it highlights the degree of autonomy; nevertheless, it cannot entirely explain the quality of daily life. First, labor days did not spread evenly over successive stages of the agricultural cycle. There were stages when the peasants faced labor bottlenecks and had to ignore socioeconomic activities that were instrumental to normal functioning of the household. The degree of intrusion of agricultural work into peasants' lives therefore varied periodically. It was also affected by other production requirements. Households

---

1947): 26; 8 (1948): 78; 7–8 (1952): 33; 7–8 (1953): 29; *Etudes sur le marché de certains produits congolais* (1947): 54; (1948): 57; (1948): 57; (1949): 71; (1950): 78; (1951): 78; (1960): 87; J. Bivot, "La politique des transports," 29; E. Leplae, "De l'influence des cultures de coton par les indigènes sur le développement des régions cotonnières," *Congo* 7 (1927); E. H. J. Stoffels, "Les grandes étapes de l'agriculture," 842; A. Landeghem, "1921–1936," 3; *Rapports annuels, 1939–44*, 208; L. Banneux, "Quelques données économiques," 27; "Documentation sur le coton au Congo belge," A. A., Brussels. 7; E. Leplae, "Transformation de l'agriculture indigène au Congo belge par les cultures obligatoires," *Technique agricole internationale* 6, no. 2 (1936): 111; E. Leplae, "Comment les indigènes du Congo belge . . .," 176; *Mouvement géographique*, no. 22, 1919, coll. 258; E. Leplae, "La culture du coton au Congo belge, 1915–1919," *Bulletin agricole du Congo belge* 11, nos. 1–2 (1920): 99; *Rapport annuel sur l'administration du Congo belge*, 1932, 79, 197; 1931, 79.

needed to produce, in addition to cotton, at least groundnuts, millet, eleusine, maize, and usually manioc. These workdays represented, to a certain extent, what the territorial administrators and agronomists deemed normal agricultural workloads for peasants, but not always the actual work that producers performed, because cotton-monitors, government agricultural monitors working in cotton zones, very often assigned cotton plots much larger than the legally stated acreage. Second, cotton cultivation did not burden all peasants in the same way or to the same degree. Single, polygynous, and monogynous male and female cotton cultivators experienced different ranges of autonomy. Wives in monogynous conjugal units found themselves overburdened compared to those in complex conjugal units. Whereas the heads of the households, whose supply of female and child labor was guaranteed by the colonial semantic distortion and the perpetuation of the unequal division of labor enjoyed leisure time, unmarried cultivators toiled alone, or occasionally with kin, making them the most burdened group of cotton producers.

2

Forced Cotton Production and Social Control

Introduction

In the past two decades, researchers have demonstrated the extent to which growing crops under colonialism was based on policies and practices that resulted in extreme brutalization of local populations.[1] Whatever role the African police, state-appointed chiefs, and colonial armies had in forcing peasants to follow agricultural instructions, they were only one facet of a wide range of colonial mechanisms of social control. Force, as B. Lincoln aptly put it, "remains something of a stopgap measure: effective in the short run, unworkable over the long haul."[2] This was certainly relevant in regard to forced cotton production in colonial Zaire.

In this chapter I argue that to carry out cotton cropping successfully, the colonial state and cotton companies imposed a system of social control involving not only the threat and use of force, but also structural reforms, material incentives, and propaganda. As allies, the colonial state and its cotton companies sought to "manufacture" docile peasants who would create labor time from an imagined surplus of leisure time, divert labor from the food economy, and bow to a variety of overseers entrusted with the mission of enforcing agricultural instructions. Between 1917 and 1935, the objective was to force peasants to accept economic exploitation. Beatings, fines, and prisons were used to expand the cotton economy in almost every region that offered any prospect of growing cotton. From 1936 to 1957, however, the overreaching concern became an attempt to control the rhythm of peasants' daily lives, minimize dissent, and maximize output. Structural reforms, handouts, and propaganda or entertainment became part of a program intended to shape peasants' perception of their self-interest and create a new work ethic. For all its effort to rationalize the system of social control and win over the hearts and minds of peasants, the state was not entirely successful. Regardless of the handouts and persuasion, skeptical peasants understood the meaning of the exploitation permeating their daily lives and measured it by the buying power of the prices they received and the improvement of their standard of living. The daily control of their lives highlighted their lack of self-determination, however, and was universally perceived as an intolerable humiliation. During the last two effective years of the colonial regime (1957 to 1959), this led to a system that combined coercion with incentives.

Force and Social Control, 1917–1935

It is not an intellectual development that brings our indigenous people to share our ideas and conform to our moral principles. The driving principle of life remains the law of the strongest. They submitted after they experienced our superiority. They remain disciplined because they have been firmly convinced of our force.[3]

Creating a servile labor force proved a complex and difficult process for the colonial administration. First, it involved reaching a relatively small number of cultivators scattered over a large area. Those forcibly incorporated into the system had to be carefully supervised. Though company and state agents worked together, as late as 1951 each agent still had to supervise between 3,000 and 6,000 cotton cultivators.[4] Second, the difficulty of supervising a large number of peasants was compounded by the nature of the environment, the state of the physical and administrative infrastructure, and the patterns of land use. Third, cotton production competed with peasant food production, which often offered higher prices. Fourth, taxation proved noncoercive because peasants often collected at low costs products whose prices allowed them to pay their taxes. Finally, agronomists shared the belief that Africans were a drag on commodity production. These factors convinced officials that force alone could make peasants decide to produce cotton.

Though social control varied from region to region between 1917 and 1935, the threat and use of force remained the defining feature of the cotton economy. Naive colonial economic planners thought at first that when male and female cotton cultivators were preoccupied with the required fieldwork, they were distracted from thinking of their plight. As the Council of Katanga Province explained as late as 1945,

"When the people are busy, they talk very little."[5] After 1945, however, the main argument of planners was that cotton cultivation would allow Africans to become self-sufficient farmers who would be satisfied as they benefited from rising standards of living. This reasoning resulted in a range of policies and practices that deprived peasants of physical mobility and kept them working. In 1917, at the very beginning of cotton cultivation, the state decreed that territorial administrators could prohibit peasants from dispersing and settling within the remotest parts of their chiefdoms. From about 1920, policemen began to patrol villages regularly and sometimes forbade people in some territories from playing cards, drinking beer, and traveling.[6] Travel had been forbidden outside the chiefdom since 1910 without a pass. As the following warning illustrates, patrolling people's movement developed into terrorism:

> Policemen must no longer search through the bags of native travellers, planting some hemp in the bag of a woman who refused to have an affair with them some days before, or who refused to sell them, at a depressed price, a bunch of plantains that she went to buy at some distance to feed her family. Women who desire to go through our posts in the evenings, as they have the right to do so, must no longer find a road toll, identical to what Saint Mary the Egyptian asked from the inhabitants of the Nile river, arbitrarily and odiously imposed on them by the policemen.[7]

By the 1920s the colonial presence intruded into every facet of peasants' lives in village communities. Indeed, the official prohibition of night dances and most rituals like Matamba, a dance traditionally associated with the ritual killing ceremony in Luisa, was strictly implemented. From the point of view of the colonial state, rituals, religious activities, and large social gatherings were the sites both of dissipation of energies better devoted to cultivation and of potential "subversion." Some territorial administrators viewed them as the source of what they called "congenital laziness."[8] Leisure and entertainment were believed to decrease productivity.

Unlike colonial northern Nigeria and Malawi, where state power was exercised at the market, colonial Zaire was controlled by the state and cotton companies both at the market and at the point of production. A growing coercive administrative apparatus of agricultural officers, crop supervisors, local chiefs, and (as we shall see) cotton-monitors made this efficient control possible at the point of production.

The use of the *Fiche de contrôle et surveillance* was one mechanism that locked peasants into production. This booklet, issued to each male cotton cultivator, recorded the number of his wives, the amount of seed issued to him each season, annual yields, and his district, territory, chiefdom, and village of residence. Of critical importance were the remarks and observations written down by the administrators, agricultural officers, and personnel from the cotton companies.[9] The latter, who outnumbered state agents in many areas, "travel[ed] up and down villages repeating the order to 'produce and work more.'"[10] They described the extent to which peasants were satisfying production schedules, and aided in establishing the secret list of "offenders" subject to punishment.[11] Furthermore, during buying sessions, the district commissioner instructed the market supervisors to document how much each peasant household produced. This data was added to the peasants' registration booklets and duplicated in special registers which were copied and transmitted to the territorial administrators. Those households which failed to sell sufficient amounts were often subject to retribution. Thus, while receiving minimal remuneration, cotton cultivators provided the regime with the very information it used to control them, at the time they least expected to be watched.[12]

These systems of control and supervision fostered a sort of colonial "penal code" that justified the use of violence against those who, willingly or unwillingly, failed to satisfy the production requirements. The courts in such cases were chiefdoms or sectors courts. This code permitted territorial administrators, agronomists, crop supervisors, chiefs, policemen, and cotton monitors to use force against resisters. Although the 1917 decree establishing the forced cropping system made no provision for penalties against those who failed to grow crops, it did not prevent the territorial administrators from punishing those who refused to follow agricultural instructions. The 1918 legislation which legalized the use of force at the point of production reinforced this punitive power. The state decreed that failure to comply with the colonial law would result in a penalty of seven days of hard labor and a fine of 200 francs. Though a 1933 decree reduced the fine to 100 francs, it still maintained the seven-day prison sentence, thus furthering the legal basis for repression. In 1942, an ordinance replaced the seven-day prison sentence with a one-month prison sentence. Backed by this legislation, cotton supervisors often spread violence into rural communities. For failure to cultivate required crops, the sentence was generally fifteen days in prison and a fine of 100 francs.[13]

This repressive legislation, which supported the actions of officials and their African subordinates, transformed the system of control into a legal means of bringing violence and brutality into peasant communities. Violence became the way of running the day-to-day bureaucracy of economic exploitation. The account of Sumba drastically depicts the use of violence against insubordinate cotton cultivators in Kongolo in the late 1940s:

> Whoever had not finished clearing the land was punished. How? By being whipped on the spot. . . . I saw with my eyes my maternal uncle whipped. . . . His brothers, who were beside him, were very angry. Very angrily they began to say provocative words to excite his anger as well as that of others who underwent the punishment. They effectively excited his anger. He cursed the white man who ended up by slapping him on top of the whipping he received.[14]

Several factors explain the intervention of territorial administrators at the point of cotton production. First, the philosophy that underlay the administrative ethic held that "in Africa, the greatest art for an administrator is not to work so much, but to have people toil, especially the indigenous people."[15] Second, an administrator's promotion depended in part on the agricultural production achieved within his territory; this generated numerous abuses because what mattered to the administrators was "production first, if I do not want trouble."[16] Third, some territorial administrators were on the cotton companies' payrolls, and some hoped to be hired by the cotton companies when they retired from state employment. An article published in *L'informateur,* entitled "Les scandales du Congo: les monopoles en taches d'huile. Sus aux accapareurs!" suggested that this practice was common in 1936. It complained that two cotton companies, Cotonco and Cotanga, were receiving the best cotton zones in the Kabongo area, helped by territorial administrators who were preparing for their retirement: "One favor brings another; and the position of a company administrator is always easily given to a high ranking retired official! This would only be one more familiar person in the house. And this is what one can name an administrator: 'benefice causa.'"[17]

These considerations had a bearing on the way some territorial administrators performed agricultural tasks, winning them a reputation for terror that sometimes echoed the horror of the earlier "red rubber" regime. Writing in 1937, A. Rubbens concluded,

> It has become increasingly evident that the basis of a major part of our economic success in the Belgian Congo is forced labor in the strictest sense of the word. Those who have known the two regimes confirm that our entire administrative personnel is drawn into a kind of blind belief in cotton. As in the past with rubber, an official thinks only of exceeding the results he has obtained in previous

years; if he takes the job for the first time, he would be somehow dishonored if he did not reach previous production levels.[18]

Territorial administrators were not in charge of the implementation of the cotton regime. Officials from the cotton companies, with the assistance of state agronomists, oversaw its implementation. Yet company officials and state agronomists could not implement the cotton regime by themselves. Without African collaborators, their actions would have been ineffective. Their policy was to get the leading members of local communities into the lower colonial administrative positions. These were the agricultural monitors appointed by the state and cotton-monitors appointed by the cotton companies. These agents were trained to impose a rigorous work schedule and to use a wide array of punishments against peasants who failed to perform work obligations. The function of these new agricultural agents, known as agricultural monitors, cotton soldiers *(soldats-coton)*, cotton messengers *(messagers-coton)*, and cotton-monitors *(moniteurs-coton)*, was to stimulate production of cotton and to perpetuate the whole colonial society. The continuous increase in their number indicates their importance. Theoretically, the cotton monitors explained to cotton cultivators how to grow crops and checked to see if they had actually done so. In practice, they forcibly imposed a myriad of tasks that increased cotton output and reinforced the regime of force. Cotton-monitors measured the plots and instructed peasants when to clear and prepare the land, seed, weed, and harvest; they conducted crop and livestock censuses within their circles; and they constantly passed information between high-ranking agricultural officers and peasants.[19] The actual exercise of this latter function caused many to go beyond the law. The agricultural monitors were spies, which made the local situation very conducive to bribery by the local people.

Many of the cotton-monitors were ex-soldiers of the Force Publique, policemen and workers, and they tended to rely on intimidation by the threat of force to enhance production. Very few had formal agricultural training. In 1947, for example, only one agricultural agent out of sixteen was trained. As late as 1957, there were twenty-four untrained agents for each trained agricultural agent, and this ratio marked an increase in the extent of violence. Some allotted plots that were far beyond the legally specified acreage in hectares. The immediate result of this practice was twofold. First, households were unable to provide the required labor, which meant either prison, whipping, and fines or the bribing of the cotton-monitors to avoid such punishments. Second, cotton-monitors became *de facto* policemen. Former soldiers, messengers, and workers started their new careers with "a police mentality and greedy outlook," leading to abuses and scandals. The complaint of a cotton-monitor against a peasant usually resulted in the latter's imprisonment.[20] Court registers for chiefdoms or *secteurs* are replete with cases of cotton-monitors prosecuting cotton cultivators who failed to perform the agricultural work properly. These registers show that cotton-monitors were the force *par excellence* that maintained and extended colonial rule.[21]

Whatever their background, most cotton-monitors used their power to enhance their social and economic positions, and regularly abused their authority by engaging in the rape of female cotton cultivators, bribery, injustice, and brutality. These aspects of social history are not difficult to verify. Oral data and the chiefdoms' court registers, which were also avenues for rural negotiation over what would and would not be accepted by the local population, provide substantial evidence illuminating the misconduct of cotton-monitors. A high magistrate inspecting Dungu's courts in 1934 said, "Gangolenzi, a cotton-monitor takes advantage of the men being in the fields to have affairs with their wives."[22] In 1952, when the state and cotton companies had modified abusive features of the cotton scheme, another magistrate observed that "cotton-monitors' actions, all of us know, are often illegal and iniquitous, and even a bit dishonest."[23] The brutality of cotton-monitors is still vividly remembered by peasants in Doruma: "A refusal to grow cotton? Prison and whipping. We went to work while receiving lashes on our backs. The cotton-monitor was also an administrator. His job: to force us to do the work on the fields; he whipped us. Never were we left alone and free."[24] It also emerges in the following poetic song:

> Hunt, fish and enjoy good food,
> Always remember to dry something for *Matala-tala*'s man,
> Drink and go drunk,
> Always remember *Matala-tala*'s man,
> Whether there is rain or sun, you will seed, you will weed, you will
>   cut old stalks under his eyes,
> If you miss the roll call, you will be on the list of *Matala-tala*'s man,
> The list will make you undress,
> The list will show your hanging scrotum,
> And if you are not lucky, you will see the "red lips."[25]

Territorial administrators, aware of the situation, reduced the role of illiterate cotton-monitors to "harassing 300–400 cultivators within their sectors with continuous orders to work, . . . providing rudimentary technical knowledge . . . and . . . indicating to chiefs cotton cultivators unwilling to grow cotton."[26] In fact, it was the prosecutors, or *greffiers*, who defined the offenses after the judges of the local courts had decided. Hence the powerful position of the *greffiers*, who could also point out to judges things that could be done.

In cotton areas, state and company officials also targeted chiefs who, from the very beginning, played a critical role in forcing their own people to grow cotton. This reliance on chiefs sprang from the belief that "he who has the chief on his side, has also his followers."[27] Agronomists gave chiefs production instructions and seeds, which they transmitted to headmen, who in turn mobilized the cultivators, managed conflict to keep the law and order necessary for production, and supervised the cotton warehouses.[28]

The chiefs' integration into the colonial social ladder had important social and economic consequences. It heightened the segmentation of the countryside by making chiefs a relatively privileged subordinate segment within the colonial social aggregate. In sharp contrast to forced cotton cultivators, chiefs were exempt from taxation and forced labor. As the labor recruiters' collaborators, the chiefs received bonuses from the recruiters and could use recruitment to rid themselves of insubordinate individuals who defied their authority and threatened to ruin their prestige. As production supervisors, chiefs received production premiums; combined with bonuses these premiums fueled economic and social inequality between chiefs and commoners. During the 1930–1931 season, for example, while a cotton-producing household in the Uele-Nepoko district made as little cash as 66.50 francs after taxes, Chief Gilima received 21,000 francs in cotton-production premiums alone.[29] These economic advantages, which enticed chiefs and headmen into cultivation, help explain why the chiefs' attitude toward compulsory cotton cultivation differed from that of peasants. They also explain why these leaders dealt harshly with their own people.

The chiefs' production premiums were proportional to the number of kilograms of cotton brought to the market by their subjects. Thus, the larger the number of cultivators, the greater the potential amount of reward. As chiefs and headmen could not increase the population density in their circles, the only way they could augment revenue was to force people to increase production. Their tactics generated a great deal of hostility. By the 1940s, peasants in the Lomami district would sing the following lyrics: "White man does not have anything to do with us; the worst person is the chief. White man does not know what we were doing; it was the headman who told them to chase us."[30]

Formal state policy supported the territorial administrators, chiefs, headmen, and cotton-monitors, using native courts, policemen, and the Force Publique to instill fear, compel obedience, and expand the cotton cash economy. The colonial metaphor for local tribunals was *véritable machine à punir,* "a real machine for punishment." Initially the tribunals were created in 1926 to settle conflicts between Africans, but colonial officials as well as African leaders gave them punitive power. Along with fines, whipping, and prison, native courts formed a structure capable of countering open resistance to forced cotton cultivation. The local courts became the incarnation of repression. As the Council of Orientale Province explained in 1955:

> The practice has demonstrated that local courts already played a predominantly repressive role. To generalize the capacity of these local courts to enforce the T.O.E, [educative works] is going to intensify their repressive character. And we must fear the abuses. Local courts already work under the influence and authority of the agricultural agent, the territorial administrator, the missionary, and the agent of Cotonco. Local courts have become institutions of repression instead of being institutions designed to settle family matters.[31]

Using the local courts, territorial administrators, agronomists, chiefs, and cotton-monitors prosecuted men, women, and even children who were unwilling to show their cotton fields to policemen and quarrelled with them instead. They also prosecuted those who threatened cotton-monitors, refused to harvest cotton, or bypassed the prescribed market. They also used harsh methods against men and women who reduced the specified size of their plots. The definition of crimes, offenses, and penalties was left to the whim of the prosecutors. The consequences were beneficial for the extension of cotton, but ravaged peasant communities: a couple of weeds in the field could be punished with a whip. A couple of cotton plants not lined up led to a fine. Late seeding could mean months of prison.[32]

Imprisonment was surrounded with many myths to frighten peasants. The oppressive nature of a colonial prison extended beyond its physical boundaries and affected the psychology of rural populations. Convicted peasants were often brought to prisons in chains with their arms bound behind them, suggesting they were reduced to impotence that could be overcome only by removing the attitudes that kept them from adjusting to colonial society.[33] Prisons meant physical suffering and a hostile environment, and were built to house outlaws whose view of the world was to be reshaped to fit colonial economic exploitation. They incarnated the structure of oppression. In addition to being whipped, prisoners performed a broad range of forced labor. In Dungu Prison, especially in 1933, prisoners mostly cut firewood for colonial officials.[34] Mugaza wa Beya's life history sheds a great deal of light on the nature of colonial prisons. He described his experience in Kalemie prison, the main prison of the Tanganyika district:

> Every morning, we were split up and each person was assigned a task. Kalemie was [a] . . . very bad jail. [We had] to fetch water in Lake Tanganyika in half a barrel and pour it into pans for governmental officers. . . .
>
> At times, they asked me to do different work. I was a bit lucky. My friend was not. He was sent to cut wood. This [indicating his shoulders] was completely darkened by carrying water. . . .
>
> At noon we came back to the jail in order to eat; at 2 P.M., we returned again to work. There were fields on the hills we had to weed; they were cassava fields. . . . This was what we were doing in jail.[35]

He speaks also of conditions inside:

> In jail, there was no light, it was dark and in this darkness, people bumped into each other. The prison on the inside was like a barrel of shit. Those who made noise at night, usually the innocent, were stripped and in the morning, after the report had been sent, the white man came to order whipping—four lashes. Every morning, the white man came, divided up the line of the prisoners and designated those who were to be whipped. No one was allowed to watch; everyone looked down.[36]

Prisoners also suffered from poor diets. The evidence is thin, but strongly suggests that prisoners were underfed. The case of Titule Prison highlights the quality of their diet. A magistrate inspecting the prison in 1946 wrote that "meat and fish supply for prisoners is absolutely insufficient. Twenty-one kilos of meat were bought during the third quarter [of the year] to feed as many as 460 people."[37]

The *chicote*, a hippopotamus-hide whip, was widely used to discipline cotton cultivators both in prison and in the fields and was an integral part of the culture of terror. Both oral and archival evidence illustrate the extent to which the whipping terrorized the people of the cotton-producing areas. As a former cotton cultivator recalled it, the whip was a scourge for the colony. For "poorly maintained fields," cotton cultivators received as many as twelve lashes. To be seen traveling or in the village during work time was a crime, punished mainly with the whip. Generally, "men were whipped in the fields in the sight of their wives and children. They were whipped naked by the policemen."[38] Whipping was associated with sexual insults. It is said that some resisters were beaten undressed and purposely at their lumbar muscles until they ejaculated, forcing them into the epitome of humiliation and shame.[39] Although flogging women was illegal, stories about women who were whipped are numerous and frightening. Policemen whipped overworked women who failed to cut off cotton stalks and neglected to weed the entire plot. "While on tour with cotton-monitors for ensuring control, policemen committed rape and many lived by plunder."[40] More than a decade before, the administrator of Poko Territory reported to the district commissioner: "[W]omen . . . have been whipped . . . because they refused to provide corvée labor on chiefs' fields. . . . The maximum has been twelve lashes."[41] Writing in 1939, a colonial official acknowledged that in many areas "it is simply a shame to see that almost entire villages of people were whipped before they went to work the fields!"[42] The administrative report of Dungu Territory for 1945 noted similar treatment: "During my visit to Bokoyo chiefdoms, I was told that a newly appointed Cotonco propagandist in Biodi has committed many assaults on cotton cultivators: he illegally gave up to twenty lashes to over 200 people."[43] The experience of Lufundja Mbayo, a former policeman of Mambwe chiefdom, is illuminating:

> [Let me tell you] one thing. If you failed to cultivate your field and feed your wife, we had to give you lessons. Those who were troublemakers and refused to work on their fields were arrested. This was our job to arrest them. Those who refused to grow cotton were jailed. After they had spent days in jail they were free but if they continued to make trouble, we whipped them—nine lashes.[44]

The whipping was in fact ceremonial, a horrible spectacle whose objective was twofold. First, it inflicted pain on the resisters; colonial officials hoped to stop them from repeating the actions and thus negatively affecting the others. Second, and most important, it instilled fear in the mass of spectators and made plain the nature of the treatment they would endure themselves if they attempted to block cotton expansion. Behind the whipping ceremony was a clear message to spectators: "The only way to avoid confrontations is to grow cotton. . . . Growing cotton is the only way to be in peace."[45] Cotton production and a culture of terror, therefore, went hand in hand.

A 1931 ordinance legitimated whipping as a disciplinary measure in prisons; it remained in force until 1959. In the colonial situation, the whip was an integral part of prison experience. A look at the registers of prison punishments in cotton-producing areas reveals that few, if any, of those who went to prison came out without having been flogged. Verdicts rendered in 1931 in a Bambili prison indicate that, apart from paying fines, jailed cotton producers received twelve lashes each. The whip was used regardless of gender. What was important was the forced socialization of "raw cultivators" in order to make them submit to economic exploitation. The Boemi chiefdom's records testify that both Azande and Mangbetu women sentenced in 1949 were flogged.[46] Other prisons within cotton-based economies followed similar practices. Records show that in 1953, every one of the 1,044 prisoners in Buta Prison received on average three lashes, while in 1954, each of the 331 prisoners was flogged ten times. The register of punishment of Titule Prison in Bambesa for 1946 shows that 931 prisoners received eight lashes, 46 received six lashes, 60 received four lashes, 16 received two lashes, and 14 prisoners were kept in solitary confinement.[47]

Prison, fines, and whipping affected only a portion of the peasants who refused to grow cotton. Because the objective of cotton schemes was to reach every producer and increase the cotton output, the state enforced a new tax policy. Two tactics were used. First, the state increasingly raised the rate of taxation in cotton-growing areas. These tax hikes forced peasants to increase production. Taxation rose from a minimum of 2.30 francs in 1922 to 17.50 francs in 1930. Although a calculation of tax increases in real terms which takes purchasing power and devaluations into account has not been made, it is still clear that the burden of taxes during the depression and the war (1930–1945), when prices for cotton and other produce first collapsed and later rampant inflation affected imports, were in fact far higher than they had been.[48] Second, where peasants showed hostility to cotton cultivation and had access to other resources, the state required that they pay their taxes in specified amounts of seed cotton.[49]

As reflected in table 4 (acreages), the threat and use of force played a major role in expanding cotton cultivation from 1917 to 1935. However, these tactics did not always bring about the desired results. Beatings, fines, and prison terms did not reduce the Africans to fearful cultivators ready to bow to territorial administrators, agronomists, and African subordinates. Repressive threats and fines, intended to instill fear and reduce the wealth of peasant households, produced contradictory results. What was intended to compel obedience often caused radicalism. The harsh treatment produced wrathful peasants who articulated their grievances and created an oppositional ideology. Prison became, in V. Drachousoff's words, "a potential site to spread the spirit of resistance."[50] Colonial officers recognized that jail, by its very nature, was counterproductive, inasmuch as "jailed cultivators produced nothing and so were a burden for the state."[51] Furthermore, force led to clandestine outmigration, a phenomenon that threatened the continuation of the cotton economy. The administration, therefore, sought to win over the hearts and minds of cotton producers.

Winning Over Hearts and Minds, 1936–1957

Let us go back to our village, those people bring us good things.[52]

The crop [cotton] is becoming less unpleasant to local people thanks especially to an increase in price. . . . Besides, the presents that chiefs and headmen are receiving are certainly part of the reason.[53]

Handouts and propaganda were used periodically between 1917 and 1935, even though force was the predominant feature of the cotton scheme. From 1936 until 1957, however, structural reforms, incentives, and propaganda assumed greater importance as instruments of state policy. Most colonial officials adhered to the adage, "It is necessary to build up force in order not to have to use it."[54] The shifting strategies sprang from colonial economic planners' recognition that force alone was insufficient. In fact, force caused clandestine outmigrations and heightened local opposition in cotton-growing regions, leading to the colonial fear of collective revolts. Cotton cultivators were not a mass of docile workers who could simply be moved into cotton fields through any mechanical exercise of force. As A. Landeghem correctly explained, cotton cultivators "had, despite what some have said, *the soul of a culti-vator* [my emphasis]; they know how to choose their land, whether for a plot of plantain, manioc, rice or cotton; and some would be surprised to see . . . that with their poor tools, they get successful yields from a soil that gets no fertilizers, and that they must constantly struggle to keep clean of invading weeds."[55] It was this *soul of a cultivator* that the state and cotton companies sought to colonize beginning in the 1930s, using a variety of incentives, including structural reforms, material rewards, and propaganda.

Structural Reforms, Handouts, and Social Control

Unlike their counterparts in Uganda and Malawi who received high producer prices, cotton cultivators in colonial Zaire received artificially depressed prices before 1936. By nominally raising producer prices, decreasing tax rates, and distributing material rewards, the state and cotton companies sought to create new attitudes toward the work of cotton cultivation. New incentives gave peasants new perceptions of their self-interest and attempted to convince them of the advantages of cotton in order to keep them from developing a consciousness of exploitation. From the mid-1930s, these incentives demonstrated the colonial state and cotton companies' perception of the peasants' mentalities and economic and social needs. Increases in producer prices and reductions in porterage requirements also showed a new sensitivity to what moved peasants to anger.

In 1936, the state restructured the cotton market by establishing a *potentiel* formula, which created a price stabilization fund that raised prices. Whereas in 1937 cotton cultivators received 1 franc per kilogram of seed cotton, in 1941 they received 2.77 francs, and in 1950, they received 17.55 and 19.72 francs in the north and south respectively.[56] At the same time, the state reformed the unpopular system of porterage. First, beginning in 1930 the state urged cotton companies to increase the number of trading posts. Trading posts increased from 254 to 508 in 1934, almost doubled again in 1937, and reached 1,200 in 1940.[57] Second, the state and cotton companies created *marchés volants*, that is, "mobile markets," authorizing buyers to purchase cotton outside administration-controlled posts in remote areas. Third, the state began instructing cotton companies to locate their trading posts 20 kilometers away from one another to reduce the distance peasants had to travel. In practice, however, many cotton cultivators still traveled more than 20 kilometers to find the nearest market to sell their cotton. Those forced to do so received some cash, a machete or hoe, and a small amount of salt. At the same time, the state began to provide transportation allowances. Theoretically, transportation allowances were a benefit, as weight and distance were remunerated, but the real value was minimal. These allowances represented nothing more than one franc per 20-kilogram bag of cotton, 10 grams of salt per kilogram to carry, and a machete or hoe for carrying a 50–100 kilogram load of cotton.[58] Poor transportation allowances decreased the transport costs of cotton companies. More important, they obscured the perception of exploitation among cotton cultivators.[59]

The system was effective only as long as the outputs remained low. For large-scale production, the system proved counterproductive. Examining the situation in the Maniema district, one official reported that peasants abandoned over 10 tons of cotton on the roads because they had to walk long distances. The ineffectiveness of the system may explain why the 1936 reform focused on expending and constructing roads and bridges, and creating the Messageries Automobiles (transportation by trucks) in each cotton-producing district. The construction of roads and additional trading posts subsidized by peasant production were among the highest priorities of the 1936 reform. In fact, the 1936 legislation authorized the state and cotton companies to withhold paying cotton cultivators in order to construct, maintain, and repair roads they aptly called *routes cotonnières*. The main goal of these "cotton roads" was "to reduce porterage of cotton outputs."[60]

Beginning in the 1930s, the state also modified its taxation policy. Colonial officials periodically reduced the tax rate to encourage peasants to grow cotton. For example, whereas the tax rate for the colony stood at a maximum of 12.15 francs, any Alur household cultivating a cotton plot of 50 ares paid an amount as low as 5.15 francs. Since tax rebates reduced state revenue, they were not widely adopted. Elsewhere, the state stopped collecting taxes during the hoeing and seeding of cotton as a *modus vivendi*. This measure allowed Azande tax defaulters to have a field of cotton before tax collectors passed through the village:[61]

> In the beginning when the white man asked us to grow cotton, we used to flee to the forest. We also fled at the arrival of a tax collector. Then we were told that the *bakumba* [official] would not collect taxes when we were seeding our fields. Many of us who did not want to pay taxes, remained in the village and cultivated a plot of cotton, because we knew that we would not to be jailed. After the seeding we fled to the bush.[62]

These structural reforms, initiated by the state and cotton companies to end the most abusive features of cotton cultivation, were not the only means used to reach the hearts and minds of peasants. The colonial apparatus also constructed a vocabulary that twisted the meaning of *matabishi* (gifts) to include the premiums that were given to peasants. To those who produced exceptionally high yields, the state and cotton companies granted premiums, including bicycles, sewing machines, and gramophones. To cotton growers who produced average yields, they provided hoes, axes, machetes, a colorful piece of cloth, or a small amount of salt. These goods created an illusion of wealth among peasants, meanwhile serving to translate exploitation into the redistribution of wealth. The use of the word *matabishi* to describe these transactions was blatantly duplicitous because the companies deducted a certain amount per kilogram of cotton from peasants' pay to cover the cost of these items. This abuse of a local term attempted to mask peasants' perception of their crippled social existence. Gifts of hoes, axes, and machetes were an effort to provide unproductive and ill-equipped peasants with tools. Though these tools only marginally improved the working conditions of forced cotton cultivators, the "community looked at those who received them as hard workers, women and men everybody admired and sought to marry; gradually, we asked for axes and machetes as part of bridewealth."[63] This practice became very common in the 1930s and continues today in the northeast areas where metal objects had been bridewealth. Generally, while the number of people forcibly incorporated into the cotton scheme increased, the number of tools given out decreased, suggesting that the objective was less to provide the technology needed to produce cotton than to manipulate consciousness.[64]

Bicycles, gramophones, and sewing machines were rare production premiums carrying a great deal of prestige. In the words of Nduba Mosaka, a descendant of a former cotton cultivator, "Someone having a bicycle in a village was distinguished from the rest. It was like someone owning an airplane."[65] These special objects went only to a few highly productive households. Property relations within households channeled these luxury items to husbands, leaving wives outside the distribution circle. "Where is my husband? I want to use his bike," was a verse from a song sung by Mangbetu women, indicating that though women enjoyed the use of cotton-generated luxury items, they did not own them.

Salt was the only item that every household received; it was given primarily to women. A colonial official first suggested that "a portion of the remuneration be paid in salt" because "it would be much appreciated by cotton cultivators' wives."[66] Officials thereafter became convinced that distributing small amounts of salt would keep women within the system. From the time of cotton imposition in 1917 to the 1950s, salt was either still made by women in the dry season or bought when people could afford it. Hence the salt campaign was specifically directed at women and acknowledged their role in farming, harvesting, and transport. In fact, one woman said that they accepted salt because "it freed us from making our own salt. . . . As you know the art of cooking is an asset for a woman. . . . If you cook well, you improve your rank as a co-wife."[67] In 1928, Cotonco and its associates distributed 165 tons of salt worth approximately one million francs as production premiums. In 1932, they distributed as many as 350 tons worth twenty-one million francs. The share of each household varied across districts and time. During the 1935–36 season, women in Kasai received 25 grams, while women in the Maniema district received 10 grams of salt per kilogram of seed cotton.[68]

The impact of salt in stimulating cotton production went far beyond its intrinsic value. In summarizing the impact of gifts of salt and tools, an agronomist stated, "These production premiums fuel the enthusiasm of people, especially the women. We cannot envisage replacing them by a major increase in producer prices."[69] Indeed, the distribution of salt and periodic gifts of cloth to women were perhaps the most efficient means used by the state and cotton companies to control labor at the household level. Here are the words of a song sung by Azande women when returning from the marketplace: "Salt, you have neither bone nor flesh . . . but you make me walk long distances. . . . You make me carry heavy cotton just because of your saltiness."[70]

Propaganda and a New Work Ethic

At the same time the state and cotton companies were implementing structural reforms and offering handouts, they were also trying to instill a new work ethic and new values through agricultural exhibits, cotton festivals, films, and plays. The reasons behind this colonial propaganda using popular culture lie partly in Europeans' preconceived ideas about Africans. Some colonial economic planners claimed that though "Africans had no creative will to find solutions, they had the will to accept them."[71] Others agreed with E. Leplae, the architect of forced cotton cultivation, who put it bluntly: "The native does not think, the authority must think on his behalf."[72] Furthermore, some believed that the Africans knew "how to observe Europeans . . . and . . . willingly imitate them." Thus, colonial propaganda using African popular culture was a means by which to "capitalize on this gift of imitation."[73]

During the mid-1930s, the state and cotton companies began to emphasize the use of agricultural exhibits and cotton festivals, thereby using symbolic discourse to teach peasants rudimentary agricultural techniques. The ultimate objective was to introduce new images; while creating a new life style, these images also created expectations predicated on hard work in the fields. One problem frequently encountered by the colonial state was that not all administrators shared the official view, and when the state and cotton companies collided, some officers were caught between divergent interests. For the state, cotton festivals offered a way to generate a "team spirit" among territorial administrators, agronomists, and crop supervisors:

> During these agricultural festivals and meetings, you will have to discuss of course serious matters, but you will have to combine the useful with the agreeable and the serious as well; you will remember that many difficult problems often are solved more easily during enjoyable activities rather than around the table or when sitting face to face in an office.[74]

An analysis of the Bambesa agricultural exhibit, a typical exhibit which took place on December 4, 1938, illustrates how the state used these events as pedagogy and propaganda. The Bambesa agricultural exhibit was a feast day. The approximately six thousand participants included three segments of the colonial social aggregate: European territorial administrators and agents, state agronomists, and company agents; chiefs and headmen; and the peasantry, including men, women, and children. The exhibition included agricultural and commercial sections, divided into five stands. The agricultural section represented the cotton labor process, and each stand presented a phase of work. Strategically, each of five stands of the exhibition transmitted agricultural knowledge to peasants. The first demonstrated hoeing, done by Van Dijck, a state agronomist. The second presented drilling and the best way to seek the best soils; it was performed by the same agronomist, and repeated by subordinate African agricultural agents. The third stand demonstrated seeding, thinning, earthing, sorting, and harvesting. The fourth included a showing of maize, groundnut, millet, and cotton crops; and the fifth stand showed the ideal crop rotation in meticulous plots. Harvested crops were also exhibited to convince the most recalcitrant of the planters.

This section of the exhibit attempted to deny the hardship of agricultural work by idealizing the farming life. Indeed, the showcase farm exhibited "a nice house, a cowshed, a sheepfold, a henhouse, a granary and a rock to dry cotton. The entire complex was very well thatched; there was also a wheelbarrow to transport cotton."[75] A price was posted, misleading many spectators into believing that their cotton would be used to buy the farm. Clearly, this farm complex was a new image that the cotton companies used to promote a new rural life attainable through cultivation.

The commercial section of the fair was even more important. It displayed a motor bike, a sewing machine, bicycles, and loincloths. Beside each item, a certain quantity of seed cotton showed the price. The last stand in this section embodied the social ideology the cotton companies intended to convey to cotton cultivators. It was an artful whole, whose symbolic discourse invoked and associated positive values with cotton. On approximately 150 square meters stood two contrasting allegories, one presenting a "culture of survival" and the other a "culture of progress." The first allegory showed a tiny and miserable peasant with a pile of dirty, gray, and yellow cotton that no one would want to buy. He was obviously poverty-stricken. Next to him, there was another staged allegory illustrating a robust peasant living comfortably in a house with a bed, bedding, a mosquito net, table, chairs, and other items, thanks to the well-harvested and sorted cotton for which he received a good price. To mark the contrast, placards with inscriptions in Lingala stressed the profit which awaited a careful cultivator.[76]

The performance of first-fruit ceremonies was yet another strategy to expropriate elements of African popular culture to promote commodity production. In many African societies, first-fruit ceremonies were political rituals designed to guard society against socially disruptive forces.[77] In 1937 the cotton companies began appropriating this African cultural form to promote cotton cultivation in what they referred to as a "cotton festival" (*fête de coton*).

Cotton festivals took place in Uvira, Niangara, Kanda-Kanda, Kibombo, Lusangi, and Kasongo. When the Niangara cotton festival was held in 1937, peasants, chiefs, territorial administrators, and state agronomists attended the ceremony. The organization of numerous leisure activities, firecrackers, games, plays, movies, and offerings made cotton festivals more playful than agricultural exhibits, which primarily stressed the communication of agricultural knowledge. A. Ravet remarked that those cotton festivals were "a marvelous means to begin a cotton season" as they released tension, playing the role of a safety valve.[78]

The Kasongo cotton festival, which took place on March 4, 1938, was revealing. In addition to its adaptation, appropriation, and imitation of the local social environment, and its dances and orchestra, the festival included the distribution of production premiums to chiefs, elders, and the most successful cotton producers by Stradiol, the Maniema district commissioner. The festival emphasized this public distribution of production premiums in order to create a spirit of competition within the peasantry, no doubt, that would stimulate production. Indeed, as A. Ravet expressed it, "Whereas those who had high yields were admired and applauded, those who got small production premiums were booed by the crowd."[79] To instill a similar spirit of competition among chiefs, the trophy of a green cotton sateen flag embroidered with a flower of cotton was handed to the chief whose people had obtained the highest average production.[80] Green is the color of Islam. The green sateen flag in this Islamic area indicates again an effort to appropriate a local cultural form to boost production.

Films and plays in an African *lingua franca* supplemented agricultural exhibits and cotton festivals. These forms of propaganda also spawned symbolic discourse, contrasting the existing material conditions of peasants with the ideal conditions that would unfold once they agreed to cultivate cotton. More than any administrator's orders and instructions, a genre of film presenting "some bands of poor pygmies sitting near their miserable huts" was intended to have direct effects on peasants' thought. *Cultivons du Coton,* a one-act play by Jérôme, a Marist Brother of the Buta congregation, was performed by the local people on the occasion of an agricultural exhibit held on November 4, 1939. It is worth quoting at length.

The stage represents a corner of a local village: a few houses, and a village's yard. A group of people come out of their homes and sit down at the yard . . . they are talking . . .

One person: Hey! My friends, what are we doing here? We pay taxes every year, and it is becoming unpleasant.

All in chorus: You are right friends, taxes are a nuisance, but anyone who does not pay these taxes goes to prison. Does he not?

One person: We cultivate rice, maize, and groundnuts but this does not bring in a lot of money and, after we have paid our taxes, "all our francs are finished."

All in chorus: You are not lying friend!

At this moment, a noise is heard from the stage; everybody looks in that direction. A man bringing a sack arrives in front of the group. Everyone looks at him . . .

He: Hey, what is going on here? Are you lazy? Why are you standing around doing nothing, is there no work for you?

All: What work?

A person: We have planted rice, groundnuts and other crops and they are growing.

He: Well, they may be growing, but have you planted cotton?

The first person: Does anyone eat cotton? *(general exclamation)* We do not want to cultivate it. We produce foods, partly for our consumption, and partly for sale; so we have something to pay our taxes.

All: Yes, that is it!

He: Hey! You are not smart!

All: Watch out! Do not make fun of us!

He: I am not making fun of you, my friends! Cultivating cotton and food crops is smarter because cotton brings in a lot of money! Thanks to it, I can pay my taxes and have money left over.

All exclaim: Ah!

He: That is the way, friends! See, I have with me a basket containing cotton seeds which I will sow.

All get up and look at the cotton seeds. Who taught you how to cultivate cotton?

He: Was it not the white man?

At this moment, brassy music is heard from a distance. All listen to the music and talk in low voices.

He: Hey! Friends, there will be a big feast in Buta for cotton, I forgot to tell you about it.

A person: What is the purpose of the feast?

At this moment a well-dressed guy arrives.

All people: Wow! Look at this clerk!

The guy (surprised): I am not a clerk. I am simply a hard-working peasant.

A person: How can that be? You are not a clerk! Do you work the land? Can someone who works the land wear such a nice suit?

The guy: No, dear friends, I am not a clerk but a hard worker; during the last months, I cultivated cotton, I planted a lot of it with my wife and children. When I sold it, I earned 500 francs!

All exclaim: 500 . . . !

The guy: Comrades, 500. . . . I paid my tax, that is 57 francs; with other francs, I bought clothes for myself and my dear ones. Believe me, I assure you that cotton brings in a lot of money . . .

All (convinced): It is true, it is very true.

A person: Who then taught you to be so smart to cultivate cotton?

The guy: Was it not our white man, the white in charge of cotton? Truly, do you know nothing about cotton?

All: Are we not idiots? Are we not vulgar people?

The guy: Well, friends, do not talk that way, you are not vulgar natives. Absolutely you are not. These days, there are no more vulgar people.

At this moment, the brassy music seems to come nearer. All listen then. Suddenly, the people dance on the rhythm of the music.

The guy: This music of Buta is surely not ordinary music.

At this moment, a group of cyclists (about twenty), well dressed, arrive on the stage. The natives look at them amazed.

A cyclist: Hey! Friends! How do you not know that today is the great feast? How come you are poorly dressed and isolated like natives in the past?

A person: Hey! *(indicating his group)*. Friend, do not make fun of us. Are we not sad and poor people? You, you are rich men, you are the white man's men.

A cyclist: Well, how come you are saying that!

A person: Yes, you are not a clerk as compared to us?

All the cyclists look at each other: We, clerks! *(guffawing)*. We are clerks!

A person: I am not lying while saying this, you are rich men, you have nice clothes for the feast and nice machines!

All cyclists (laughing): Hey! Friends, these are not machines, they are bicycles!

A person: Its name is a bike, is it not?

All cyclists: Surely you are a "uncivilized native," you do not know what a bicycle is!

All people: Are not we vulgar taxpayers? Is not a taxpayer's lot to bewail?

A cyclist: Hey! Hey! Why is a taxpayer to be bewailed? Look, friends *(showing the handsome group of cyclists)*. Do we all not pay taxes?

All cyclists: Yes, but we also cultivate cotton, we prepare large fields and if God helps us, we have large harvest. So we earn big sums: Some have 700 francs *(here, all cyclists speak at once)*. I have 800 francs, another 1,000 francs, [and so on].

The people (stunned): Well, do not tell us jokes, you are making fun of us!

The guy: Why do you not cultivate cotton? Anybody who desires to have a lot of francs cultivates cotton and this is the reason why we of Uele, we have a lot of money. *(everybody agrees)* Well, today is the big feast in Buta, the feast of cotton!

A person: Tell me friends what is this feast for?

A cyclist: Why do we have this feast? Because the white man wants at the same time to show us all the benefits from cultivating cotton and a showcase farm where cotton is best cultivated.

A person (turning toward his friends): Friends, let us go. . . . We will also cultivate cotton. We will no longer be idiots. We will also have nice dresses and bicycles.

At this moment the brassy music arrives at the side of the stage, playing a military parade.

A cyclist: Well, friends, let us go! Let us march behind the music, now the big feast has begun.

All leave the stage: The cyclists ride their bicycles and run after the music while the natives are dancing around the musicians who parade in front of the platform where the authorities are.

Commenting on one film he watched, A. Ravet noted, "What will undoubtedly remain in the memory of the audience was the contrast between the poverty of the pygmies and their wives and the comfortable life in larger communities."[81] Plays performed by cotton growers in an African language played a similar role as they explained the advantages of cotton cultivation.

Cotton festivals, agricultural exhibits, plays, and films were supplemented by pamphlets and comic books written in African languages. Illustrations in these books showed phases of the cotton labor process, indicating the appropriate care to be given to the crop at each stage. As one agronomist put it, the idea behind comic books was less "to teach people real agricultural knowledge, than to induce them to work in a cotton plot."[82] Agronomists or African cotton-monitors explained the technical requirements of cotton to peasants during public meetings to clarify what the pictures failed to communicate.[83]

While material incentives and colonial propaganda were primarily designed for adults, schools prepared younger generations for farming life in the cotton-growing zones. Schools integrated lessons on manual work and gardening in their curricula, thereby playing a critical role in instilling a new work ethic in children. In addition to the instruction they received in the classroom, students were asked to cultivate demonstration fields and develop skills they would use throughout their lives. Sometimes, cotton cultivation was more than educational. In missionary schools, students living in dormitories were forced to wake at

5:00 A.M. to work. If they could not finish their tasks, they returned in the afternoon.[84] Cotton production in demonstration fields brought benefits for schools, but the primary reason behind that course of study remained to prepare young people for farming life.

Material incentives and propaganda generated mixed results among the peasantry. Some men and women developed a vision that favored the expansion of cotton cultivation, while others began to articulate a radical ideology. Evaluating the impact of incentives, agricultural exhibits, cotton festivals, plays, and films in shaping the way peasants perceived forced cotton cropping, one colonial official said, "Agricultural exhibits, as well as plays performed in an African language by blacks, which explain the advantages derived from the annual revenues which cotton generates, wield an effective indoctrination favoring the expansion of that crop." Cloth, tools, ornaments, and small amounts of salt exerted *de facto* indoctrination, veiling economic exploitation: "They [the state and cotton companies] handed out salt, *marecani*. When they arrived in a village, they gave it to the chief who distributed it to the villagers. People saw this and they were pleased with it. Those people are bringing us very good things, they said."[85] Some cultivators simply wondered, "Why should we worry? Cotton is money."[86] Gift-based persuasion convinced even those who had fled to the forest to escape the system temporarily. As one peasant suggested,

> When the policemen began to do their propaganda, they usually hunted them [peasants], arrested them and forced them to grow. Then when these people became used to growing cotton, they found that they could make money; they began to say "Hoo, we were ignorant, let us go back to our villages, this is 'rewarding work'".[87]

The perception of cotton cultivation as "rewarding work" was far from the truth before about 1950. This comment indicates the success of the methods and the power of the colonial social ideology surrounding gifts and propaganda. Indeed, for nine months of work during the 1932 season, a cotton-producing household in Doruma Territory made 14.12 francs after taxes, an amount worth just a *kaniki*, a piece of calico.[88]

Accepting the vision of cotton cultivation as rewarding work was one of the numerous ways that peasants coped with the cotton scheme. Officials did not understand that this kind of peasant acceptance of the cultivation of cotton was a tactic to be left alone:

> We were asked over and over to tell what we thought of growing cotton by the *commandant*. He wanted to know how we felt. We knew that we all did not like to cultivate cotton but we lied because

some officers yelled at us. We called them lions. We felt like we had to answer that we liked growing cotton because this was the easiest way for them to leave us alone. We thought we were to give that answer to avoid confrontation with colonial officers.[89]

The Registre du Contrôle de l'Activité Individuelle, 1957–1960

For all the effort to rationalize the system of social control and win over the hearts and minds of peasants, the companies were not entirely successful. Regardless of the material benefits and persuasion, skeptical peasants understood the meaning of this exploitation permeating their daily lives. The most convincing evidence of the limited success of these methods intended to control peasants at the point of production was the continued use of forced registration by the state in 1957 at a time when it was gradually ending the most abusive features of the cotton economy. Referred to as the *registre des planteurs* or the *registre du contrôle de l'activité individuelle*, this registration was intended to focus on the "growing number of cultivators whose outputs fell far below the average." The objective was "to check the activities of each adult man in order to separate insubordinate cotton growers with a real bad attitude or seeking to escape any regular activity from good ones."[90] This forced registration combined coercion with incentives. Mechanically, the system proved to be an effective way of controlling cotton cultivators. The register provided the territorial administrators and state agronomists with critical information such as the cotton cultivator's census identity number, copied into the notebooks of the cotton-monitors and the cotton companies' personnel; the number of wives and children; tax status, to ensure that the peasant had paid his tax; the size of the plots and yields of the principal cash crops; the evaluation of cotton growers; and diverse observations such as the physical aptitude of the peasant and hiding places for refractory cultivators. "What is mentioned in this column" as a territorial administrator expressed it, "must give a precise idea of the state of the spirit of the cultivators and corroborate the evaluation they received."[91]

The system was also designed to allow the network of colonial officials to control the minds of peasants. Keeping notecards in itself does not control the minds of peasants, but the classification of producers did. Indeed, this system classified male members of the household as outstanding, good, bad, and recalcitrant cultivators. While outstanding cultivators did their work perfectly, good cultivators were those who at times required the intervention of the agricultural agents to work correctly. Bad cultivators were peasants who always had such failings as putting off agricultural work and neglecting the care of fields. Refractory cultivators were people who had no cotton fields and were known as *awayawaya* in Kamina.[92] This classification of cultivators was associated with discriminatory treatment intended to generate differential perceptions of cotton cultivation. Only for the first and second categories of cultivators would the state and cotton companies reserve some favors, such as permits to buy hunting guns, rights to gifts of gunpowder, and rights to participate in the competition for awards. The last category was reserved for what was generally called *corvée* labor, or unpleasant work, and "prestations": porterage, repair of bridges, roads, and warehouses. Writing in 1957, A. Goffin, district commissioner of the Haut-Uele district, stated, "In the future, we will resort only to bad cultivators for non-agricultural work; for this reason, the village chief must draw up a list of them to be inserted into the register."[93] It was believed that when separated out by preferential treatment, cotton cultivators would develop differential visions of cotton cultivation and offer differentiated responses to it.

3

Sharing the Social Product:
Peasants and the Market

Introduction

We must understand that the mentality of the local people is altogether special. . . . When we buy their products at higher prices, as it is the case today, we offer a reward to their laziness; the natives then produce less.[1]

Fighting nudity and staving off the poverty of African peasants were, in colonial rhetoric, the two major moral claims for the imposition of cotton production in the Belgian Congo beginning as early as 1917. However, African producers to this day still say that cultivating cotton did not generate a flow of resources into their households. In reality, peasants had been trapped in a marketing system based on an economic logic that propounded two contradictory premises. On the one hand, state administrators planned for an economic development based on increased cotton production, while on the other hand, they held a view that handsome prices paid to producers would "offer a reward to laziness," and subsequently decrease productivity. Certain factors helped government officials translate their view into policy. First, whereas the local handicraft industry in West Africa created parallel markets that shielded cotton producers against brutal colonial exploitation, cotton companies in the Belgian Congo were the only outlet for peasants; cotton itself had no intrinsic value for the producers except in the Kasongo area and in the district west of Lake Tanganyika where cotton had been woven before. Second, the protests of peasants hardly altered the highly regulated cotton-marketing system, and for all their resistance to low prices, cotton producers remained outside the process of pricing. This resulted from the state's control at the point of production as well as in the market. While control over production shifted the costs of production to the peasant households, control at the markets pumped out wealth for cotton companies, establishing what J. Berger has called a "culture of survival."[2] Precisely, low cotton prices encouraged peasant migrations to corporate plantations and mines when they were needed, and this excess of available workers reduced the value of peasant labor.[3] As we will see, generosity and the desire to accumulate profits did not go hand in hand.

In this chapter I examine the mechanisms that the state and cotton companies used to appropriate their surpluses. I explore how these forms of material appropriation changed over the two distinct phases of the marketing system of cotton: the free market and the monopsony phase. In the free market years, dating from 1917 to 1920, though the agents of trading companies periodically handed some cash to peasants, barter dominated exchange relations and generated robbery. As territorial administrators took control of the marketplaces in 1921, the monopsony phase began and continued throughout the cotton economy until 1960. In the initial stage of monopsony, peasants were exploited not only because high prices were not available on the world market, but because the administration failed to oversee the market transactions, leading to exploitation of cotton producers beyond approved means and authorized levels: cheating on weights, misreading and rigging of scales, and manipulation of cotton grades all contributed to defrauding the producers. While these practices increased the profits of cotton companies, the Great Depression, extending through the years 1929–35, prompted changes in the economy and compelled the state and its allies to rationalize their tactics in order to maximize profits. The *barème de prix* (scale of prices) and the *avance provisionnelle* (advance system), which started in 1936 and 1946 respectively, expanded the cotton companies' take. During this stage of monopsony, also known as the stabilization period, the companies' dividends soared, and the value of their shares and capital increased.

Free Markets and Surplus Extraction, 1917–1920

The Belgian Congo was, with French Equatorial Africa, the major area of monopoly trade in the late nineteenth century. As a result, there was rarely a need to establish a very rigid and regulated marketing system. In colonial Zaire, the lack of market organization lasted until the second decade of this century. Indeed, between 1893 and 1918, no legislation regulated the marketing of African gathered commodities. African gathered products were traded in free markets. Trading companies' agents, moving widely from village to village, bartered cheap European manufactured goods for various African commodities. Much of the few kilograms of cotton produced during this experimental period was bartered.[4]

From the fall of 1917 to the fall of 1920 attempts at cotton cultivation were still experimental and in the hands of state officials. Illegal barter rather than payment for cotton provoked peasant resistance. After the first year, the government was forced to pass the August 7, 1918, decree which defined conditions under which cotton was to be traded. Summarized, these conditions stipulated as follows: the organization of markets, wherein territorial administrators scheduled periodic sale sessions, specifying when peasants had to sell their cotton; that any cotton buyer had to hold a special license issued by the administration, possess gins, and either own or rent sufficient warehouses to store ginned cotton; and that the state reserved the right to set a stipulated minimum price. State control at markets had four purposes: to secure regular sale sessions, to maintain the high quality of cotton, to ensure at least some minimal incentives for cultivation, and to generate revenues through control of exports.

Although this embryonic legislation tried to protect peasants, they did not derive an appreciable income from growing cotton. The free markets based on barter often led to injustice and robbery; where mercantile activities had expanded the cash supply, and the traders handed out cash to peasants, the former accumulated extraordinarily high profits at the expense of producers.[5] Consider the disproportionate ratio of producer prices to prices on the world market. At the very outset of the cotton scheme, the traders bought cotton for .20 franc (reduced price) per kilogram and later sold it at .75 franc (275 percent higher) in the colony.[6] In 1917, whereas a kilogram of cotton sold at 5 francs on the overseas market, Tetela and Zimba cotton cultivators in the Sankuru and Maniema districts were paid a price averaging between 1.20 and 1.80 francs per kilogram of lint cotton.[7] The figures for 1918 provide more evidence; in that year, while the selling price of cotton on the Antwerp market was 6 francs, local peasants were paid only 1.80 francs.[8] The blatant impoverishment of peasants, due to free markets and barter, quickly led to the suppression of barter in 1917 and the creation of state-controlled markets. These measures were taken to protect the cotton producers, but ultimately they failed.

Monopsony and Surplus Extraction, 1921–1935

After the short phase of free markets, the state granted monopsony to cotton interests. This reorganization had far-reaching effects. The role of the territorial administrators in pricing became strictly limited; the market was highly regulated, and so was the size of returns to peasants. This section discusses the implications of monopsony on the economic destiny of peasant communities.

Monopsony on Paper

While the 1918 legislation simply laid the foundation for free markets in which peasants could sell their cotton to any owner of gins, the 1921 decree granted monopsony to cotton companies, and transformed trading posts into company-controlled markets.[9] Now peasants found themselves forced to supply their cotton to a single holder of a cotton zone and gins. To be sure, this arrangement suppressed competition and, unlike the earlier situation, always maintained the producer prices at minimal level. Although the state maintained the right to set minimum producer prices, monopsony narrowed its freedom in doing so. During the free market phase, the absence of companies with explicit interests in cotton enabled the state to enjoy great autonomy, which it gradually lost. In 1920 powerful holdings, especially the Société Générale, industrialists, public subscribers, and the state, capitalized six million francs in the cotton economy by creating the Compagnie Cotonnière Congolaise (Cotonco). In that year, the state became an investor whose economic interests were now the same as those of the cotton companies, and its central administration sided with cotton companies. The Société Générale, which now invested in cotton companies, controlled most of the Belgian economy and now extended its reach to the colony.[10] Cotonco and its affiliated companies directly controlled well over half of the cotton-producing areas and hence controlled all those local markets as well. This was exceptional, even for the production of cash crops, and a regulated marketing system existed only for cotton. In fact, from 1921 to 1935, while other agricultural products—except for palm products, which were controlled by the Huileries du Congo Belge—continued to be traded in free markets, the system of cotton zones guaranteed monopsonic prices to the cotton companies.

The creation of the Comité Cotonnier Congolais (CCC), itself dominated by Cotonco, was yet another factor which further reduced state autonomy. Until the Great Depression, each of these cotton companies operated on its own. The zoning regulation of 1921 established a *modus vivendi* that minimized competition among the holders of cotton zones. However, the regulation did not unite the cotton companies nor coordinate their activities in dealing with the state or other adverse interests in the colony. This lack of coordination enabled the state to arbitrate competition between cotton producers and cotton companies, as well as between the latter and other capitalist trading firms. Cotonco reinforced its control over all the companies by creating the Comité Cotonnier Congolais in 1929. The onset of the Great Depression, which in general strengthened the hold of the major trusts over the independent smaller companies, assisted Cotonco in this maneuver. The resulting elimination of significant competition among the companies further limited the ability of the local colonial government to set minimum producer prices.[11] As part of its stated objectives of seeking "to maintain a close link and identity of view with the administration in the metropole and in Africa," the CCC "centralized issues of general interest about the cotton industry in its relations with the government," and pushed to achieve many new advantages. They secured from the government the abolition of a tax and duty on cotton exports in 1930; a reduction of freight to a symbolic rate of 1 franc per ton on any boat taking cotton from any place of production to Kinshasa, the capital; 43 million francs in loans from the Belgian government to purchase cotton and avoid bankruptcy in 1931 and 1932; and most important, they reformed cotton marketing in 1936 by applying the principle of *potentiel* which underlay the "price-scale system." As the state's power in mediating between producers and cotton companies diminished, the cotton companies became almost self-controlled enterprises despite the opposition of the governor-general. As a result, cotton companies shifted as much of the operating costs and risks as possible onto the peasants when they set producer prices. The compensation they paid was as low as seemed feasible without provoking either general sabotage or insurrection.

Markets on the Ground—The Actual System in Operation, 1921–1935

The reform of 1921 provided, in theory, some measure of security for peasants, including minimum cotton prices set by the administration, control of the markets to reduce blatant cheating by company agents, and the elimination of middlemen; yet peasants were still exposed to economic abuses. We have seen that marketing based on zoning regulations precluded competition and maintained uncompetitive prices. Moreover, the colonial administration's failure to monitor cotton sales caused peasants to suffer losses.

Peasants suffered losses on cotton production beyond the approved means and authorized level in many ways, including cheating on weight, the misreading and rigging of scales, manipulation of cotton grades, the marketing of worthless consumer goods, and by dishonest use of *paniers tarés*—the system by which the companies intended to pre-vent cheating by requiring the standardization of basket weights. Cheat-ing on weight was widely practiced by company agents responsible for buying seed cotton from peasants. Examining commercial agriculture from 1920 to 1940 in the Lulua district, Nkala Wodjim Tantur concluded, "A lot of cheating was committed, many villagers were paid a price far below the value of the product presented to the buyer because a good and constant supervision of the marketplaces had failed."[12] Failure to prevent cheating by posting officials in trading posts seemed inevitable because of the swelling number of trading posts and the reluctance of the colonial administration and cotton companies to shoulder any costs of the cotton economy. The colonial administration moved to having peasants assume the greatest risk. This was the logic that led the ad-ministration to tailor a system, which it called *achat par paniers tarés* (sale by [using] standardization of basket weights), to reduce these malprac-tices. The system required peasants to make uniform baskets of a specified size to contain a standard weight of cotton and from which the buyer deducted a prefixed tare, the constant weight of the empty basket. Though the system was intended to protect peasants against the losses, the cotton companies' agents turned it into a tool for misrepresenting the kilograms of cotton peasants actually brought to the market by over-stating the weight of the tare, thus withholding resources which would have benefited cotton cultivators. For example, during the 1947 cotton sales at Malgbe trading post, company agents deducted 6 kilograms of seed cotton per load that a peasant brought to the market, while in fact the emptied basket that represented the tare weighed only 5 kilograms. The market operation in the village of the Azande Chief Adala was sim-ilar: company agents deducted a tare of 3 kilograms per load, but the ac-tual weight of the baskets was 2 kilograms. Such dishonesty generated substantial surpluses. At the Bafuka gin during the 1946–47 sales, for ex-ample, the surplus was 89,395 kilograms.[13]

In addition, the state and the cotton companies' agents misread the scales and rigged them to defraud peasants. These practices were well attested to by such measures as the use of automated scales and the posting of young, literate men in the market to check weights. Asked if Hemba peasants who did not know how to read the scale were cheated, Lwaka Mukandja, a former cotton grower, said, "The buyer diminished the weight of the load. The actual weight of the product was always lowered. The idea of posting young literate men was intended to deal with all this and it came from the peasants themselves."[14] In addition to posting young literate men at the market to reduce the practice, Vice Governor-General A. Moeller proposed that cotton companies' agents weigh cotton on automated scales and hand out to peasants tickets showing the weight of the basket and information necessary to identify the buyer. These modifications "aimed at impeding cheating or at least having the buyers get the fear of the sanctions they could expose themselves to."[15]

The state and company agents, enticed by bonuses, did not fear these sanctions, and went on to manipulate cotton grades, often grading cotton below its true value to maximize profits. In 1922, E. Fisher found that a Cotonco agent working among the Azande producers "bought most of cotton as second quality cotton."[16] Former Ngbandi cotton producers told me that "the first harvest was not better paid than the cotton they supplied just before they cut the bush," meaning that the buyers hardly took into account cotton grades. The lack of efficient control of the markets contributed to spreading the practice, even though young literate men in the village were there to check. Whatever measures were taken failed to stop these abuses because the state's effort to reduce porterage by adding trading posts resulted in a shortage of officials to monitor the sales in every market. On the basis of firsthand observations gathered by market administrators, Vice Governor-General A. Moeller reported, "Under the prevailing system, the proof of infractions of the law on the remuneration of cotton is possible only when the representative of the authority is present at sale sessions. This, however, is impossible. In this matter, cheating is quite commonplace and because there is no control on the spot, the proof difficult to find."[17]

As administrators entirely failed to monitor the markets, some cotton companies began to sell overpriced, cheap manufactured goods in the same markets where they bought cotton. This allowed them to practice a form of indirect barter in which they reaped additional profit. The accounts of Nieuwe Afrikaansche-Handels-Vennootschap (N.A.H.V.) operating among the Amadi cotton producers is typical of these economic extortions. In 1924, for example, this Dutch company "sold to the Amadi goods such as drums, big boxes and caps. . . . We see in these items . . . the unrewarding role of our personnel stimulating cotton cultivation among our natives. . . . Cotton bought from our population with cheap and nasty goods is cynically decked with a [Dutch] flag and dearly sold in Amsterdam."[18]

The tax rate, which varied according to cash influx within a territory, also reduced the income peasants derived from cotton cultivation. Out of 42 million francs that cotton growers received in 1934, as much as 60 percent was swallowed up by taxes; for that year, tax receipts from cotton producers represented 27 percent of the total tax receipts in the annual budget.[19] Witnesses agreed that the price of cotton was relatively low as compared to tax hikes and the cost of living. Continuous decreases in productivity made even the little benefit that the native got from cultivating cotton meaningless. Simultaneously, territorial administrators diverted peasant resources through export duties that, while filling up the coffers of the state, were an indirect tax on peasants. This *taxe cotonnière*, money the state extracted for every kilogram of ginned cotton, was instituted in 1924. The rate started at .25 franc per kilogram of ginned cotton, rose to .35 franc in 1925, and remained fixed until 1929, when it rose to .36 franc. It was abolished in 1930 to shield cotton companies against bankruptcy in the Great Depression years. For example, this tax duty allowed the state to extract 175,000 francs in 1925 and as much as 225,000 francs in 1926. From 1930 to 1936, the state had received 28.65 million francs in taxes and export duties, and in 1938 tax and duties on cotton exports procured 12.48 million francs for the state.[20] By 1935, the state had partly achieved its stated objective of generating resources through cotton exports.

In summary, cheating on weight, the misreading and rigging of scales, manipulation of cotton grades, the marketing of worthless consumer goods, and the system of *paniers tarés* drained peasants' earnings outside the conventional market. Therefore, these practices offer a strategic entry point for gauging exploitation beyond the calculation of prices and in expanding our understanding of what happened to peasants at the markets.

The combination of these practices with monopsony and tax withholdings kept cotton producers from accumulating any wealth. From the beginning of the scheme, "a native [could not] afford either a pair of pants or a shirt."[21] A vast body of evidence indicates that as early as 1921 cotton producers "were unhappy about the buying price of cotton."[22] In 1923, "cultivation of cotton was dragging primarily because the lowest prices were paid to the producers."[23] Seven years later, "the economy of forced cultivation was not expanding because people didn't find a satisfactory return [for] their work."[24] Here is the testimony of cotton producers in the Maniema district, collected in 1928 by a colonial official:

> On numerous occasions, people have expressed to us their discontent about the prices of cotton which they estimate are insufficient. In some places I was told that they profited much more from growing groundnuts than cotton. It must be noted that they are not completely wrong and that among most crops, cotton is certainly one which compensates less the sum of labor needed to produce it.[25]

In addition to losing the opportunity to grow the more valuable crop of peanuts, peasants lost income due to the Great Depression. During the depression years, they were the most impoverished segment of the rural society integrated into the colonial economy. In 1932, in fact, "buyers of cotton discounted the time devoted to the cultivation and transportation of cotton, and paid a price lower than the lowest salaries of workers within the same areas."[26] The Boa producers at Titule in the Lower Uele area, considered to be the most prosperous cotton producers, provide a good illustration. In the early 1930s, workers toiling for capitalist enterprises were receiving, in addition to food, a monthly average wage of 500 and 600 francs; after taxes, their net earnings ranged from 470 to 570 francs. Over the same period, the Boa cotton cultivators were making between 82 and 120 francs after they had paid their taxes. These incomes were very high as compared to the average of 40 francs that the Alur cotton producers were earning in the northeast of the country. And among the Mangbetu cultivators, the income dropped as low as 14 francs.[27] Income among the Mangbetu was 61 percent lower than the average income they earned in 1924, and among the Amadi producers, income fell 83 percent. Outside these groups, cotton producers in the northern area worked twelve times harder to earn what they made four years before the Great Depression. The same pattern in income variations and fluctuations appeared in the southern area, except in the Tanganyika district, where household income was 90 francs and increased to 146 francs in 1936, after the price reform of that year. These figures were optimistic estimates, however, since tax collectors often neglected to report the so-called voluntary contribution and polygyny tax.[28] Variations in income in different locations were linked to soil fertility, the efficiency of control over the markets, the cost of transportation, and people's response to incentives, as documented in chapter 2.

The conclusion emerging from this analysis is that, contrary to Bauer's misleading thesis that "people get from the market what they deserve" and that "poor resources, poor skills, and lack of initiative make poor people," supplying cotton to the colonial markets for accumulation was, according to a metaphor that peasants used, "a run behind the horizon," meaning that increased household production created illusions of wealth.[29] E. Leplae, the director general of the Department of Agriculture and the most noted advocate of compulsory cotton cultivation, acknowledged the exploitation of peasants by cotton companies. Analyzing data gleaned over more than ten years, he concluded in November of 1929 that "cotton companies are taking very great advantage of high prices of cotton; they have been buying it from the natives at reduced prices; their benefits per kilo have increased to 3 or 4 francs; and the value of their shares [has] increased six-fold."[30] The conclusion reached by a member of the Commission Permanente pour la Protection des Indigènes, writing nine years after E. Leplae, indicates that until 1936, cotton cultivation impoverished African producers. For the people of Lualaba and the shores of Lake Kisale, for example, he estimated that a crop of cotton yielded an income worth just two nights of fishing.[31]

Reforming the Cotton Marketing System, 1936–1959

Though cotton companies enjoyed monopsony, the Great Depression revealed their vulnerability and predicted a gloomy future for the cotton economy. The collapse of prices on the world market resulted in the fluctuation of producer prices, leading to the closing of many remote cotton zones because the high cost of transportation reduced profits. The fluctuation of producer prices caused peasant resistance and signaled that monopsony would be worthless if peasants stopped growing cotton. Controlling price fluctuations and improving conditions of production became the highest priorities in stabilizing the cotton economy. To achieve these goals, the Comité Cotonnier Congolais and the state mapped a new price-setting arrangement in 1936, called *barême de prix*, which established the price stabilization funds. The Second World War compelled the alliance to further modify the setting of prices by creating the Comptoir des Ventes des Cotons Congolais. This marketing organization, completely under Cotonco control, changed the method that would henceforth determine the profit margin of cotton companies and the returns to peasants for their work. Both the 1936 and 1946 legislation stabilized producer prices and expanded, through the Fonds de Remploi (Stabilization funds), the network of roads that reduced porterage. The profits of cotton companies, however, exceeded these benefits.

Stabilizing the Cotton Economy, 1936–1940

To avoid price fluctuations, provide tools, and construct roads and bridges, the Comité Cotonnier Congolais and state officials set up the *barême de prix* as the first step in consolidating the cotton economy. The *barême de prix* was a "scale of prices" established each year on the basis of an average selling price and the total amount of cotton produced in the preceding year. The average selling price involved export surcharges, cotton companies' net benefits, industrial costs, and the so-called *potentiel*, an amount of money per kilogram of lint cotton that a cotton company should make available for later purchase of cotton within its concessions.[32] This *potentiel* included not only the remuneration of peasants, but also various expenses that directly affected their pay. The *potentiel* comprised funds added to the existing budgets of chiefdoms, most notably the salaries of agricultural agents, propaganda expenses, costs of cotton selection and breeding, transportation costs, money for building local courts and prisons, which were necessary for social control, and money for tools and books that enabled colonial manipulation. The *potentiel* also covered charges which would have increased the cotton companies' operating costs.[33]

At first glance, the *potentiel* played a positive role; most important, it contributed money to the stabilization funds, successively named Fonds de Remploi (1924–36), Fonds de Réserve Cotonnier (1936–42), and Caisse de Réserve Cotonnière (1942–60). As noted earlier, these funds were first established by a portion of the *potentiel*, and after 1946 by the difference between the actual prices on the world market and the low annual price estimates set in advance by the Comité Cotonnier Congolais administrators and approved by the administration. In 1942, after the Fonds de Réserve Cotonnier had become Caisse de Réserve Cotonnière, the management of the funds was entrusted to a committee, named the Comité de Gérance du Fonds Cotonnier (Cogerco), which included four state officials and two representatives of the cotton companies. In 1947, the membership of the committee was brought to ten: six state officials and four representatives of cotton companies, whose first stated goals were to seek the best way to raise funds and to use and share cotton-generated profits in a manner which would benefit peasants.[34] In practice, their highest priorities were to build a reserve in order to avoid the fluctuations of producer prices, to provide peasants with hoes, axes, and machetes, and to repair and maintain the roads called *routes cotonnières*.[35] Finally, they raised peasants' incomes compared to those of earlier years. In 1937, for example, cotton producers in northern cotton zones made 175 francs per year. The following year, peasants received 200 francs, and in Buta they enjoyed 360 francs; in certain communities of the Buta area, the annual income reached 800 francs.[36] Income increased in similar proportions in the southern cotton zones. Consider the household incomes in the Tanganyika district: whereas in 1935, peasants there received 90 francs, their incomes rose to 201 francs in 1937, 253 francs in 1940, and 602 francs in 1946.[37]

These incomes, though higher than before, were still below value of peasant labor. In fact, income growth was first linked, as I will show, to larger household plots rather than to higher prices. The way the amount of *potentiel* was calculated could hardly insure a fair distribution of the cotton-generated wealth. In the first five years, the administrators of the Comité Cotonnier Congolais responsible for setting the *potentiel* allotted a fixed rate of 13 percent of the adjusted revenues from sales of the

annual crop to the cotton companies after deductions of all except purchasing costs. Thereafter, they claimed that cotton companies obtained
15 percent of the gross revenues and that 85 percent went to the producers. These figures would have us believe that from 1940 on, the
households enjoyed the largest proportion of cotton-generated profits.
Yet differing rates of gross revenues in favor of peasants did not actually shift profits from the cotton companies to households. The figures
seemed to be only a device to pacify the critics who opposed the exploitation of the producers.[38]

Similarly, the structural linkage of peasant remuneration to price pro-
jections affected the distribution of wealth among the producers and
cotton companies. When either the prices on the world market or production declined, or when the operating costs increased, as was often
the case, the administrators of CCC diminished the amount of money
they made available for peasant remuneration. As a result, cotton producers suffered while cotton companies remained completely protected, even if the margin of their profit shrank. For example, when cotton companies' average operating costs increased by 43 percent from
1939 to 1945 due to raises in the salaries of European employees "the *potentiel* remained low and this did not allow [them] to adequately reward
local people."[39] When prices were good on the world market, the CCC
administrators maintained the rate of the *potentiel* unchanged. From
1936 to 1943, prices on the world market rose by more than 100 percent,
but the average producer prices rose only 25 percent, and even declined
from 1939 to 1941. The wealth extracted from producers was channeled
into stabilization funds, which withheld peasants' resources in good
years for political purposes, thereby turning the stabilization funds into
a joint savings account for the state and cotton companies. Overall, the
stabilization policy provided its administrators with a legal financial
institution to dispossess cotton producers of any income beyond the
guaranteed level. In fact, after World War II, much of the income that
peasants were entitled to went to the funds.

The major concern of company administrators was to figure out ways
to pass on their operating costs to producers. They succeeded in their
efforts because the companies' bookkeeping involved many entries that
the CCC administrators were unable to monitor. This exacerbated the
extraction of wealth from peasants to the extent that one colonial
official stated that the policy objective was "to have cotton cultivators
depreciate cotton companies errors and investment."[40] This view was
shared by Governor-General P. Ryckmans from the very outset; he
pointed out in a 1936 letter that "Cotonco allocates 30 percent of the
benefit per kilogram, this is to say, a bit more than 2.7 francs per kilo-

gram to depreciation. Is this a regular depreciation repeated every year or a way to depreciate errors made in the past? And once these errors are corrected, must 2.7 francs be devoted every year to depreciate gins?"[41] In addition to the costs of depreciation, the companies also passed on to peasants expenses such as the costs of transferring funds from Europe to Africa, insurance, and at times, interest on bank loans and the expense of paying off capital costs.[42]

The construction of roads and the distribution of axes, hoes, and machetes to cotton producers in order to foster a hegemonic integration into the cotton economy could hardly mask the predatory nature of Cogerco. In fact, although Cogerco's indiscriminate allocation of funds to peasant "development projects" had some political benefits, it angered many territorial administrators, who further exposed the exploitative character of the institution.[43] A typical letter from the district commissioner of Uele in 1946 reveals one hidden rationale behind stabilization policy:

> The government had, in its policy of building roads, made a difference between the roads of general interest and the private ones. To make the *caisse de réserve* supply the funds to maintain roads serving to transport cotton was only a decoy to mask the excessive contribution of cotton cultivators to road maintenance as it is an exclusive burden put on their backs for the construction of new roads.[44]

The same official highlighted the gap between the stated policy and the actual use of the funds, revealing another hidden side of the stabilization policy. He stated that the money deducted from the income of peasants in Uele, a cotton-producing district in the north, was used to construct roads and bridges in Sankuru, a cotton-producing district in the south, enabling cotton companies to compete with other capitalist companies during price fluctuations. Finally, Cogerco's substantial extraction of funds from cotton producers enabled the state to maintain through this stabilization policy a fixed, exorbitant tax rate that would apply to the producers, regardless of bad harvests. The state justified this extra robbery by insisting that the cotton producers' income was generally higher than income outside cotton-growing areas. Once this assumption was stipulated, the state saw no reason beneficial to itself or the cotton companies for allowing the tax rate to fluctuate according to crop viability. Thus, Cogerco raised money that served cotton companies and state interests as well.

It is not surprising that from the very beginning, in April 1937, the minister of colonies reporting on the financial situation of cotton companies concluded, "The *barême* does not establish a fair share of benefits between cotton companies and cotton growers. . . . Wisdom keeps us from increasing too quickly the remuneration of the countrypeople but fairness is not to be overlooked."[45] Two years later, Governor-General Ryckmans wrote,

> The *potentiel* as I have approved its calculation so far has permitted to set up a reserve of 131 francs per ton of seed cotton and poured into Fonds de Remploi, but the *potentiel* has also permitted to build up reserves which amount, for some companies, to 217 francs per ton of seed cotton. This amount consciously makes me wonder whether the scale of price which I have accepted without discussion of its elements ensures a fair share between the producers and cotton industry.[46]

Even in the best of times, a fair share was illusory. From 1936 to 1947, though peasant incomes had increased, they contrasted remarkably with the lavish profits of cotton companies, the handsome dividends that cotton companies and shareholders enjoyed, and the huge surpluses transferred to stabilization funds. This exploitation of peasants was the outcome of an antipeasant policy that most territorial administrators shared about returns for peasants and the manipulation of the *potentiel* described earlier:

> Prices which cotton companies must pay to producers must be set by considering the margin of benefits necessary to pay the cost of industrial facilities and various charges, and to enjoy benefits which the sales of the product can generate. Of course, we do not wish that the industrialists make superprofits, but it would not be wise to jeopardize the stability of the companies by setting producer prices too high in proportion to actual prices on the world market.[47]

This policy undoubtedly increased the cotton companies' dividends and profits. Take, for example, dividends and profits made by Cotonco, Cotonnière du Nepoko, Cotonnière du Bomokandi, and Compagnie Cotonnière du Tanganyika. At its foundation in 1920, the start-up capital of Cotonco amounted to 6 million francs. This capital, uncorrected for devaluations and inflation, rapidly rose to 10 million in 1924, 30 million in 1928, and jumped to 60 million francs in 1929. During the Great Depression, peasants received prices next to nothing, but Cotonco's capital gains increased from 60 million francs in 1929 to 70 million in 1931, and reached 300 million by 1947. Similarly, dividends paid on Cotonco's shares of the first and second series, worth 50 and 10 francs in 1935, respectively, doubled their value in the following year.[48]

One explanation of Cotonco's soaring capital gains and dividends is that the company was an offshoot of the Société Générale. This relationship made the company a corporation which dominated local markets. At the beginning, as we have pointed out earlier, Cotonco was granted monopsony over nine economic districts, each with a 40-kilometer radius around a gin. In 1936, Cotonco was also granted monopsony in four free zones. These economic districts were such large concessions that Cotonco began increasingly to control the whole local market. Whereas Cotonco and its subsidiary Nepoko bought 59 percent of seed cotton produced in 1929, one year later, Cotonco, Nepoko, and Bomokandi controlled 70 percent of the colony's total production. In the early 1940s, Cotonco alone bought 60 percent of the total national production; together with its associates, it controlled 80 percent. From the 1940s to 1960, Cotonco had 70 percent of the market.[49] By controlling most seed cotton, the company was able to carry off the wealth of the communities to its coffers. This control of the markets generated capital gains which the company reinvested in subsidiaries and other cotton companies within and outside the colony. In 1927, Puppa and Sabbe, two Greek cotton entrepreneurs, were granted two concessions in the valleys of the Uele and Nepoko Rivers and created the Société des Anciens Etablissements Puppa et Sabbe with a start-up capital of 3 million francs. Two years later, Cotonco became a shareholder and invested 3 million francs in the venture, which brought the total capital to 6 million francs. Out of .8 million francs of the Comptoir de Vente des Cotons Congolais, a marketing company, Cotonco and its subsidiaries alone held .4 million francs. Outside the colony, Cotonco prospered too.[50]

Such a command of the markets secured Cotonco's prosperity beyond a doubt. But available evidence shows that even companies which bought cotton from limited markets made profits. This is one more indication that the companies made money at the expense of peasants, keeping them in poverty. The prosperity of cotton companies created higher returns on cotton investments. The following figures, though not adjusted for devaluation or inflation, indicate this. While dividends of 35 and 7 francs paid to A and B shares of Cotonnière du Nepoko in 1935, they rapidly rose to 100 and 20 francs in 1936, respectively. The net profit of the company increased from 2.5 million francs in 1942 to 3.04 million francs in 1943. Over the same period, the dividends of Cotonnière de Bomokandi rose from 100 francs to 200 francs, though its profit increased by only .45 million francs. From 1939 to 1942, producer prices did not increase, while cotton companies' profits rose by over 230 percent per kilogram of seed cotton.[51] The increased profits of Cotonnière du Tanganyika (Cotanga) in the Tanganyika district also highlight the impoverishment of rural people by cotton companies. In 1941, Cotanga earned 1.8 million francs in profit. The following year, its profit jumped to 2.76 million francs, and to 2.85 million francs in 1943. Cotanga's profits did not come from an increase in the volume of seed cotton purchased from peasants within its zones; rather, the company's total purchases declined. The amount of cotton it purchased rose only from 7,296 to 8,026 tons in 1941, and to 8,775 tons in 1946.[52] This company extracted profits by paying low prices to the producers while production and prices on the world market were expanding.

Moving Peasants to Increased Economic Insecurity,
1940–1959

During World War II, cotton companies lost their markets. The war made it plain that, monopsony notwithstanding, cotton companies could suffer losses during cyclical crises and wars. As many former markets for colonial Zaire's cotton exports were closed, more problems arose for the cotton economy: cotton companies owned only a limited number of warehouses, and they foresaw the difficulty of storing their ginned cotton, totaling 40,000 tons annually for some companies; even with adequate warehousing, storing cotton over a long period was a serious concern. The abolition of cotton cultivation looked devastating for the economy, and Great Britain, the major market for cotton exports, wanted to buy at once, at fixed prices, enough cotton to cover annual needs, a requirement which no single cotton company was able to meet.

At the beginning of the war, cotton companies formed the Pool de Vente, a marketing pool, whose ambition was to find ways to sell cotton in the best interests of the cotton companies while still adhering to government policy.[53] This pool sought new outlets for cotton exports in South Africa, India, and Austria; it proved so efficient that it reduced cotton stocks. Their successful sales of cotton combined with the lessons of the war, as well as the expiration by 1946 of the monopsony that cotton companies had enjoyed since 1921, transformed the pool into a permanent organization named Comptoir des Ventes des Cotons Congolais (Covenco) in January of 1946. Summarized, Covenco's functions ranged from technical operations to actual cotton sales in the world market. It took lint cotton from the gins and assured transportation and storage. It graded, sampled, and classified cotton bales. Paying the bills of carriers and forwarding agencies, handling duties, selling cotton, receiving payment, and sharing profits among its members were also its tasks. Cotton companies worked together through this marketing company.

This institution changed the previous price-setting arrangement. Now peasants found themselves paid advances, named *avances provi-*

Table 3.1. Money (francs/kg) transferred to Cogerco, 1948–1953

Year	A	B	C	D	E	F	G
1948	15.30	15.30	8.55	8.55	6.75	44%	44%
1949	16.80	16.80	11.55	11.55	5.25	31	31
1950	27.55	29.72	17.55	19.72	10.00	36	34
1951	28.50	29.95	21.30	22.75	7.20	25	24
1952	27.55	26.65	20.55	19.05	7.60	28	29
1953	—	—	14.25	19.05	—	—	—

Source: G. Depi, "La Caisse de Réserve Cotonniére," *Bulletin de la banque centrale du Congo et du Ruanda-Urundi*, 1957, 65. A and B are the total amounts of money that peasants in the north and south were entitled to. C and D are the actual amounts paid to peasants in the north and south. E represents the positive difference transfered to Cogerco. F and G are the percentages of the difference for the north and south, respectively.

sionnelles, when they brought crops to the trading centers. Company administrators proclaimed that advances were paid to peasants because "they no longer sell their crop to a merchant or a gin owner; they remain the owners of the product until it is sold both on the local and world market."[54] In fact, this meant that the risks of transportation and sales were now shifted to the producers; moreover, the interest on any positive difference between advances and final sales figures was a windfall for Covenco.

The legislation's implementation moved peasants to the front line to absorb the shocks of price fluctuations and assume more costs and risks. In reality, it was a setback for the cotton-producing households. First of all, Covenco avoided state control altogether and directed resources towards cotton interests. Indeed, after sales of cotton on the world market, it deducted first the profits of cotton companies and then operating costs and previous advances paid to peasants. The remainder was transferred either to Cogerco or cotton cooperatives. These transfers to Cogerco's funds generated large sums that many state officials warned "were beyond the need of a policy destined to support production."[55] These transfers to Cogerco of money that peasants were entitled to (see table 3.1) reduced household resources, and continuously increased Cogerco's assets. By the end of 1945, the Fonds Cotonnier held about 225 million francs, and in 1947, the Caisse de Réserve Cotonnière had approximately 450 million francs. These amounts rose to 1.0025 billion francs in 1950, and reached 1.003 billion francs in 1955.

Second, more often than not, the prices of cotton exported to Belgium were set lower than the prices on the world market, reducing peasants' income even further. In 1951, 1 kilogram of colony cotton was worth 88 francs, but cotton companies sold it directly to the Belgian textile industries in Belgium and in the colony for 60 and 45 francs, respec-

Table 3.2. Producer and world prices (per kg)

Year	Producer price (in francs)	Selling price
1916	0.20	0.60 F
1917	0.50	1.00 F
1918	0.60	6.00 F
1924	0.37	3.651 gold F
1925	0.46	2.830 gold F
1926	0.37	1.870 gold F
1927	0.34	1.840 gold F
1928	0.39	2.311 gold F
1929	0.48	2.325 gold F
1930	0.52	2.160 gold F
1931	1.05	6.17 F
1932	0.60	6.25 F
1933	0.60	8.7 cts/lb
1934	0.60	12.00 cts/lb
1935	0.70	11.60 cts/lb
1936	0.85	13. cts/lb
1937	1.00	10.00 cts/lb
1938	1.00	10.65 cts/lb
1939	0.90	8.70 cts/lb
1940	0.90	10.96 cts/lb
1941	0.92	11.00 cts/lb
1942	1.09	18.31 cts/lb
1943	1.25	20.14 cts/lb
1944	—	20.65 cts/lb
1945	0.48	21.46 cts/lb
1946	1.12 (north)	
1947	2.75	36.65 cts/lb
1948	8.55	31.16 Fob Matadi
1949	11.55	33.02 F
1950	18.63	40.32 F
1951	22.02	52.14 F
1952	19.80	47.33 F
1953	16.65	37.22 F
1954	—	39.56 F
1955	19.50	38.82 F

Sources: "Agri (386) 120." G. Depi, "La Caisse de Réserve Cotonnière," *Bulletin de la banque centrale du Congo belge et du Ruanda-Urundi,* 1957, 65. *Bulletin agricole du Congo belge,* (1924), 15; (1926), 15; (1929), 21; Cotonco, "Rapport 1930," annexe ii; "Agri (369) 1/2," "Agri (378) 17, FI 5, no. 2381," "Agri (378) FI 6/144," E. Gordia, "Culture cotonnière," le 24 juin 1946; "Agri (378) H,"; *Etudes sur le marché de certains produits congolais,* (1939–1946): 54; L. Banneux, *Bulletin d' information de l'INEAC,* série technique, 1 (1938): 13.

tively.[56] One year later, the colony cotton was sold to textile industries both in the colony and in Belgium at 30 to 55 percent below the world market price (see table 3.2). Often, as happened in 1953 because of a fall in price, cotton growers did not receive the remaining balance to which they were entitled. This reinforced, from 1948 to 1955, the difference between producer prices and the prices that cotton companies reaped on the world market, which were between 137 and 268 percent higher.[57] The appropriation by Cogerco of from 25 to 44 percent per kilogram of what would have gone to peasants impoverished the latter; until 1955, however, administrators claimed that peasants received between 43 and 45 percent of the sale of every kilogram of lint cotton sold on world markets. Evidence from the Tanganyika district shows that cotton producers' average income rose 20 percent in 1948, declined 9 percent in 1949, and increased only 2 percent the next year.

Peasant household income increased significantly only under the *paysannat* scheme in the 1950s. In 1957 for example, households in the Kabinda district made an estimated income varying between 1,300 and 2,327 francs. Households which grew cotton, corn, groundnuts, beans, manioc, or other crops made between 13,411 and 10,326 francs, to which cotton contributed 12–17 percent.[58] Obviously, this augmentation of household income stemmed primarily from an increase in output and from diversification in productive activities rather than from higher prices of cotton alone. Moreover, the prices often quoted as indicators of prosperity contrast with contemporary observations that took into account the rising cost of living for rural dwellers. A colonial officer made this plain when he stated, "Among the natives, there is a discontent: we have failed to make the crop as popular here as in Uganda. The remuneration is inadequate and the Blacks are growing the crop only under the pressure of the administration." When I asked a descendant of a former Hemba cotton-producing household whether people benefited from cotton, he bluntly said, "Wealth! I do not see it."[59] While households suffered income shortages, companies prospered at the expense of the producers, as the records of Cotonco show. In the 1930s, Cotonco's shareholders were paid annual dividends that represented 20 percent of the value of their shares. In 1948, a 125-franc dividend was paid on each share; this rose to 150 francs in 1949 and jumped to 240 francs in 1952. Although the gross profits of Cotonco dropped slightly in 1953 and 1954, dividends of 280 francs continued to be paid to each shareholder from 1956 to 1958; shareholders' assets grew because the Caisse de Réserve, Cogerco and Covenco artificially diminished the revenues of peasants.[60]

4

Cotton and Social Inequality

Introduction

In the past two decades, researchers have moved away from the conception of the peasantry as a homogeneous and undifferentiated group. Most researchers agree that African peasants included both exploiters and exploited. From Mozambican data, Isaacman has demonstrated that social differentiation took place between chiefs and cotton producers as well as among peasants themselves. Concerning intracommunity differences, he argues that "preferential treatment at the market, commodity production based on unpaid labor, and a variety of other incentives all combined to enhance the economic position of the chiefs."[1] In his study of the Malawian peasantry, Mandala documented a similar process, showing that prosperous Zunde landowning peasants, hiring migrant labor, accumulated more appreciable resources than poorer peasants.[2] Nayenga and Vincent have pointed out that chiefs in Uganda diverted *luwalo* labor (unpaid labor) from public work for private use on their lands and used their coercive power to collect fines and taxes, which further differentiated the social structure.[3] Finally, in a study of the formation and stratification of the peasantry in colonial Ghana, Howard concluded that "it was debt relationships, incurred by the mortgage of crops or by usufruct, which provided the dynamics in stratifying peasants."[4]

This scholarship is a corrective to the center-periphery dichotomy that, while appropriately emphasizing the exploitation of the productive unit, ignored unequal relations within the community and household. Still for all its contribution, overemphasis on social differentiation shares the ideological parti pris of the underdevelopment theory when it overlooks the role of international factors. Internal social differentiation has real meaning only when the transfer of wealth from the household to

the center and the colonial state are explicit as well. Despite their entrepreneurship and ability to take advantage of the economic opportunity
opened by cash crop production, the so-called "rich" peasants, the
Zunde landowners and cocoa planters, ultimately experienced the collapse of their economic ventures, and uncertainty quickly replaced their
prosperity. This is even more true for chiefs whose economic prosperity
was based on their continued loyalty to the colonial regime and services
to different fractions of capital. Evidence from Zaire shows that despite
the privileged position these African subordinates occupied within the
colonial social aggregate and despite the substantial material wealth this
yielded, they remained a fragile and exploited class. In spite of their
seemingly important revenues, chiefs' incomes remained insufficient.[5]

In this chapter I examine the roots of inequality in the cotton-producing regions by focusing on the social gap between chiefs and cotton producers. The social differentiation that emerged between the two groups
was a conscious and controlled process that primarily benefited the state,
although it did channel substantial amounts of wealth to chiefs, which
they did not necessarily transform into capital. I argue that the sources of
inequities between chiefs and peasants included the appropriation of unpaid labor for commodity production, the pricing system, which withheld portions of peasants' income to pay chiefs' bonuses, the reinforcement of chiefs' power through the judiciary, and the chiefs' exemption
from taxes. In the second part of the chapter I explore inequities within
the household, pointing to the unequal allocation of agricultural tasks
and scarce resources. To assess the level of household inequality, I examine the process of decision making, the expenditures of the household,
and the sites of investment and priorities. Central to this section is the
view that the head of the household, by controlling the levers of power,
reproduced historical inequalities in the division of labor and allotted
most of a household's poor earnings to his priorities. I argue that because
of poverty, inequities within the household deserve to be described not
as exploitation, which implies the accumulation of wealth, but as the
unequal distribution of poverty. The gap between the prosperity of the
cotton companies and the poverty of cotton producers was the most
important form of social differentiation created by cotton cultivation.

Exploitation and Intra-Community Inequality

Colonial Zaire's cotton economy paralleled that of Mozambique, where peasants to this day proclaim that "cotton is the mother of
poverty." Rodney's statement that "Africans got into colonization with
a hoe and came back with a hoe" is as true of cotton producers in Zaire

as it was of Tanzanian peasants. The assessment of the plight of peasants in Luba Country by the members of the Council of the Province of Elisabethville illustrates this point: "We have . . . demanded much of these rural peoples: recruitment . . . construction and maintenance of roads . . . cultivation of cotton and food crops . . . and gathering of rubber . . . but we have done nothing or nearly nothing to ameliorate their lot."[6] Even in 1927 a colonial official in Orientale Province was quick to point out that "of all crops, cotton is certainly the one which pays badly for labor needed to produce it."[7] In numerous areas of Zaire, cotton cultivation symbolized, to borrow a graphic phrase from Bill Rau, the passage from "feast to famine." The Lulua cotton cultivators are a good example. According to an agronomist, they were, in 1932, "less robust. Diseases and undernourishment have made these blacks weak and delicate."[8] Although soil productivity, weather, and plant diseases caused regional income variations of up to 70 percent in some years, poverty among cotton-producing peasants remained constant in all regions of Orientale Province.[9] Because of this poverty, rural differentiation was most noticeable between chiefs and peasants, and appears to be one result of the exploitation of rural people.

Chiefs, Peasants, and Social Differentiation

The most visible inequality in the community was the unmitigated poverty of peasants, especially when contrasted to the wealth that it was possible for chiefs. Many of the factors that generated interhousehold differentiation in other cotton-growing parts of Africa were absent in cotton-growing areas of colonial Zaire. Belgian agricultural policy inhibited the African initiative that created substantial differentiation among peasants in Malawi, Senegambia, Uganda, and Ghana.[10] The nature of the cotton labor regime, the retention of land tenure, and low population density precluded the hiring of a sizeable labor force; every potential agricultural worker was a forced cotton producer. Cotton seeds, which were a scarce resource and a stratifying factor in Uganda and Mozambique, were readily available in colonial Zaire. In fact, the colonial administration and cotton companies granted 20 kilograms of cotton seeds to each household yearly. While these factors reduced the possibility of differentiation among peasants, several factors—the appropriation of peasant labor for production on chiefs' cotton fields, the breakdown of the social mechanism for the redistribution of the social product, production premiums given to chiefs, the exemption of chiefs from taxes, and their power to extract fines from peasants—widened the gap between chiefs and peasants.

Labor Appropriation for Production and Social Differentiation

Unlike the situation in the Teso district of Uganda, where chiefs illegally diverted corveé labor intended for public works to employment on their own lands,[11] the chiefs' access to African labor for cotton commodity production was an official policy in colonial Zaire. Until the 1940s the colonial administration and cotton companies did not dream of transforming local chiefs into capitalist farmers. Yet they encouraged chiefs to combine their moral authority with new administrative coercive power to tap the labor of their subjects. The appropriation of labor by chiefs leading to social and economic differentiation did not emerge for the first time with forced cotton cultivation. Labor appropriation was widely practiced in precolonial societies.[12] But forced cotton cultivation expanded the scale of labor appropriation and changed the destination of the product. Formerly, collective labor on chiefs' fields produced material wealth, but some of it had a collective use value. Colonial policy not only maintained precolonial collective labor on chiefs' cotton plots and restricted intrahousehold cooperative work, it broke down the mechanisms of social redistribution, making room for individualism and some private accumulation. One has to bear in mind, however, that collective labor on a chief's plot went against individualism and that the restriction of intrahousehold labor was mainly a problem between the genders. As noted earlier, accumulation was often less than it was imagined to be, given the short tenure of office of many chiefs. As a result, only a minority of chiefs appropriated peasant labor, which exacerbated the division between the two groups. A song sung to me by former Luba cotton growers comments on this process:

We grow, the chief reaps.
We sweat, the chief reaps.
Our hands have blisters, the chief collects cash.
In old days, he would have provided the food.
In old days, he would have provided drinks.
Nowadays, chief eats where our eyes cannot see.
The chief is stingy![13]

Chiefs took full advantage of the opportunity and made use of collective labor to produce cotton. Inspecting the vast southern region of Lonkala, Lusambo, Tshibala, Kabinda, Maniema, and Lusambo, E. Fisher observed in 1921 that cotton cultivators "planted and cultivated for their chiefs larger fields, at times, of several hectares and even of up to five or six hectares larger."[14] Two years later, the same cotton expert noticed a similar exploitation of peasant labor by chiefs in the

Table 4.1. Chiefs' and peasants' plot sizes (in hectares)

Chiefdoms	Households	Chiefs' plots	Household plots
Kole	2,876	8	0.35
Banguma	2,353	4	0.32
Gengete	2,112	6	0.25
Alipae	1,321	4	0.40
Yaura	918	4	0.30
Samara	532	1	0.20
Dekwe	296	1	0.40
Senepako	110	1	0.25

Source: District de l'Uele-Itimbili, "Compagnie cotonnière 1927–1928."

Lower and Upper Uele districts. There, he recorded, "Chiefs and notables make the community prepare their lands and once their own fields are prepared, these dignitaries lose interest in the work of their people and so the work advances with difficulty."[15] In 1930, U. Blommaert, a leading cotton agronomist, alerted the public to the exploitation of peasant labor by chiefs, saying, "Where the custom requires the people to cultivate a field for a chief, it is advisable that they start earlier in order to allow them to prepare their own fields. It is an important point: numerous chiefs, greedy for money, abuse their people who then run out of time to establish their own fields and are thus obliged to reduce their size."[16]

The appropriation of peasant labor increased the chiefs' cotton outputs. The size of the labor force is reflected in table 4.1, which illustrates a typical situation in the Uele-Itimbiri district. It indicates that the size of a chief's plot was proportional to the size of the population under his authority and was up to 22 times the size of a household plot. It also demonstrates how the size of the population under their control and supervision created inequality among chiefs. Nevertheless, the fact that Chief Yaura with a small population obtained a cotton plot as large as that of Chief Banguma, who ruled more than twice the number of households, indicates that the differential coercive power of chiefs to extract peasant labor added to the gap. Thus, the use of collective labor on the chiefs' cotton fields from one season to the next and the lack of remuneration to communal workers increased chiefs' wealth.

Chiefs often abused their power, causing many cotton producers to resent their chiefs rather than the colonial state or cotton companies. They would say, for example, "The white man does not have anything to do with us; the worst person is the chief."[17] A group of Mangbetu peasants said the people "might smile at [the] chief's face, but their hearts were always in war against him, and whatever he would do, nothing will ever keep them from recalling their hardship."[18] Within sectors, local politics limited the exactions of chiefs; not only might the people run away or refuse to work, but they might back other candidates for chief and claim to the territorial administration that the chief was a usurper. In some areas (e.g., Tanganyika district) this led to great instability among chiefs and hence less coercive power over villagers.

Pricing, Incentives, and Social Differentiation

Pricing was another significant stratifying mechanism. When setting producer prices, especially after the reform of 1936, the state and cotton companies withheld a certain amount of cash per kilogram of seed cotton to pay for propaganda and the chiefs' production premiums. Though the amounts of these premiums varied in some years by 50 percent from district to district, they generated cash and created inequality everywhere. In the 1920s, chiefs in Uele region received 20 francs per ton of cotton, while chiefs in the Maniema district were given 10 francs per ton. The figures from the 1930s reflect similar trends. In 1936, most chiefs received 60 francs per ton of ginned cotton, although in Kasai, Colocoton paid chiefs and headmen production premiums of 10 francs per ton. In the Ubangi district, the state and cotton companies gave production premiums of 20 francs per ton to headmen, agricultural monitors, and "deserving" cotton growers.[19]

Compared to the transfer of cash to cotton companies and the social responsibility of the chiefs to improve the cotton economy, these production premiums may seem negligible, and chiefs may seem to be an exploited segment of the colonial society. Nonetheless, the premiums channeled more money to chiefs than peasants received for growing cotton, thereby differentiating chiefs from peasants, changing lifestyles, and provoking antagonism within communities. We have seen that while northern cotton growers suffered harsh exploitation during the Great Depression, their chiefs received production premiums ranging from 7,000 to 21,000 francs, amounts far beyond the annual income of peasants. In 1931, while peasants in Uele-Nepoko earned only 66 francs as annual income, Chief Gilima received 21,000 francs in production premiums alone. Nor was Gilima an isolated case.[20]

Production premiums fueled inequality in the south, too. In the Sankuru, Kasai, and Lomami concessions, although chiefs and headmen received production premiums of 10 francs per ton of unginned cotton, only half the rate of premiums paid in the northern concessions, these premiums nurtured social differentiation. In 1936, Colocoton and Cotonco paid Chief Mutombo Katshi 1,000 and 8,000 francs, respectively, during the same season, the headman Musongeye received 1,800 francs. The income of peasants, in contrast, was estimated to be about 120 francs.[21] Thus pricing designed to induce chiefs into production as labor supervisors fostered social differentiation because it transferred a portion of proceeds from producers to chiefs.

Taxes, Fines, and Social Differentiation

In remarkable contrast to chiefs, who were exempt from impoverishing taxes, cotton growers paid taxes, fines, and surtaxes called *centimes additionnels.* The rate and increase of taxes in cotton zones caused an overall drain because they were proportional to the cash influx and higher than in non-cotton-growing areas. From 1921 to 1930, the cotton economy brought to peasants approximately 116.45 million francs which, as a proponent of cotton cultivation bluntly put it, "represented just enough money to pay partly or entirely their taxes." During the first decade of cotton production, the amount of taxes, though not adjusted for devaluation and inflation here, rose from a minimum of 2.30 francs in 1922 to 17.50 francs in 1930. In the Bondo area, taxes rose from 12.45 francs in 1923 to 25 francs in 1927, and 43.50 francs in 1930. In 1930, while cotton producers paid a minimum of 17.50 francs, their counterparts outside cotton-growing areas paid an amount as low as 9.50 francs.[22] While taxation reduced the income of peasants, it increased the earnings of chiefs, who received a percentage of the money collected. This further widened the gap between the cotton-growing peasantry and chiefs. Tax increases forced peasants to increase cotton production and to neglect food production, which directly affected nutrition and the general state of their health, and also prevented them from pursuing other lucrative activities, thus locking them into poverty.

Chiefs and other leaders justified their status by claiming to be guardians of their societies. Their appointment by the colonial state altered their roles so that they could collect taxes, recruit labor, supervise forced cultivation of cash crops, and preside over Native Tribunals. This diversification of roles detached chiefs from their own subjects. On some issues, some chiefs sided with their people, but even then, the state used powerful means to foster loyalty: removal from office, suspension or reduction of salaries, and deportation compelled cooperation and transformed chiefs into administrative agents who carefully observed the balance of force and sided with the powerful party. Cotton production premiums and the extension of their punitive powers especially changed the role of chiefs.

The new powers of chiefs served to reduce the incomes of peasant households not only through taxation but also through the extraction of fines, which were one of the main colonial means of repressing peasants who refused to produce cotton. In Shaba, "in any chiefdom, at least one man out of five was condemned for infractions of the system of forced cultivation,"[23] and was fined by his chief; thus it is apparent that fines were a systematic way of extracting cash from peasant households, which widened the gap between peasants and chiefs. Chiefs kept a portion of the fines as overhead for the operation of the Native Tribunals, which provided them with a certain amount of patronage.[24] These tribunals reinforced their power and became a basis for private disposition of public funds. The ability to extract surplus through fines depended on the coercive power of chiefs. Regarding the Bena Tshiofa, an officer in 1943 pointed out how the misuse of chiefly power screened out peasant resistance. The officer referred to it as tyranny, noting that "the defender is not heard and finds himself condemned for dirty or stained cotton, and for not having a cotton store and grill. We can judge that this stems only from his [the chief's] administrative power which is based neither on the custom nor the written law. It is created for current needs to reinforce the authority of the chief and is simply arbitrary."[25]

Chiefs, using the judiciary, pumped cash out of peasant households whenever they challenged cotton production. In other words, they commercialized peasant resistance. In an analysis of over one thousand cases cited in inspection reports from 1945 to 1954, a failure to cut old stalks of cotton, for example, resulted in a fine of 50–300 francs. Peasants who refused to harvest their cotton, from 1932 to 1945, faced fines of 20–100 francs.[26] Peasant labor had become a commodity to the extent that any absence of labor came to be precisely evaluated in money. The chiefs and the Native Tribunals together set the prices for unperformed work and hence put a precise price on various forms of refusal or resistance to fully carry out allotted tasks in cultivating cotton.

Even though chiefs did not keep the fines they collected for private use, they ultimately benefited from them. The fines were used in large portion to pay the salaries of the local policemen and the hired personnel of the Native Tribunals. Chiefs targeted not only peasants who refused to cultivate crops, but those who defied their authority. From 1938 to 1952, the sample shows that a refusal to obey a chief or elder, or a dispute with a cotton-monitor or policeman, cost peasants up to 100 francs. For refusing to obey a policeman, or for fleeing from one, the penalties amounted to 25 and 100 francs respectively.[27] Each amount taken away from the household, though it did not go to the chiefs, deepened the gap between chiefs and peasants.

The impoverishing nature of these fines is clear when compared to household incomes. Though household income varied greatly, depending on soil fertility, the vagaries of climate, the cost of transportation, and above all the cost of living, fines ruined household finances. For an Azande head of household making 47 francs per year in 1931, and forced to pay 20 francs for not selling his cotton at the prescribed market, the household financial situation was precarious. When the income of cotton producers rose after 1936, fines also rose. Moreover, fines were almost always combined with prison sentences, which diverted labor from production. Overall, it is clear that because fines affected a large proportion of peasants, they reinforced the social gap as they transferred resources from households to the state apparatuses of oppression. In general, these fines partly explain a perpetual circle of small debts in the household at the end of World War II, at the nadir of the so-called *effort de guerre*. This was an extreme situation but indicative of the kinds of stresses that existed at other times too. As V. Drachousoff noted in 1947, the "fines are profitable but to coffers of the state," and because they were big, "money always ends up in the hands of the Boula-Matari [the colonial state]."[28]

Chiefs and Peasants: Differentiation in Practice

Communal labor and production premiums enhanced the chiefs' financial position, and fines and taxes reduced peasants' household income. This inequality in accumulation affected the lifestyles of the two groups; between chiefs and peasants, there were differences in clothing, housing, and food consumption.

Going naked is not by itself an indication of poverty, since cultural and climatic conditions may dictate the act. In the United States, for example, people lie on beaches half-naked to get tanned in the summer in a manner that European explorers of the nineteenth century would consider indecent. Nor is manner of dress a reliable indication of social class, but in the context of cotton imposition, whose moral justification was the desire to fight nudity and stave off poverty, the contrast of the half-naked with the well dressed reveals social disparities. This is well illustrated by photographs taken in various cotton zones of the Ubangi, Uele, Maniema, Sankuru, Kasai, and Lomami districts. A salient feature of these pictures is the dichotomized social universe they present. Wherever they were photographed, chiefs were well dressed, smiling, and seemingly happy, while peasants were half-naked, emaciated, and appeared discontented.[29]

Likewise, housing revealed inequalities. Although households transported cotton in rotation and organized small crews to fell trees, and despite the colonial introduction of high-yielding varieties and plant rotations, cotton cultivation greatly diverted labor from other household activities. Thus peasants, unlike chiefs, lacked time to maintain their houses. For example, in 1926, many peasants in the Kibari-Ituri district continued to live in small homes, while chiefs and headmen were very well housed, sometimes in houses made of bricks. Territorial administrators urged chiefs and headmen in Niangara to have "cotton growers use their few non-labor peak weeks before the harvest of cotton to repair villages of which so many are in ruins"[30] in 1945.

Ecology, economics, politics, and culture determine the production of food in a community. The patterns of food consumption, however, indicate the material conditions of life and the social relations of production. Some foods, such as manioc, were associated with low social strata, and others were indicators of wealth and prestige. In many African societies, cultural mechanisms were used to limit the consumption of some foods, which became the prerogative of ruling elders. Differentiated access to foods of different nutritional value and the varying patterns in the consumption of specific kinds of food are evidence of social stratification. Differences in food consumption among cotton-growing communities resulted from the cotton economy. "We cannot draw attention enough to food imbalance of these populations who are lacking not only animal and vegetable proteins but who have a diet less varied due to a gradual extinction of traditional crops which have no longer a place within the agricultural cycle as new cash crops have been introduced."[31] G. Malengreau struck a similar note when, in 1952, he said, "Anyway one cannot compare a worker with a poor man of the interior who is underfed."[32] Even though proponents of the cotton economy claimed that peasants derived important resources from cotton, evidence indicates that these resources were mythical: "With all the money which fell in his hands, the cultivator, because of the low prices he receives on the markets, has nothing with which to buy for himself and his family additional foods of which he disposed in old days and which he does not produce any more."[33] This food scarcity affected peasants but not chiefs and other privileged members of the colonial aggregate. In 1930 for example, vegetable food was sufficient in the Uele-Itimbiri district, but meat was scarce. Despite this meat scarcity, the consumption of the poultry was high among chiefs, headmen, *capitas vendeurs* (salespersons), and clerks to the court.[34]

Production-Oriented Polygyny and
Inter-Household Differences

"Polygyny had added [to] the list of its other advantages that of allowing its practitioners to avoid judiciary sanctions without coercing them to work."[35] The cotton labor regime, as we have seen, precluded wage labor, as everyone was forced to produce cotton. The alternative available to expand household labor was marriage, especially polygynous marriage. Access to marriageable women, therefore, divided peasants not only from chiefs, but also among themselves. Historically, having several wives ensured a high rate of reproduction and was a mark of prestige, wealth, and power. Forced cotton cultivation exacerbated the competition for wives, and polygyny became increasingly production-oriented. People used wives to increase their profits. Thus, in the context of commodity production, many wives provided labor, and a large pool of wives further stratified the community.

The impact of polygyny on differentiation was complex because it interacted with preexisting rural social differentiation, generational inequality, and gender. Within the complex household, polygyny shifted most of the burden of cotton production to wives' shoulders and enabled male heads of household to enjoy more time for social activities and more leisure time. Explicitly, it established the male's right to a larger pool of female agricultural labor and permitted the male head of the household to divide the agricultural work between co-wives. The most convincing empirical evidence to support this assumption is the report that "almost the heads of the polygynous households alone exceeded the standard size of the mandatory acreage."[36] A 1942–43 production survey from Luboya village in Kabinda indicates that eight out of ten households were polygynous; two to four wives married to one husband would control from 0.90 to 1.65 hectares of cottonfields. The survey of a Ngefu village community echoed this trend. All six households surveyed there were polygynous, and each of these productive units cultivated between 1.21 and 2.70 hectares; the household composed of three to five wives produced the highest yields.[37] These acreages were beyond the capacity of single and monogynous households.

Chiefs were able to resort to polygyny more than other members of rural communities. The chiefs in the Tanganyika district, specifically in the territory of Mwanza, are a good example of those who used production-oriented polygyny. Here, Chief Banza Nzoloko Lekoymani had nineteen wives, and Chief Ngoyi Kazimu had twenty, while Chiefs Ilunga Kabole and Mafinge had ten and forty wives, respectively.[38] Yet access to the labor resources of women was not a privilege exclusive to chiefs. Elders and affluent peasants also used these institutions. In Uele, cotton-growing heightened polygyny among seniors so much that it deprived social juniors of the opportunity to marry at all. Writing in 1947, a territorial administrator said that because of polygyny "numerous young men do not find wives."[39] This may explain the rise of cases of adultery in the Native Tribunals. Elders did not have the same coercive power as chiefs, but they had the means to control young men and women, even though these mechanisms did not always lead to the desired result. In many societies incorporated into the scheme, elders continued to control access to wives by requiring bridewealth instead of the cash which young men could obtain. Where cash crops had expanded the cash available, elders steadily raised the brideprice. Consider, for example, the swelling amount of the brideprice in Kanda-Kanda area, where it ranged from 1,000 to 1,200 francs in 1935, oscillated between 1,500 and 1,800 francs in 1936, and reached 2,000 francs beginning in 1937. Elders also participated in the definition of sexual conduct and moral codes used in Native Tribunals. The sanctions surrounding adultery and elopement, for example, show the chiefs' preoccupation with social control over young men and women. For adultery and elopement, Boa offenders paid as much as 200 and 750 francs respectively, plus damages to the former husband, which ranged from 500 to 800 francs. Increased outmigrations of young unmarried men from the 1940s onwards are an indication that many of them failed to marry as a result of elders' control. Equally, migrations explain why elders failed to entirely control the countryside. A study conducted in 1948 by L. De Koster indicated that many peasant communities lost up to 60 percent of their able-bodied men.[40]

For young males, therefore, marriage as a strategy to control labor and accumulate wealth remained a limited option. The widespread practice of polygyny monopolized by chiefs, elders, and affluent peasants restricted teenagers' access to wives; this difficulty was compounded in some areas by prebridewealth payments provided by wealthy men to prospective parents-in-law for a young woman before she reached the age of marriage. This practice prevented parents from accepting another prospective son-in-law, and reinforced polygyny among already polygynous men. In Sankuru, a pioneering cotton-growing district, a large proportion of the married women were co-wives probably because of this practice. The 1955–57 demographic sample indicates that polygyny reached its peak there in the 1920s and 1930s, when over 40 percent of the married women in the 45–54 age group shared a husband.[41]

Though there is thin evidence that in some years monogynous conjugal units produced as much cotton as polygynous ones, high outputs in monogynous households were the exception rather than the rule. Cotton output was proportional to the labor pool at the disposal of the household, and the outputs channeled cash and material rewards accordingly. This differentiated access to labor generated rural inequality and caused migrations of the young men, as I will show in chapter 5.[42]

Polygyny allowed the head of the household to avoid working harder on cottonfields, but it also was a benefit to co-wives. In fact, it decreased the workload of female producers more than monogamy did. In other words, cotton cultivation placed a burden on women, but it did not do so equally. Indeed, contrary to the tenet that equates polygyny with the exploitation of female labor, my analysis shows that it reduced women's workloads because it split agricultural work between several co-wives. Wives in monogamous conjugal units found themselves overburdened compared to those in complex conjugal units. This was especially true until the 1940s, when the size of the plot remained equal regardless of the marital status of the household head. In this context and by comparison to monogamy, polygyny represented the household structure best adapted to cope with labor bottlenecks caused from forced cotton cultivation.

In summary, it can be stated that cotton cultivation did not uniformly structure daily lives in the countryside. Single male, polygynous, and monogynous male and female cotton cultivators experienced different ranges of autonomy. Indeed, of the many factors which differentiated rural societies, control of the youth and polygyny were the most significant, because they determined the amount of labor available for cotton production.

Intra-Household Inequality

Cotton impoverished, but it did not impoverish evenly; it created inequalities both among and within households. Splits within the households occurred along marital status, gender, and age lines. Inequality in the household was manifested in the allocation of agricultural work as well as the distribution of scarce resources.

Men, Women, Work, and Social Inequality

Feminist literature tends to assume that women were victims of exploitation. Many researchers, failing to recognize the colonial capitalist systems of production which exacerbated the exploitation of labor, blame the exploitation of women on African patriarchy and men. Although the structural subordination of women led to the exploitation of female labor in many societies before the introduction of cotton production, Africa offers a variety of experiences that cannot be reduced to a monolithic cultural form. Early anthropological literature had documented that there were, in precolonial as well as in colonial Africa, three patterns of division of labor. In some societies, men and women worked together; in others, men undertook the bulk of agricultural work; in others women alone did field work, except the clearing of the land.[43] In areas which became cotton-growing zones, the situations were as follows around 1890. Men cut the trees, women cleared underbrush, prepared land for planting, planted, tended, and harvested; on fields without big trees, women did all the farm work. There were a few exceptions (like the Kuba and Alur) where men participated in all the phases of farming except weeding. Women did all the food processing everywhere. In Kivu (Nyanga) men did however cultivate banana groves by themselves without women's input, and men everywhere took care of cutting the trees. The field products belonged to the women (see court cases), and the property of husband and wife was kept sharply separate. When cash crops like cotton came in, men supposedly owned them (as for palm trees or coffee trees); even though women did more work on cotton fields, the proceeds now all went to men. Women, however, could and did claim money for clothing and school expenses for the children, as well as hospital expenses, from the men. In some cases, however, men claimed that schools and health were women's responsibility and did not assist them. Whatever the situation, by controlling money, husbands now had much greater control over their wives.[44]

Through an examination of the allocation of agricultural tasks along gender lines in households of colonial Zaire that were forced to cultivate cotton and of the conflicts between husbands and wives that resulted from the distribution of the scarce cash resources that cotton generated, I argue that the subordination of females is not a universal occurrence. Forced cotton cultivation caused unequal division of labor and resources between men and women, but the inequities are also notable between single and married men, and between both the male and female members of monogynous and polygynous households. These inequities were based on the colonial imposition of the administrative classification of the healthy adult male. The methods used to share the communally earned cash within the households (as documented by the judgments of Native Tribunals) reflects differentiation in resource control and access. The intrahousehold conflicts that resulted as women struggled against the inequities imposed by husbands and colonial institutions of social control demonstrate the different degrees of subordination they suffered in various spheres.

Regardless of variations among ethnic groups, married women worked more days than their husbands, as illustrated in charts established by agronomists in the Kasai district. Table 8 shows vast discrepancies between a wife's workload and her husband's.[45] For the three years (1929, 1930, 1932) analyzed here, the average workload for females was 38 percent heavier than the average male workload, without taking into account tasks such as collecting firewood and cooking, which represented over 60 percent of the total household workload.

The division of agricultural work was rooted in the social ideology that associated "hard work" with men and "soft work" with women. This conception emphasized that clearing the land was men's work and the subsequent stages were women's work. However, seeding, weeding, harvesting, and transporting cotton, phases seen as "soft stages," required more labor than the "virile" ones. As a result, "Apart from felling the trees, it was [she] who did most of the work."[46] After observing women's involvement in cotton cultivation in the Kabinda district, Lesage concluded in 1943, "The greatest part of agriculture work, if not the totality, is performed by women."[47] The conclusion reached by the Katanga Province Council for 1944 is equally illuminating. Though the members acknowledged that "most of agricultural work is done by the whole family," they specified that "usually, women and children participated massively." They stated, "This is the case with cotton cultivation where, except for the clearing of the land, almost all the preliminary works, notably making wraps, harvesting, sorting, and carrying cotton to the market are entirely performed by them."[48]

Not only does table 4.2 underestimate the number of days required to transport cotton to market, it represents the task as one shared by men and women, so we can conclude that the average workload of females was in fact more than 38 percent greater than the average for males. In addition to the Katanga Province Council's report, which lists carrying cotton to market as the responsibility of women, we find further support in the photographs that colonial governments used to show happy peasants participating in state projects. Despite their probable intention as propaganda, these photographs reveal aspects of peasants' experiences and other information otherwise unavailable. They show, for example, that most carriers and sellers of cotton were women and older children. Most husbands "had their wives travel considerable distances to bring their cotton to the trading stations."[49]

Cotton cultivation, it should be remembered, generated labor bottlenecks. These seasonal labor peaks intensified the unequal division of labor within conjugal households. During the land clearing and harvesting bottleneck, while men cleared the land, women and older children harvested cotton and carried the yields to trading places. The Alur cotton growers used *koya*, a form of collective and reciprocal work which lasted throughout the cotton cycle, but in other areas, only limited cooperative labor occurred among households during these peak periods.[50] Male cultivators organized small work crews to fell large trees collectively. Others recruited labor from unmarried youth, younger

Table 4.2. Share of agricultural work in the household (days per year for selected years: 1929, 1930, 1932)

Type of work	1929			1930			1932		
Workers	Man	Woman	Child	Man	Woman	Child	Man	Woman	Child
Clearing	20	—	24	110	—	—	110	—	—
Hoeing	80	—	—	24	80	10	24	80	10
Seeding	35	—	—	—	25	10	—	25	10
Weeding	—	30	6	—	20	5	—	25	5
Harvest	—	32	8	—	32	10	—	32	10
Carrying	—	9	—	10	50	10	10	50	10
Cooking	—	350	—	—	200	50	—	200	50
Construction	—	—	—	10	—	—	10	2	1
Porterage	—	240	—	150	40	—	—	150	40
Total	135	661	38	304	447	95	154	564	136

Sources: "Rapport sur l'agriculture," district du Kasai, 1929, 6; 1930, 6; 1932, 6, 7, 1.

brothers, and in-laws. In the southeast of the country, still others asked their prospective sons-in-law to perform bride-service in the cotton fields. Though in some households, the head of the household, wives, and older children all traveled many kilometers to sell their cotton, in others, women carried cotton in rotation to avoid strangulation.[51] Whatever rotation was adopted, however, and despite the state policy to expand the network of trading stations and roads, "carrying cotton remained difficult in the colony"[52] as late as 1947 because "increasing output placed cultivators in front of new difficulties."[53] Such strategies to overcome the labor bottlenecks broadened husbands' autonomy more than wives' and reflected rigid gender inequalities. Labor derived from juniors reduced the workload for men, but transport in rotation offered women only moral support in enduring the harshness of porterage labor. Similarly, crop rotation, because it stressed multiyear use of plots, freed men from clearing land yearly, but increased women's work and tied them to the cotton fields; prolonged use of the same plot encouraged the proliferation of weeds, and cutting weeds remained a woman's task.

Cotton and Allocation of Scarce Resources in the Household

Between 1917 and 1935, cotton cultivation yielded only enough for peasants to pay their taxes partly or entirely. Because of these exploitative taxes, differentiation in resource accumulation in the household was not visible; there were no substantial cotton-generated resources to be shared. The main source of inequality remained the disproportionate allocation of the agricultural tasks, and the main expense was taxation. The remainder of cash served to buy basic utensils for the daily functioning of the household: blankets, clothes, and kitchen items. Taxes and low prices for cotton eroded any purchasing power of cotton producers and made it nearly impossible to accumulate any wealth.

Inequality in resource allocation was visible only in highly productive households that received a few prestigious manufactured goods. This differential access to prestige-carrying goods was the outcome of colonial policy: while the periodical allotment of bicycles, sewing machines, and gramophones went to *healthy adult males*, the colonial administration and cotton companies allocated, in their effort to reach the hearts and minds of producers, a small amount of salt to women.[54]

As household income increased after the reform of 1936, further differentiation between household members emerged, and the sites of investment were increasingly gender-diversified. For many male cotton producers, marrying more wives to augment production became the main site of investment. Observations of contemporaries and testimonies of former cotton growers show that cash flowed from cotton companies to husbands. Among the members of the colonial social aggregate, missionaries were certainly those who intruded most into the intimate life of indigenous people. Sister Marie Françoise, supervising a dispensary funded by Cotonco, pointed out in 1936, "The heads of the household are the most docile cotton growers, [because] their wives work while they will have a very well-lined purse at the end."[55] Sensitivity to the plight of female cotton producers was not confined to female missionaries. A humorist, writing in the *Essor colonial et maritime* in 1937, observed, "For the well-off who have bought wives, . . . cotton is a blessing because their wives toil while they reap the benefit."[56] In 1951, an administrator of the Mangbetu cotton producers assessed their plight: "The use of bicycles [had] greatly increased"[57] among men, and women and children had more clothing. Differentiation is further captured in the song sung by women of the same area, striking a chord that is still remembered today: "Where is my husband, I want to use his bicycle." Bicycles and clothes did not carry equal prestige; as a descendant of a former cotton grower reminds us, "Someone having a bike in the village was like someone owning an airplane."[58]

Intrahousehold inequality is further revealed in the wives' search for access to cash. The division of labor, as we have seen, shifted much of the agricultural work to wives. Women sought parallel cottonfields, beside family plots, illustrating that females accepted inequality without challenging male control over the allocation of resources.[59] Actually, their accommodation was only one facet of the story; as we shall see, tensions surfaced over this very issue.

The concept of the healthy adult male hid, as we have seen, the central place of women in growing cotton, and had far-reaching implications for the flow of resources into the household. It established that the household head was the owner of the plot and had ownership rights to its proceeds, whereas before, the one who planted and tended the field usually owned its yield. Thus, the concept contributed to the view that male producers alone had the right to the money earned from cotton. This view has survived until today. When I asked a descendant of former cotton growers, a professor of history, why husbands controlled the use of money, he quickly replied: "Anyway, it was mainly men who were to grow cotton. Every man has a cotton field and when you look at the list of Mambwe chiefdom, it cites individuals who are men and not women. A man could of course get help from his wife or wives."[60] The Hemba view that a woman who provides help does not have ownership of the product affected the distribution of cash in the household. As a Mangbetu saying goes, "Helping somebody build a house does not make you its owner."[61]

From the foregoing evidence, two major conclusions emerge. First, the most significant differentiation that took place in cotton-growing areas was between chiefs and peasants. It arose because of the appropriation of unpaid labor for cotton production on chiefs' plots, production premiums deducted from peasants' remuneration, and the chiefs' power to extract fines and taxes, which further reduced the already low earnings of peasant producers.

From the beginning of the cotton economy to the mid-1930s, taxation remained the principal expense. Inequality appeared as more and more highly productive households received prestige items, which went to men. From 1946 to 1959, as peasants' income increased, men controlled the levers of power and diverted scarce cash to gramophones, bicycles, and sewing machines. These items remained their property; wives received only items for daily living, such as clothes. In all these social inequalities and social injustices, the heavy hand of the colonial situation is evident. For cotton companies, increased profits through increased cotton production was the only goal. The state and the companies imposed a patriarchal world view through the administrative category of the healthy adult male, and intensified preexisting social differentiation in order to exploit all Africans. Peasants, however, were more adversely affected than chiefs, and women were more exploited than men.

5

The Infrapolitics of the Cotton Cultivators

Introduction

The African initiative literature of the 1960s and 1970s paid attention to large-scale social movements, including open rebellions, social banditry, and religious movements, which negated the reality of colonialism as well as the connection of these movements to nationalism.[1] These forms of struggles, however, were only one facet of peasant political behavior. Because these forms of rural struggle were open, they resulted in severe repression, forcing peasants to conceal their hostility and hatred. Peasants, as we will see, engaged in various forms of hidden resistance which obliged colonial officials to change agricultural and labor policy and make concessions to producers.

Peasants resisted cotton production in several ways. They rarely engaged in open collective rebellions, because the dangers of reprisal were great. Only occasionally, in a fit of anger, did they attack cotton monitors, rude chiefs, policemen, crop supervisors, territorial administrators, or agronomists. Instead they protested clandestinely. Peasants undermined the production cycle, prevented the cotton economy from diverting all their labor from housework and food production, and fled into deep forests. Still others migrated to neighboring cities and countries. Peasants also engaged in calculated silence or concealed their hostility and kept colonial planners from impinging further into their intimate life. Cotton cultivation created social inequality within the households, against which women and the young struggled. The market was also a place of struggle. Here, peasants used three major tactics. Some mixed their cotton with heavy materials, hoping to compensate for prices forced below the value of their labor. Others did what they aptly called "taking back one's own cotton" from the company warehouses, selling it in the second or third sale sessions. Others left their cotton to rot on the stalks when they received bad prices during the first sale sessions. Finally, peasants used closed associations to restore social harmony and recover local autonomy.

Struggle over Control of the Production Process

At the very beginning of cotton production, territorial administrators associated the "infrapolitics" of cotton producers with "African laziness." "African laziness" probably stemmed from a body weakened by malnutrition and endemic diseases such as malaria. Weak and sick people cannot work as fast and hard as healthy persons. Hence the cotton system itself, which led to malnutrition, may have caused "laziness," but it was also in part a form of the infrapolitics of cotton producers: a form of disguised, low-profile, undisclosed resistance, whereby peasants disguised their efforts to thwart the appropriation of their labor, their production, and their property.[2] More astute colonial officials realized the ramifications and the meaning of this hidden resistance. They became aware of the cotton cultivators' subtle ability to artfully avoid work obligations, and they reported that "the blacks, artful observers, are quick to discern diverse ambitions of the whites and, in turn, make the most of them by using various forms of flattery, to spare themselves maximum exertion."[3] Most territorial administrators began to report that "peasants were not willing to cultivate the crop."[4] Pointing out the causes of a decline of production in 1921, De Meulemeester, the governor-general of Orientale Province, observed that the main one was the "little good will that most local people show for maintenance that cotton requires from the seeding to the time of harvest."[5] This absence of enthusiasm on the part of the peasants was found in every cotton-producing community. In 1928, Brenez reported the limited enthusiasm of the Luba and Songye for cotton cultivation.[6] What Brenez observed in the Lomami district was also happening in the lower Uele district. Commenting on that district in 1924, Sparano reported that "other indigenous peoples, once they received their seeds, either planted only a portion, or did not seed their fields."[7] Women were targeted as well as men. Native Tribunal records of Bokapo chiefdom reveal that as late as 1945, some women were sentenced to seven days in prison and fined because they had refused to work in their cotton fields.[8] These examples illustrate the peasants' hidden hostility to cotton cultivation, despite the use of force and innumerable attempts at the hegemonic incorporation of cotton cultivators.

The ubiquity of these forms of resistance was rooted in the structural organization of the cotton economy itself. The paucity of cotton markets forced peasants to walk distances of as much as 100 kilometers, thereby meeting and walking along with others from other communities. During these trips and long waits at the marketplaces, they shared experiences that became part of a collective memory. Prisons, where dissident peasants met, were another site for the exchange of personal experiences. The similarity of these experiences contributed further to the spread of modes of hidden resistance.

Fleeing Coerced Toil

"The first reaction of Africans when an agent approached their village to organize the forced cropping system for the first time was to flee into the forest: the village either became empty or only a few old men remained. We see these flights again today in the backwater regions which remain untouched by Europeans."[9] Many peasants avoided cotton cultivation by fleeing into the deep forest and bush, where they built innumerable "camouflaged villages" *(villages camouflés)*, comparable to the maroon communities in the Caribbean Islands and the Americas, and to Quilombo in Brazil.[10] The village of Loho in the Ubangi district, probably a unique case, is a prime example. Loho is an area stretching between Banzyville, Gemena, and Bosobolo Territories in the Ubangi district. As early as 1934, territorial administrators noted Loho as a "hiding place for African out-laws" in their reports, a role it continued to play until 1955. In 1938, peasants from some chiefdoms had retreated into this remote place, where they had erected refuges, viewed by the colonial order as shelters for fleeing professional criminals. In colonial semantics, outlaws were not people who were dangerous to their fellows, but men and women who opposed submission to colonial rule. Among those who "sought insistently to settle in isolated refuges" were peasants who had attacked crop supervisors, tax-collectors, chiefs, cotton-monitors, and policemen. There were also alienated cotton cultivators who had refused to pay their taxes, those who had escaped from prison, and those who refused to perform forced labor obligations in agriculture, road construction, and bridge maintenance.[11]

Peasants could flee only as long as the administration remained weak in the countryside. Beginning in the 1930s, as the state and cotton companies expanded the local transportation network, the forest and bush gradually ceased providing a lasting shelter to most of those seeking freedom.[12] Indeed, the appropriation of peasant income financed the construction of roads connecting peasant communities to colonial centers of power. These roads allowed rapid movement of troops to intimidate peasants, establishing a culture of fear. The state undertook a number of military campaigns against these camouflaged villages, dispatching soldiers to terrorize peasants in Gemena territory; while in nearby Banzyville Territory mostly among the Ngbaka (Bwaka) people, police operation's took place.[13] Of the many reasons that led the state to undertake military operations against these outlaws for ten months in 1937, an officer singled out the need "to bring back the natives to do legal obligations in growing cotton and peanuts."[14] Thus, though by 1936 the state had moved away from the use of violence, it often strengthened control through repression to substantially reduce peasants' free social spaces. Celebrating the results, another officer wrote, "Passive resistance diminishes, the natives gather bit by bit along the roads, taking census is in progress, the natives rebuild their houses and grow cotton."[15] The power of colonial military force demonstrated to cotton cultivators that as a group they could only live within the system and that a complete withdrawal from the cotton economy was open only to individuals. Collective withdrawal was impossible—an attempt, as an old man aptly put it, to "run behind the horizon."[16] Nevertheless, as late as 1955, almost two decades later, peasants were still fleeing into the forest when colonial officers arrived, finally forcing officials in Bosobolo to adopt less brutal action toward these "outlaws": "Only patience and persuasion will get the better of this deplorable attitude. Acting otherwise would incite the indigenous people to flee to French Equatorial Africa, like what is happening in Banzyville Territory where migrations are frequent and difficult to stop."[17] Migrations were another "weapon of the weak" that withdrew labor from the realm of production. The viability and outcome of this mode of struggle depended on the cotton cultivators' ability to use the resources at their disposal, notably the environment, ecology, vital information at critical moments, and the relative weakness of the local administration.

Whereas internal migration was used especially by peasants who lived far from international borders, those located near international borders combined internal migrations with flights to neighboring countries. For example, Loho's location near an international border offered a definite advantage; when its inhabitants were hunted by the Belgian military force, they could flee to Ubangi-Chari, where an ethnic network offered relative anonymity.[18] In 1938, many peasants in Bosobolo fled to French Equatorial Africa. When counting Bosobolo's population for 1955, territorial administrators found that as many as 2,550 peasants had crossed the border to settle in Pandu, a village in French Equatorial Africa. And as late as 1957, Belgian officials were still complaining that there were flights from Libenge and Bosobolo to the Ubangi-Chari. "The border here is a line which stops nobody," said a Belgian official who was frustrated by flights of Azande peasants to Sudan and of the Alur cotton growers of Mahagi to Uganda.[19] Available quantitative data do not allow an analysis of the phenomenon before 1940, yet territotorial administrators allude to the "usual" migrations to the Sudan prior to that time. A colonial inspector in the Dungu Territory in 1947 discovered that in the Renzi chiefdom, approximately 150 to 200 peasants had migrated to the Sudan; two years later, the seasonal and "family" migrations escalated in the same region to 2,661 people. Whereas 931 Azande, Alur, and Logo people of Zaire fled to the Sudan in 1955, as many as 2,904 Sudanese crossed the border into Faradje, Mahagi, and Dungu.[20]

Two-way migrations occurred also between Zaire and Uganda. In 1955, as many as 3,500 people deserted Zaire to migrate to Uganda. Three years later, 715 people fled to Uganda, while 7,300 peasants of Zaire moved back and forth between the two countries. What prospect could a flight to Uganda offer to dissident peasants from neighboring Zaire? Current scholarship on Uganda has exaggerated the so-called prosperity bred by cotton. Researchers, isolating high prices paid to peasants and failing to look at cotton cultivation as a total process, have incorrectly associated the cotton scheme in Uganda with prosperity.[21] High prices notwithstanding, cotton cultivation in Uganda was based on tenancy, which is a system of exploitation. Of course tenancy allowed a certain flexibility in organizing labor compared to state-controlled production, but it did not free workers from the exploitation of their labor and the extraction of surpluses by those who owned land. Here is an excerpt from the *Cotton Trade Journal:*

> The normal tenant farmer in Buganda pays a rent, known as Busulu, to his landlord, which amounts to Shs. 8/50 a year plus Shs. 1/50 for land tax, irrespective of the size of the holding. In addition, he has to render a kind of tithe, known as Nvujo, which amounts to Shs. 4/ for a plot of cotton not exceeding one acre and a further Shs. 4/ if it exceeds an acre. Nvujo was also levied on brewing of beer.[22]

In the final analysis, movement from one hostile environment to another involves several factors—not just resistance, but also ethnic networks, colonial labor forms in different countries, local politics, and the hope for free social space. The traditional territories of the Ngbandi, Azande, and Alur peoples stretch across Zaire, the Central African Republic, the Sudan, and Uganda. The encapsulation of these peoples within colonial borders did not coincide with ethnic boundaries. As they had in the past, people still moved back and forth across borders. To temporarily avoid colonial demands, peasants used ethnic ties that facilitated their movements. While colonial demands motivated peasants to migrate and ethnic ties paved the way, the structural conditions and social organization of work in migrant-receiving countries shaped the cotton cultivators' perception of exploitation and influenced their choices. Explaining why peasants fled to the British Sudan in the late 1940s, a high-ranking colonial official from colonial Zaire pointed out the recruitment for the militia and the Force Publique, the abandonment of the village system there, and a weakening of control at the Sudanese border.[23]

Flight to neighboring countries was not just the result of forced cotton cultivation. At times, local politics was the direct catalyst. Tensions surfaced between state officials, chiefs, and local representatives of the Church, and these power struggles in local communities precipitated flight. One of the best known examples is the case of Subchief Bitima who, after having attracted thousands of peasants to join him to the Sudan to avoid forced labor, went back after the war with a good number of his followers. Conflict between this Azande headman and a Catholic Church catechist led the latter to subversive preaching that caused international migrations. The catechist exhorted his Christian followers to oppose recruitment, to desert to the Sudan, and reject traditional labor levies and colonial forced labor. His discourse, combined with a weak system of imposition in the Sudan, influenced many peasants. In another case the flight of Chief Bobwandera to the Sudan in 1943 drained his large following.[24]

While labor drafts, tax collections, local politics, and difficult access to women's labor contributed to migrations, the centrality of cotton cultivation in the rural economy and its intrusion into the very fabric of social life was the major cause.[25] Poor people, especially young men who were unable to marry and thereby unable to share their obligations, were most likely to migrate. Some young men married if they could as soon as they were driven into cotton cultivation. Married cultivators, relying upon their family labor, found their workload lighter and became more tied to commodity production. As a result, men sought to have more wives. Those who failed to find a wife opted for migrations, because for them "life in the villages meant poverty, and often undernutrition."[26] An excerpt from the 1937 *Essor Colonial et Maritime* illustrates this:

In villages, there are two types of Blacks. The have-nots, who are bachelors, and the well-off, who had bought wives. As for the former, the establishment of cotton plots which they must plant, reap

and carry themselves and which give them a little benefit for all the
work they do, cotton is a calamity. For the latter, cotton is a blessing
because their wives will toil whereas they reap the benefit. The
well-off, relaxing in a deckchair, enjoy good life in cotton zones.
The have-nots, on the contrary, will have only one idea: *y jouer la
fille de l'air.* [to flee][27]

Sister Françoise Marie wrote in the late 1930s that "in general, the heads
of the family appeared to be the most docile producers."[28] Unmarried
cultivators were also more likely to migrate because of their lack of social ties. Furthermore, moving with large families increased the danger
of being captured by the police. By the end of World War II, there was
an overall consensus that bachelors were becoming rare in the countryside; most of them had gone to urban centers and to the mines. As a result "the population of the countryside became aged."[29]

Large migrations from cotton-growing areas began as early as the
1930s. These migrations were different in that they involved choosing
an alternative and playing off one European interest against another. In
1937 for example, 2,000 cotton cultivators from the Malonga area fled to
the mines, and approximately 3,500 others left other territories to migrate to upper Katanga mining centers.[30] There were significant reductions in the number of cotton cultivators in Colocoton zones; of the
20,737 peasants cultivating the crop in 1939, only 12,507 were still cultivating in 1945. Thus, in six years, Colocoton suffered a 39 percent loss of
cotton producers within its zones.[31] The Cotonco zone of Mwene Ditu
went through a similar crisis. The number of peasant households that
cultivated cotton dropped from 16,034 in 1940 to 10,195 in 1945. Over
the same period, the number of peasants in Cotonco zones in the Lomami district dropped from 51,028 to 39,309. From 1939 to 1945, as many
as 49,000 cotton cultivators in Kasai, Lulua, Kanda-Kanda, and Kabinda
voted against forced cotton cultivation with their feet. As late as 1955,
territorial administrators in Uele still reported that young Mangbetu
men continued to migrate to find jobs in European enterprises. The
Council of Orientale Province observed a gradual decrease in the number of cotton cultivators, and the land under cultivation dropped from
121,085 hectares to 107,246 hectares in 1958.[32]

The effects of migrations were mixed. On the negative side, migrations intensified the workload for those who remained, usually women.
Increased colonial demands fell on a fewer remaining peasants. Moreover, migrations in some areas undermined the food security of the
peasants. Evidence from Kanda-Kanda, Kabinda, and Tshiofa shows
that peasants were forced to buy food that they could no longer pro-

duce. Beside producing cotton, the remaining peasants maintained roads, provided forced labor, and supplied food to the mines and urban centers. Migrations distorted communities and households and had particularly adverse effects on women. For example, the small communities in the Kabinda and Tshilenge territories located along the right bank of Lubilashi river had 16,503 men, 27,186 women, and 29,559 children in 1940. It is worth recalling that in addition to their other work, women shouldered the majority of the household work. On average, one woman supported at least 1.6 people, and in the Bena Shimba chiefdom, one woman supported two people.[33] Therefore, in both the short and long term, migrations disrupted colonial economies, and stopping them was a necessary condition for the continued commoditization of African labor. The colonialist solution came in July, 1945, when two ordinances were passed to stop further migrations of rural populations. The new legislation regulated conditions under which permission to move could be granted to peasants and empowered local courts to force the return of those who had illegally migrated to urban centers, thus regulating the movement of rural populations.[34] The ultimate measure to stabilize labor was the establishment of paysannats which were intended to increase households' income and stop migrations. On the positive side, migrations and threats of flight forced the state to reduce workdays for unmarried peasants, and they altered the authoritarian social organization of production. In 1944, the Council of Elisabethville Province proposed to reduce a bachelor's workload to two-thirds that of a married household.[35] Forced cotton cultivators, then, despite their subordinate class position, affected policies and the direction of change in the countryside.

Hidden Struggle against Coerced Toil

"The owners of cotton fields are in general invisible and cannot be found. . . . The Alur is very peaceful but gifted with a harmful idleness and knows how to avoid artfully and easily his work obligations."[36] From the beginning of cotton imposition, peasants located cotton fields on poor land, reduced the size of plots, boiled, roasted, and discarded seeds, or cut the roots of the plants to avoid a total immersion into production and convince the authorities that another crop would be better. In the early years, the Azande, Boa, Luba, Ngbandi, Songye, Tetela, and Mangbetu peasants deliberately located their cotton plots in exhausted or less fertile lands and reserved the most fertile soils for food crops.[37] The practice was widespread enough to attract colonial officials' attention. Writing in 1930, a state agronomist stated, "What we can confirm is that there are some well cleaned fields, cultivated on time in good terrain and which yield between 600 and 700 kilograms and even more. In contrast to these, there are also fields producing less than 700 kilograms because they are purposely established in less fertile soil or exhausted terrain in order to block European effort."[38] Another agronomist indicated that in the Ubangi district opposition came from the headmen who advised peasants to put aside good land for food staples and to grow cotton on exhausted lands that gave an additional advantage of being easier to clear.[39]

Available evidence shows that Tetela peasants in Sankuru boiled seeds before they planted them from the beginning of cotton imposition. As early as 1925, people on the southern plains of the Lubefu River told a state agronomist in broken Tshiluba, "Buloba kutamba kapia," which means, "The soil is burning the cotton seeds."[40] Peasants knew that open refusal and direct confrontation would be suicidal, while their tactics of thwarting germination frustrated the cotton economy and brought a lower degree of suffering.[41] By using such "weapons of the weak," cotton cultivators hoped to convince the state and cotton companies that the land was not appropriate for cotton cultivation, even though this was not an easy way to struggle against a system that closely controlled them. Studying the African response to the forced cropping system in Kamina, Nkulu Kalala explains, "In Nkingo, peasants had agreed to grow cotton but at the same time, they found a subtle device: They boiled the seeds before they planted them." In 1924, Sparano observed similar sabotage among the Azande and Ngbandi cotton cultivators in Bondo. "Other indigenous people, once they received the seeds, either planted only a portion of it, or did not seed it at all." Explaining decreased production in 1930 in the Uele-Bomu district, Sparano pointed out, "these unsatisfactory results are due to the fact that local people abandon a portion of their seeds." U. Blommaert, a cotton expert in the Uele noted, "In general, the sowing in native agriculture necessitates 20 kilograms per hectare because we must take into account the fact that a great deal of it is wasted." Roasting cotton seeds was widely practiced; because African producers knew that Colonial officials were aware of such tactics, they commonly nicknamed them *matala-tala*, meaning "wearing glasses," to mean an officer who carefully checked seeds and cotton fields. The Azande producers called a careful state agronomist or crop supervisor "he who looks at the manure heaps," and "he who checked if the seeds planted had been burned and thrown out negligently in the waste."[42] It was not only peasants who burned, boiled, and discarded seeds. Chiefs and elders whom the state failed to support in local political disputes engaged in similar acts. Early on,

Stocker reported that some Mangbetu chiefs in Niangara Territory, "instead of sowing the seeds, hid them and kept them from the villagers."[43] Cotton producers, especially in the Uele, also deceived officials by reducing the sizes of their plots. Sometimes two or three households worked together in one plot instead of two or three as required by the administration.[44] Like their husbands, wives resisted state control at the point of production by sabotaging the process of production. They refused to cut off old stalks and weeds or to cut roots when weeding; they boiled cotton seeds before seeding them. Colonial annals are replete with stories of "women who were whipped because they have refused to provide corvée labor on chiefs' cotton fields, preferring to work their own gardens."[45] Boa women, for example, "opposed the extension of cotton plots because they shouldered much of the weeding."[46] Whippings, fines, and jail sentences were the most common punishments for "insubordinate" women. However, the scattering of small plots supervised by a small number of crop supervisors over a huge cotton-growing area made resistance viable.

Another tactic primarily used by peasant women to undermine production was to weed late or not at all. Mascart, an agronomist in charge of the Bili region, found that 52 percent of fields were poorly maintained after inspecting 248 cotton fields in 1930. Sentences passed by Native Tribunals show that many women were condemned because they had failed to cultivate and maintain cotton fields. Every cotton-producing district in the 1930s faced opposition from men and women who refused to follow the orders of agronomists to pick cotton, leaving it to rot on the bush. C. Coperus, for example, noted that in 1927 cotton cultivators in Maniema, dissatisfied with low prices, engaged in this practice to oppose the expansion of cotton. As a result up to 50 percent of good cotton was abandoned in the fields. In the lower Uele and Ubangi districts, "people were not harvesting all their crop," and a colonial officer estimated that "hundreds of tons of seed cotton were so wasted." Peasants used the method as late as 1940.[47] This sabotage was in the hope that the crop would be abandoned.

Silence: Creative Adaptation

It is easy for men who work in the fields all day long to fall into the habit of silence as they mull endlessly over one thing and another. The mystery of things, their how and why, conduces to silence.[48]

So far, I have explored forms of resistance which negated the appropriation of labor, implying that working in the cotton fields was collaboration with one's own exploitation. It was collaboration in spite of oneself, and peasants resisted when they could. It is true that silence did not challenge the cotton scheme, and suggesting that it did may lead to the conclusion that everything was resistance. In spite of the difficulty of decoding the meaning of silence in the performance of assigned work, I contend that silence was an example of agency, a creative adaptation and a way of coping with the appropriation of labor. A close examination of colonial records as well as conversations with former cotton growers supports this argument.[49] Confusion about this point arose because the majority of colonial officials failed to grasp the meaning of work performance. For most of them, silence and conformity implied the absence of opposition and resistance. Likewise, whenever people worked on their fields of cotton, territorial administrators hastily concluded that "no manifestation of defiance [was] indicated." They failed to discern that the completion of assigned work concealed hostility and hatred, that the peasants' silence was active, their conformity was calculated, and that many actions which were perceived to be expressions of "African laziness" and "African incapacity to foresee the future" were actually forms of struggle against cotton cultivation. As pointed out elsewhere, laziness could be due to illness and malnutrition or to ill will. "African incapacity to foresee the future" could be merely good economic sense, that is, choosing to care for food crops first, or it could be a case of resistance. One cannot know the truth in every individual case, but given the other expressions of resistance, especially running amok, it must frequently have been a form of resistance.

Labor was as valuable to peasants as it was to colonial economic planners. As enmeshed in the system as cotton producers were, however, performing work to secure and preserve a little bit of peace had a different meaning: it was a strategy to keep colonial officers from intervening further in their intimate lives. Mangbetu cotton cultivators, to take just one example, maintained social space in this way. An astute territorial administrator realized the meaning of calculated compliance:

> Mangbetu people, naturally peaceful, seem to live beside us. Very subdued, the Mangbetu in general accept a European and his action, but they like neither. They have reached a conception of resignation, a de facto situation, and their innate opportunism leads them to do what we ask of them in order to avoid trouble. In fact, the relations between the administration and the population are not based on mutual comprehension, but it is a *modus vivendi* wherein the ward suffers in silence the authority of the guardian.[50]

Ngbandi cotton producers told me that "saying yes to a territorial administrator was a hymn to liberty" they learned to live with. Here is some of our dialogue:

Q: What did you do when you disagreed with a cotton monitor's order?

A: To whatever we heard, the best answer was to say yes.

If he asked you to take the seeds, say yes and take them, you will conceal some of them in the heap.

If he chooses to pick the land, say yes because any land is a bad land.

The hot water kills all seeds.

Q: Why did you do this?

A: We wanted them to think that we obeyed the law in order to be in peace.

Although only a few colonial officials were aware of the true significance of submission to cultivating cotton, there was shared fear. Bertrand, an army officer, said, "On the basis of my recent and personal experience, I know that almost in the entire colony, we obtain from our subjects total submission, but I also know that we are preparing a generation of rebels."[51] Of the Azande people, another officer pointed out, "The Azande people, very disciplined, [submit] by doing easily works and *corvées* the authority imposes; but it is very difficult to know what these people, who are not very communicative, think. . . . Those people obey us simply to keep us away from interfering in the intimate life of their communities."[52]

"Taking Back One's Own Cotton": Minimizing Surplus Extraction

Ah! There was a lot of cotton!
White man has just bought it,
How come I have only a little money left!
What happened?[53]

This song, sung by women while transporting cotton to the trading stations, reveals peasant understanding of the unequal exchange taking place in the market sphere and the degree to which they were exploited by the artificially depressed prices for their produce. They reacted in several ways. They refused to sell their produce or abandoned it by the wayside. They also refused to continue harvesting or harvested unripe cotton. Alternatively they would mix the cotton with debris to falsify the weight, or even go as far as raiding stores to "take back their own." In his study of forced cropping in the Tanganyika district, Kasendwe Kibonge concluded, "Reactions to low prices manifested on the market days. When prices were announced, women closed their baskets and returned home."[54] It made little difference whether the cotton was sold or not; both options were equally impoverishing. Some peasants abandoned their bags of cotton along the road to the market, which was often located far from the villages. Many others refused to continue harvesting.[55]

The practice of mixing seed cotton with stones and heavy materials was yet another indication of peasants' perception of the appropriation of their cotton.[56] This was why some peasants "picked wet cotton as they knew that it was heavier and that the benefit would belong to them."[57] Others "tended to accumulate at the bottom of their baskets all forms of debris if not heavy materials."[58] The extra weight compensated for the cheating by the buyers and for the low prices. This was a very limited option, however, since it carried serious consequences. Those who were caught suffered imprisonment, flogging, and fines. Control of loads intensified because mixing cotton with stones caused fires in gins.[59] On many occasions, company agents forced peasants to sort their cotton, spending additional days in trading stations. Agents not only refused to buy poorly sorted cotton, a punishment that impoverished households, but also intensified control at the market. As cotton was bought, bags were immediately carried to the warehouses and the contents scattered to ensure that other materials were not mixed in.[60] It was difficult to supervise all producers closely, however, and peasants often expressed their resistance in this way.

Peasants also resorted to raiding the company warehouses for cotton. To territorial administrators, this was stealing, but an old man smilingly described how peasants' saw their acts in this way: "We did not steal, we took back our cotton."[61] While the state and cotton companies viewed these acts as theft, cotton cultivators viewed them as taking back a portion of what the company usurped. There are few references to stolen cotton in colonial records. One important reason is that company warehouses were watched day and night by African guards, making it difficult for peasants to retake their cotton. Another reason is that when peasants succeeded, their acts went unnoticed. Only after the ginning operations could the companies discover any substantial loss of cotton from their warehouses. "Retaking one's own cotton" was widely practiced, even though there is little documentation of this form of resistance. As early as 1934, Azande cotton growers in Dika chiefdom were reported to have taken back a portion of their cotton from Cotonco's warehouses.[62] The best example of this tactic occurred in 1947, when territorial administrators discovered a network composed of Chief Vura, four Cotonco warehouse watchers, and twenty-one peasants. Chief Vura, explaining his involvement to District Commissioner Kreuz in 1947, said, "From the very beginning of cotton cultivation, cotton has always been stolen, not only in my chiefdom but also in all other chiefdoms." The colonial officer investigating the case described when and how the group operated:

> Such activities took place late in the night with the complicity of the keepers of cotton companies warehouses who were underpaid. . . . [I]n the countryside, warehouse keepers receiving modest salaries and guarding for thousands of francs that cotton generates, keep the key of the warehouses which are located far from Europeans and beyond any control. . . . [When cotton is stolen] the deficit can not be noticed and the causes are known only after cotton had been evacuated and ginned. Moreover, the doors of warehouses are made of temporary materials easy to remove and replace without this being noticed, remained open all night.[63]

The four warehouse keepers were sentenced respectively to thirty, twelve, ten, and six months in prison. Chief Vura got a twelve-month jail sentence, and the sentence for the peasants ranged from two to five months in jail. This system of repression may also account for the low record of these acts thereafter.

Women and Juniors Fight Exploitation

Cotton cultivation also generated tensions within households, especially between men and women, but also between seniors and juniors. Gross inequality in the distribution of agricultural tasks and in the distribution of cash provoked a growing rebellion of wives against their husbands, especially in the northeast, for in cotton-producing peasantries, cotton disrupted domestic obligations. While the social organization of production burdened wives, the distribution of cash denied property rights to women. But wives could file lawsuits against greedy husbands to obtain compensation and to redress the unequal distribution of cash. These intrahousehold tensions stemmed from the place of cotton within the global peasant economy, the conditions cotton production created, the possibility offered by local courts to mediate women's claims, and the extent to which such negotiations changed women's perception of their role in the new economy and society.

Intrahousehold tensions meant that women had to fight on two fronts. On the one hand they resisted cotton cultivation itself, and on the other they struggled against their husbands. The main means of opposition to husbands included divorce and lawsuits, to which husbands responded with negotiations, beatings, repudiations, and the elaboration of stereotypes that presented women as the real opposition against the administration and cotton interests. Lawsuits against stingy husbands were the most effective weapons wives used to restore their right to cash. Post-1946 Native Tribunal records from the northeast of the country illustrate women's efforts to obtain rights to cotton money. One verdict handed down from the tribunal of the Bakengai chiefdom in 1951 reads as follows: "Mrs. Nagugiyoko institutes proceedings against her husband with whom she has lived for five years. The reason: he had repudiated her without paying her anything despite the fact that during the five years of marriage, she worked with him on cotton fields."[64] Mrs. Nagugiyoko prevailed, and her former husband was sentenced to pay her 400 francs. The registers of the Ezo chiefdom provide further evidence. After three years of marriage, a husband broke up the union while keeping the cash earned out of cotton cultivation for himself. Bringing the case to court, his wife asked to "be compensated for cotton they had sold together," and she received 250 francs. Similarly, a woman repudiated for disobedience toward her husband demanded to be paid for "her work done on cotton fields." Again, the tribunal decided to give her half the returns from cotton cultivation.[65] Such successful lawsuits empowered women. They established wives' rights to the product of their labor. Above all, they transformed the way women perceived themselves and changed their social inferiority as the new social order allowed a woman to "sue her husband [when] he paid her nothing for her work done on cotton fields."[66]

That women gained power from successful lawsuits is reflected in the conclusion reached by a high magistrate who inspected numerous Native Tribunals of the Azande region in 1947. This officer, astonished by the number of conflicts between husbands and wives and the capacity of the latter to protect their interests successfully, urged territorial administrators "to inquire in every jurisdiction on the development which permits women to present themselves [and] their concerns about bridewealths and compensation for work on cotton fields to the tribunals and to find out why they almost always prevail and receive the payment."[67] Seven years after the publication of his report, another territorial administrator observed that "the number of affairs brought by women was still increasing."[68] An old judge told me, "Every time I had to render the verdict involving a husband and his wife about money, I had to hesitate and gnash my teeth; as I saw it, it was like every verdict made women more powerful than ever before."[69] Beside beatings, insults, and male impotence, which accounted for many disputes in cotton-producing households, lack of support in cash and goods motivated wives to leave their husbands. Evidence is still thin, but it suggests that from the mid-1930s to 1955, women increasingly used divorce to protest against their exclusion from family decision making in regard to sharing scarce cotton-generated cash. Both Azande and Mangbetu women exemplify women's struggle to gain economic autonomy through divorce. Many asked for divorce to obtain compensation for their "work on the cotton field." The annual report of Rungu Territory for 1953 recorded as many as 21 women who divorced their husbands in one quarter, and in 1955, 74 women left their husbands during the first quarter. Similarly, the report indicated that in 1953, 184 Mangbetu women deserted their households. Moreover, more and more women, contrary to the custom that holds that the bridewealth be reimbursed by a future husband, repaid bridewealths' payment themselves to their former husbands.[70] The high rate of divorce and the ability of wives to repay the bridewealth represented a new pattern in women's behavior.

The power of female cotton cultivators to deconstruct unequal relations within the household can be hardly overstated because structural limitations were so great. Stability of the household was of considerable interest in the success of forced cotton cultivation, and whenever it was jeopardized, territorial administrators advised family mediations and asked local judges and chiefs to "stop the propensity of wives to leave their husbands."[71] Local tribunals were primarily designed for social regulation, and their functioning still contained several mechanisms that controlled and subordinated women. Many cases show brothers of runaway wives jailed for having housed their unhappy sisters. Very often, fathers were coerced into reimbursing the bridewealths every time their daughters ran away.[72] Though wives technically had the right to return to their lineage when their marriage failed, these practices undermined it. The need to ensure household stability prompted colonial officials to try to use these institutions as ways to control women when commodity production was disrupted beyond economically tolerable boundaries. Marriage was an enduring social contract through which wealth and protection were exchanged between families. From the point of view of local communities, divorce, lawsuits, and repayment of bridewealth by women appeared to be serious threats to the social order that privileged men. This may explain why elopements, the most common individual way in which women sought to end subordination, were severely punished. In 1954 fines for elopement amounted to 500 francs among the Azande of Nguru chiefdom, and the compensation for the husband varied between 500 and 800 francs, amounts equal to the average yearly income.[73]

At the household level, husbands hampered women's capacity to change unhappy relations. To settle conflicts generated by cotton in the household, some husbands resorted to family mediations that prescribed female obedience and presented divorce as an option that brought shame to the family. Others used beatings, though within the limits tolerated by customary law, that is, the law of the colonial administration in a domestic matter.[74] When these methods proved unworkable, husbands had recourse to repudiations, and still others mapped out strategies which appealed to cotton-monitors, chiefs, and territorial administrators by stereotyping women as "idle wives," "disobedient wives," and "women hostile to white man cotton," thereby presenting women as obstacles to production targets. All these caricatures were keys which husbands used to open the doors of jails where their "insubordinate" wives suffered hard work and whipping.[75] Explaining why female cotton cultivators suffered repression by local tribunals, the administrator of Poko Territory reported to the district commissioner that "they have been treated so upon the complaints of their husbands."[76] The tribunal of Bokapo chiefdom recorded in 1946 many cases of "women sentenced 7 days prison and fined 25 francs" because their husbands said that "they don't work on their plots of cotton." As late as 1957, a woman named Nengombasia in Makere chiefdom "was kept in prison for two and half months upon the complaints of her husband who accused her for laziness." During the same period, Kenga, a Mobua woman, was incarcerated upon the complaints of her husband, who accused her of "not working on her field of cotton."[77]

In the war between husbands and wives, wives also used such tactics in defense. Moreover women's gossip, more or less institutionalized, provided them with a strong weapon of defense. Furthermore, prevailing beliefs in witchcraft in some areas made it the weapon of women and the weak (junior men), and in other areas a weapon of senior men. Husbands, for example, took the struggle to the intimate sphere of sexuality to ridicule and silence their wives. Sex and obscenity are social universals. Most anthropologists agree that except for "ritualized insults," which play tension-release roles, insults in general and insults of genitals in particular are aggressive behavior. In French historical tradition, where insults are primarily studied as part of an effort to grasp *mentalités*, they clearly appear as expressions of conflicts.[78] The repertoire of insults I collected indicates that husbands' insults of their wives' sexual organs were expressions of intrahousehold conflicts and a means to ridicule, humiliate, and compel wives to refrain from filing lawsuits against them. Among the Azande cotton producers, a few cases brought to the attention of officials show that angry, jailed husbands introduced grains of sorghum into their wives' vaginas, the epitome of humiliation and ridicule. Other women were labeled "manlike women," and "half-men women." These epithets meant, as one woman recalled, that "nobody would look at you; remarriage was sometimes difficult."[79] These modes of sanction silenced and intimidated many wives. However, the very fact that some women still brought the cases to the local tribunals indicates that husbands failed to control their wives through the use of insults.

Polygyny lightened the load of each co-wife, but it easily set one co-wife against the other, and cotton obligations may have aggravated this. Wealth in cash was sometimes used to increase polygyny. There was unequal distribution of cash and cloth by husbands. Among Luba cotton producers, husbands used a portion of cash to buy guns as gifts for the families of their favored wives.[80]

On the other hand, because women's struggle against their husbands was channeled through local courts, which were colonial institutions of control, they encountered limitations in entirely overcoming exploitative relations. This led to a partial victory, and the struggle became a regulated process, ineffective against the whole system of colonial exploitation. The ultimate winners were the colonial administration and the cotton interests. As a result, some women managed to cultivate a separate field of cotton beside the family plot to bring in some cash. As early as 1932 E. Leplae, the director-general of the Department of Agriculture and the architect of the cotton scheme, concluded on several occasions, "We can note that some women, without being forced, cultivate their own cotton field to get some money out of it."[81] The practice was not motivated by women's love of cotton; it was rather a choice they were forced to make to have cash for their personal needs and avoid confrontations with husbands for control over collectively earned cash. When I asked an old man why this happened, he jokingly replied, "One may say that, when in the past conflict over game has led the group to split, conflict over unequal share of work and cash people received from cotton led to having separate fields of cotton."[82] Like confrontations, accommodation through separate cotton fields pointed to the limitations on women's ability to strike at the source of inequality. Indeed, parallel cotton fields amounted to female self-exploitation that promoted cotton production. Their choice, made to create financial autonomy, provided an escape from direct subordination of husbands rather than economic autonomy, because they received prices that were below the value of their labor.

In addition to causing conflict between husbands and wives, colonial policy also intensified generational conflict. First, selected elders sought to control the labor of junior males. Given that *healthy adult male* was a loose term that allowed territorial administrators to impose taxes on young people primarily on the basis of their physical development, parents and elders circumvented this policy by falsifying the age of their children. This allowed elders to escape taxes and to exploit for their own benefit the labor of children or junior members of the village. Conflict deepened when young men newly driven into cotton cultivation sought to marry wives who would share the workload. This conflict and the effort of the junior males to free themselves from family control were demonstrated by one report: "Often, at the age of fourteen or fifteen years, young men—among whom some are not but children—are considered as taxpayers, not because of the territorial administrators whim, but because they become so voluntarily."[83] Another indication of intergenerational conflict is found in the patterns of migrations, which show that from the 1940s, young men deserted their villages to escape rigid discipline.[84] Among the many causes of this junior male exodus, colonial officials identified intergenerational conflicts whose roots were labor and access to wives, in addition to commodity production.

Closed Associations: The Struggle for Social Harmony

> The major obstacle to the diffusion of our ideas is the existence
> of so many magicians, oracles, and other *nganga* [healers] who
> maintain people's minds in fear and superstition through the
> existence of countless secret societies.[85]

Prior to colonization, there existed in many cultures closed associations which played special roles ranging from initiating young men and women into adulthood to imbuing hunters with magical powers.[86] Faced with increased economic hardship, the destruction of cultural values, attacks on daily life, and new social differentiation, noted healers, *nganga*, and inspired prophets created new religious movements. These movements aspired to maintain social harmony in spite of the destabilization of state, corporate, and African collaborators and to recover local autonomy. Because villages were controlled by state-appointed chiefs, the tactical independence of peasants was greatly reduced. Closed associations also provided ideas for awakening the consciousness of struggle and the construction of a political language.

In addition to true secret societies such as Mani or Anioto, well known before 1914, Belgian colonial semantics also defined as secret societies the African independent churches, including Kimbanguism and Kitawala, and other religious movements whose activities differed from those of validated Catholic and Protestant churches, and which propounded what colonial authorities called *superstition*. In some areas schools of initiation were also suppressed, often at the request of missionary societies, with the excuse that these activities disrupted the production of obligatory crops. From the point of view of the peasants, affiliation with such associations was not at first an act of defiance but merely an attempt at restoring social harmony. But because the colonial authorities interpreted such movements as subversive, they also automatically became a defiance of its rule, and peasants were well aware of it as soon as measures were taken to suppress these movements. From then on, enrolling in such movements became not just a rejection but a defiance of the colonial order. There were numerous closed associations across cotton-growing zones, but for our purpose, we will focus on Kitawala, Anioto, and the art of healing.

To restore social harmony and recover local autonomy, peasants engaged in many activities, which included those of ancestral cults, spirit possession, divination, and public healing ceremonies. Such activities, meaningful in the lives of peasants, were attacked because they did not fit into Eurocentric explanations, and competed with colonial values and the hegemonic incorporation of peasants in the colonial social order. When the art of healing, which colonial officials equated with superstition, successfully attracted peasants, it represented subversion and an obstacle to the progress of modern medicine. The extension of medical and social services to remote communities was in part a deliberate colonial policy to fight the art of healing and colonize people's consciousness.[87] From this point of view, healing was a battlefield between the state and marginalized traditional elites and a source of internal power struggles between the latter and state-appointed chiefs. In fact, the social function of healing allowed healers to draw large followings opposed to chiefs.[88] The story of Yangara, the headman of Gindo chiefdom and Bapaenge, the healer, exemplifies the internal struggle: "Bapaenge did his apprenticeship as a healer in Likati. When he came back to Gindo chiefdom, he attracted numerous people who believed in his talents. . . . Bapaenge claimed that people must devote their time to the work of God rather than to the work of the state and chiefs."[89] Bapaenge also dealt with the social concerns that peasants faced in their daily lives. He forbade committing adultery, smoking hemp, and drinking alcohol, which were the main causes of intracommunity conflicts.

His definition of standards of personal conduct shows that there were competing sources of order.[90]

Kitawala, also called Watch-Tower and Toni-toni, beside being Christian-inspired, was the most pervasive of all organizations and reached many peasant communities. It was a Bible-inspired movement that most attracted the attention of territorial administrators, mine managers, priests, and the weak settler class because it was propagated in many peasant communities.[91] Introduced from Zambia in 1925 in Katanga urban mining areas, it first attracted urban dwellers, including mineworkers, domestics, soldiers, and state employees. Labor migrations, troop movements, and actions taken against leaders and members eventually brought Kitawala here and there across the whole of eastern Zaire. The decentralization of its organization and the diversity of its leadership contributed to its spread, and were evidenced in the common view that "in the Congo, the movement changes as the leadership wishes." Because of harsh repression, the members and leaders of Kitawala never succeeded in building a church. This lack of an established structure allowed continuous splits in small communities and adaptation to new situations, making Kitawala effective in restoring social harmony and in the struggle against oppression.

The Kitawala movement recruited its adherents not only among the colonial elites, but from all oppressed segments. Its teaching stood in opposition to colonial ethics. In 1936, for example, using an interpretation of selected biblical verses which contradicted Catholic teachings, clerks, workers and artisans demanded social and political rights. They targeted "the state, church, capitalism, and black nationalism." Mine managers and territorial administators feared the movement when they saw "the pamphlets displaying pictures of whites being attacked."[92] Kitawala was brought into cotton-growing zones with the same militancy and vigor as cotton cultivation itself. It opposed colonial ethics which stressed docility and submission: "Wherever they preached, Watch-Tower leaders announced the coming of God, who would take over the direction of a fierce struggle against every form of established authority and give to local people heaven on earth. They also ordered the stoppage of any work."[93]

Kitawala utopian ideology was attractive to cotton producers because the leadership was able to foster hope. The activities that began in 1932 and climaxed in 1950 in the Dilolo area illustrate the impact of the Kitawala movement. That year, an Angolan Kitawala leader who was expelled from Zaire to Texeira in Angola preached forthcoming salvation. This teaching not only caused a panic in Texeira, but resulted in innumerable killings of black cattle in Dilolo, an act that was symbolic of the raising of the dead and the transformation of blacks into whites. The symbolism of black and white cattle represented a passage from forced cropping to free choice: "Whites do not grow cotton, they have us do it. In order to be able to stop working on the fields, we needed to be like them."[94] The impact of the ideology of Kitawala went beyond symbolism and could be seen in its rapidly growing membership. In Banze, a cotton-growing region between Nyunzu and Kalemie, two formerly exiled leaders mobilized approximately 200 adherents among cotton producers in a few weeks. In 1938, cotton growers as well as the *évolués* (elites) were involved in Kitawala activities in the Nyunzu-Kabalo region of the Tanganyika district. Again, the design, content, and logic of the message reflected the ability of the leadership. Because the peasantry was already stratified, the message varied accordingly: "To commoners, Watch-Tower leaders promised that the baptism would free them from the evil spell of wizards, and once the Messiah came, he would make them equal to whites. To the *évolués*, they taught the deposition of Europeans, access to independence and equality, and the possession of wealth once owned by the dominators."[95]

The promise of becoming "equal to whites" and possessing wealth found fertile soil in the minds of cotton cultivators who wished to see the end of cotton production, or, if it had to continue, wished to see prices rise. One colonial official was quick to say that peasants "adhere to the ideologies which adapt to their superstitions. . . . Kitawala attracted entire communities and even all the population of an entire region which adhered to their rites."[96] The activities of Kitawala were not confined to southern cotton-growing districts adjacent to mine camps; they reached the northern districts as well. In 1938, though the colonial administration maintained that the movement had been suppressed, Kitawala members relegated from Katanga attempted to establish the sect there. Indeed, Kitawala, taking the name of Molimo, a local Christian name for God, reached the cotton-growing district of Ubangi in the Banzyville area in 1951. Reports of territorial administrators mirror the extent to which the teaching of Kitawala shaped the political behavior of peasants there. In 1951, for example, the population of the area was "the most receptive to subversive ideas."[97] Kitawala leaders directly attacked every authority, both European and African, in their teachings. In Orientale Province, cotton cultivators who were Kitawala adherents were the most active against colonial authority. Out of 179 peasants exiled in 1943, for example, as many as 139 were Kitawala members. As late as 1956, a territorial administrator still wrote, "Kitawala remains the greatest of our concerns."[98] In 1958 the members of the Council suggested the construction of *foyers sociaux*, "institutions for cultural domestication," as a measure against further propagation of the movement. They proposed the construction of a *foyer* at Pesana in Aketi to prevent 21,700 cotton producers from becoming Kitawala adherents.[99]

Perhaps the most famous and defiant secret society was the Leopard-Man Society, known as Sua or Ngulu in the Ubangi district by Ngbandi peasants and Anioto in Ituri and in Uele by the Boa cotton growers.[100] This society formulated a response not only to the exactions imposed by commodity production and oppression, but also to internal social inequality and disruption. Anioto had already existed as a military organization using terrorism in precolonial Babali land to protect the local village against encroachment by powerful neighbors. In the rubber period of the Congo Free State, this society easily adapted to the new circumstances. Anioto attacked local collaborators and Europeans. It reached several peaks of resistance from about 1907 to 1935, after which a conspiracy of silence began to protect its continued existence. Like the Kitawala movement, the Leopard-Man Society attacked African collaborators, but it differed in its style of struggle and admission requirements. Though every man and woman was eligible to be admitted into the society, membership was selective to screen out "people who collaborated with Europeans and chiefs, in general people who could betray the organization."[101] Like Kitawala, Anioto remained hidden, but in contrast to Kitawala, Anioto violently attacked its targets. The secrecy and violence of the Leopard-Man Society, result of the need to protect its members, were demonstrated by the methods members used to attack colonial officials, chiefs, Christian elites, and African puppets. Every member of the society, while carrying out attacks ordered by the society wore (1) very sharp iron blades representing a leopard's claws in each finger, to slit the victim's throat and make deep gashes in his body; (2) a leopard skin, if the attack was made during the day or by the full moon; and (3) a 30-cm stick with a leopard track carved on the end. The claws, skin, and tracks were used to convince people the killing was done by a leopard, and in this way, the society spread terror across cotton-growing areas.

These insurgent ideologies permeated the hearts and minds of peasants. Exploiting terrorism, Anioto members became less fearful of the colonial authority. Archival and oral data provide evidence of peasants openly refusing to obey chiefs. A verdict of the Kuleponge chiefdom tribunal of March 3, 1930, reads, "Chief Yikpo called people to grow cotton but none came."[102] Vaessen, inspecting the tribunal of Niangara in 1952, tells us "Chief Misi of Manzinga chiefdom prosecutes his subjects because they refuse to obey him," and lists by name and village those peasants who refused to obey headmen.[103] Women's opposition to chiefs was equally conspicuous. Despite chiefs' instructions, women bypassed prescribed markets and refused to work their plots.[104] Songs of hatred against chiefs are still remembered by women after more than three decades. Oral data show that cotton producers sometimes ran amok when the occasion arose. The account of Kayombo, a Hemba cotton grower in Kongolo area, is illuminating:

> I saw by my eyes my maternal uncle whipped. . . . He cursed the white man who ended up by slapping him. This beside the whip he got. . . . My uncle said to the white man: If you slap me again, I am going to beat you. . . . The white man who was just behind the policeman, slapped him again. My uncle responded by seriously beating the white man.[105]

Salaries of chiefs and elders depended on production quotas, taxes collected, and road maintenance achieved in their communities. Chiefs whose subjects failed to meet production requirements suffered harsh treatment. Peasants purposely engaged in production sabotage to put chiefs' and elders' positions in jeopardy. Many Mangbetu Mavaazanga elders were fined and whipped in 1937 because cotton growers within their communities failed to work cotton fields properly. Though colonial policy advised low-ranking officials to avoid humiliating chiefs in public, evidence from the Renzi tribunal indicates that an Azande elder whose people failed to maintain a path connecting two cotton fields in 1945 was whipped in front of his subjects, losing his prestige because of this humiliation.[106] Although open hostility was perceived as a form of suicide, peasants attacked cotton monitors, policemen, and agronomists, and they refused to obey chiefs. They also gave colonial officials insulting nicknames.[107] Tensions also surfaced between peasants and African collaborators, most notably chiefs and elders, as well as within the households. Colonial archives are replete with cases of peasants fighting state-appointed chiefs, whose coercive power was resented. The most threatening challenges to loyalist chiefs' authority and prestige were the ideologies of the secret societies, which promised the destruction of the colonial society.

Studying these hidden forms of protest elsewhere, some scholars explained them in terms of the nature of the labor process and the degree of peasant autonomy.[108] Others have emphasized internal social differentiation to explain the inability of African peasants to mount collective open actions against their oppressors.[109] Still others have equated hidden resistance with the backward social outlook of peasants. In my opinion the ways in which peasant labor was organized, the composition of the labor force, and the degree to which labor for household production was separated in time and space from labor for commodity production are three important elements in explaining peasant struggle. In fact, peasants who were incorporated into different labor processes negotiated and struggled from different positions of relative strength. However, these formulations reveal as much as they obscure. First, the concept of partial autonomy is not very useful. Whatever the conditions under which peasants have worked, they have always enjoyed a certain autonomy, and this makes it difficult to determine when the peasantry will become volatile. Second, the partial autonomy/hidden resistance thesis logically assumes that the narrower the autonomy of peasants, the greater their revolutionary potential. Current scholarship and available data do not support this argument. Studies of peasant experiences point out that an inclination to resist intensified both when the forces of control weakened and when they intensified. Furthermore, peasants expressed opposition to forced gathering and cropping systems long before rigid agricultural calendars structured the rhythm of their lives; they routinely fled to the forest and bush to avoid paying taxes and transporting loads for touring officials. African peasants opposed growing new crops that they could fit in their existing systems of production.[110] This shows that the relations among hidden resistance, the workload, and economic exactions are not direct. Third, the fact that workers, peasants, and slaves engaged in similar acts of defiance requires caution in proposing that partial autonomy alone shaped forms of resistance.[111] The internal class differentiation thesis seems even less convincing. It is true that when peasants are on "The Flat Earth and Social Egalitarianism," that is, when peasants experience social equality, any state demand affects them evenly, allowing the possibility of collective action. But recent scholarship has shown that when peasants engaged in collective resistance, the colonial administration responded with violence, and when force proved unworkable, social control was effective, through gifts and semantic distortion, in reaching the hearts and minds of the peasants and frustrated radicalism.[112]

The infrapolitics of cotton producers in colonial Zaire was rooted in cotton production, but the forms it assumed were determined by a combination of communication lines, systems of social control, and repression. Everyday forms of resistance to cotton production arose from exploitation. Cotton cultivation established three-way sociocommercial relationships among village communities, the colonial state, and cotton companies that served to transfer economic risks from the state and cotton companies to the peasants. While the state and cotton companies assumed marginal productive roles—supervision of labor and imposition of work obligations—they got the lion's share of the profit.

Cotton cultivation also skewed village development. In some areas, cotton competed with and supplanted major staple food crops such as millet and eleusine. The state then forced peasants to grow nutrient-poor manioc instead. In addition to generating food shortages and insecurity, cotton production created labor bottlenecks. The expansion of the cotton market economy reinforced integration into the world market, which increased peasant insecurity. Finally, the price stabilization system was supposedly designed to shield peasants from the shocks of prices fluctuations but kept their income low. However, everyday forms of resistance are better explained by highlighting peasants' cultural autonomy, against which their experiences of exploitation were sorted and evaluated. This is reflected in their ability to nickname officials, to appropriate Kitawala, and to restructure Anioto in order to restore social harmony and recover local autonomy. Their cultural autonomy provided an understanding of how to circumvent work obligations and confront, at minimal cost, the territorial administrators, state agronomists, crop supervisors, chiefs, cotton monitors, and headmen.

In discussing the infrapolitics of the cotton cultivators in colonial Zaire, this chapter has examined the variety of ways in which the peasantry resisted and subverted forced cotton cultivation, and the extent to which their actions influenced colonial policy concerning agricultural economics. It is noteworthy that for all its volatile nature, the system of cotton production did not incite peasants to open collective rebellion, partly because the peasants themselves realized that this was a suicidal option. The cumulative effect of their hidden resistance forced the colonial state to make concessions; economic planners had to devise safety mechanisms based on differential distribution of wealth to veil the basis of exploitation.

Continued flight to the community of Loho until 1955, for example, eventually forced colonial authorities to adopt less brutal repression of the producers. To keep cotton producers working, the state first alleviated the load of peasant work and then reduced forced labor requirements after World War II. The labor requirement for unmarried cotton growers was also cut to two-thirds of that of married households. The state also attempted to ban forced labor.[113] Later, the state forced the cotton companies to improve the technical conditions of production, making fertilizers and tractors available to peasants. In 1956 for example, many Boa cotton producers used 25 tons of fertilizers, and in the following year 1,200 peasants had access to chemical fertilizers.[114] By this time farmers were totally enmeshed in the money economy because they needed money to buy inputs for the fields and not just for consumption. The constant restructuring of the market, while it increased the level of economic exactions, also modified the structure of repression, which reduced peasants' tensions. The 1936 change in state policy to replace the use of force with handouts and colonial propaganda permeated the hearts and minds of peasants. This translated economic exploitation into distribution of wealth and reduced the revolutionary potential of cotton growers.

Conclusion

The foregoing chapters have examined the cotton labor process, the effect of commodity production on rural life, and the ways in which men and women coped with and struggled against forced cotton cultivation. The imposition of cotton cultivation in 1917 constituted a landmark in the history of Zairian rural communities because the expansion of cotton cultivation changed the countryside. The autonomy of cotton producers diminished; the rhythm of people's daily lives was altered; domestic obligations were disrupted; food production decreased; and intrahousehold and intracommunity relations were transformed. From 1920 on, the state granted multiyear concessions of up to 8,000 square kilometers to each of twelve cotton companies operating in the northern and southern regions of Zaire, which were divided into numerous cotton zones. Within these cotton zones, the number of peasants involved in cotton production rose from a few hundred in 1917 to 105,556 households by 1930. Ten years later 700,000 households were involved, and in 1959, as many as 874,000 households were growing cotton, producing as much as 177,000 tons of seed cotton.

The colonial state and the cotton companies achieved this success by using force and the threat of force, as well as structural reforms, material incentives, and propaganda. While the former aimed at instilling fear from 1917 to 1936 in order to keep the cotton producers working even as they suffered losses, the latter sought to instill a new work ethic and values through festivals, films, and plays. In addition, from 1937 to 1960, the state and cotton companies improved compensation for the producers, but never in proportion to the amount of their labor. Barter, low producer prices, failure to monitor the sales, scale rigging and other forms of cheating, cotton-grade manipulation, basket standardization, zoning regulations, and monopsony all kept the producers from accumulating wealth.

The chiefs were the segment of the African population that benefited from growing cotton. Although there were regional income variations among the chiefs, they all derived wealth from the appropriation of peasants' labor for production on their cotton fields, production premiums offered by cotton companies, exemption from taxes, and the reinforcement of their power through the judiciary. Though they did not transform this wealth into capital, their accumulation created differentiation between chiefs and cotton producers. From the beginning of the cotton economy to the mid-1930s, taxation remained the principal expense for peasants. As a result, cotton production caused some degree intercommunity and intrahousehold inequality. Gross inequality appeared only in highly productive households that received prestige items, which went to men. From 1936 to 1959, as peasants' income increased, men—who controlled the levers of power within the households—diverted the cotton money to brideprice, as well as to gramophones, bicycles, and sewing machines. These items remained husbands' property; wives received only items for daily living such as clothes.

This intrahousehold inequality generated tensions, which were increased by local courts which mediated the struggle of women for their rights. Legal negotiations changed women's perception of their role in the new economy and society. The main means of opposition to husbands included divorce and lawsuits, which husbands responded to with negotiations, beatings, repudiations, and the elaboration of stereotypes that presented women as the real enemies of the administration and cotton interests. Lawsuits against stingy husbands were the most effective weapons that wives used to restore their right to cash. Women could not entirely dismantle such exploitative relations, however, because their struggle against their husbands was channeled through local courts, which were colonial institutions of control. This led to only a partial victory and the struggle became a regulated process, ineffective against the whole system of colonial exploitation. The ultimate winners were the colonial administration and the cotton interests. Thus, social inequalities and social injustices inevitably resulted from cotton production. For the cotton companies, increased profit through increased production was the goal. The state imposed a patriarchal world view through the administrative category of the healthy adult male and intensified preexisting social differentiation in order to exploit all Africans. However, peasants were more adversely affected than chiefs, and women were more exploited than men.

The measures taken to expand the cotton economy created a rigid gender inequality at the point of production. The labor of children decreased adult male workloads, but transport in rotation offered women only moral support and companionship in enduring the harshness of transporting cotton to the marketplaces. Similarly, crop rotation freed men from clearing land yearly, because the system stressed multiyear use of plots, but it tied women to the cotton fields because prolonged use of the same plot encouraged the proliferation of weeds whose cutting remained a woman's task. The most important conclusion is that cotton production did not burden all cotton producers of the same sex in the same way or to the same degree. Single, polygynous, and monogynous households experienced different ranges of autonomy. Wives in monogamous conjugal units found themselves overburdened compared to those located within polygynous conjugal units. Whereas the heads of households, whose supply of female and child labor was guaranteed, could enjoy some leisure time, unmarried cultivators were the most burdened group because they toiled alone.

Cotton production provoked resistance. Peasant forms of resistance included actions that undermined the production cycle and prevented the cotton economy from diverting all their labor from housework and food production. Some fled to camouflaged villages or across international boundaries, and others migrated to neighboring cities and countries. The market was also a site of struggle where peasants used three major tactics. Some mixed their cotton with heavy materials, hoping to compensate for low prices. Others did what they called "taking back one's own cotton" from the company warehouses, selling it in the second or third sale sessions. Furthermore, others left their cotton to rot on the bushes when they received bad prices during the first sale sessions. Finally, peasants engaged in calculated silence to disguise their hostility and impeded colonial officials from impinging further on their lives. Locating cotton fields on poor land, reducing plot sizes, and boiling, roasting and discarding seeds were all acts that reflected a veiled refusal to openly confront the state. These were conscious, political acts. Peasants knew that open refusal and direct confrontation would be suicidal; their tactics of thwarting germination frustrated the cotton economy with a lower risk of suffering. By using these "weapons of the weak," cotton cultivators hoped to convince the state and cotton companies that the land was not appropriate for cotton cultivation.

This hidden resistance to cotton production can be explained in terms of peasants' cultural autonomy. This is reflected in their nicknaming of officials, and the popularity of Kitawala and other religious movements and closed associations. Their experiences of exploitation were sorted and evaluated against this autonomy. Peasants' cultural autonomy provided an understanding of how to circumvent work obligations and confront at minimal cost the most visible state officials and African subordinates, namely, chiefs, cotton-monitors, and headmen.

Despite its importance, scholars have overlooked the significance of cotton production in colonial Zaire. The existing scanty scholarship is either excessively economistic or pays little attention to the direction of the flow of resources from peasant households to the state and cotton companies. In an effort to partially fill this gap in existing scholarship, I have highlighted not only the direction of flow of resources within and outside households and the conditions under which peasants worked, but have also drawn attention to ecological conditions, including the quality of the soil, and the technology that led to the establishment of the "culture of survival." Thus, at a national level, this study adds significantly to the social history of colonial Zaire. Similarly, this study amplifies new aspects of the history of Central African societies, especially as it departs from previous works. In 1980 Tosh pointed out that "the impression conveyed by most contributors to *Roots of Rural Poverty* is that peasants in Central Africa were able to respond to the market, provided that the colonial state did not stack the cards against them in the interests of white farming; environmental constraints and the prior claims of foods crops are generally ignored."[1] I have shown, for example, that peasants experienced differential labor demands depending on whether their plots were in the rainforest, in eight-year fallow lands, or in a savanna.

Many African cotton-growing areas were either confined to the trade-based economy, to the region of white settlement, or to peasant cotton production. However the Zairian rural economy was more complex. The cotton scheme coexisted with a weak settler class, large mining companies, corporate plantations, forced labor for "development projects," competing cash crop schemes for palm products, maize, and coffee, and a peasant food economy. While labor exports in Mozambique molded work organization there, labor competition among various sectors of the colonial economy as well as labor scarcity affected the organization of cotton production in colonial Zaire. By 1959 about one-third of the households were permanently employed in wage labor, a small percentage were traders or self-employed, and about two-thirds were rural farmers. From the 1950s onward their living standards and real incomes began to rise, especially in some of the intensive paysannat areas such as Ngandajika and Bambesa. But these developments were too recent, coercion was still too strong, and prosperity still too dependent on an overall *dirigisme* (interventionism) to be able to work on their own. Once the state structure began to collapse in 1959, the cotton economy collapsed with it.

The study of forced cotton production in colonial Zaire is a natural and corrective expansion in peasant studies. The "rational peasant model," "vent-for-surplus theory," and "African initiative school," while generally overlooking the conditions under which peasants made choices and took risks, have argued that peasants responded to cash crop production because it benefited them, viewing them as capitalist entrepreneurs who accumulated wealth. This study shows that, through concessions, the state and cotton companies transferred the costs of production to the households and forced producer prices below market value, which locked peasants into poverty. This study is also a response to both the "center-periphery" dichotomy and the current overemphasis on the internal differentiation of African peasantries. Overemphasis on social differentiation, in isolation from international factors, is an inadequate response to underdevelopment theory. To move away from this vicious circle, this study shows that the primary goal was increased profits for the cotton companies through cotton production. To help companies achieve this goal, the state imposed a patriarchal system through the use of the administrative category of the healthy adult male, and intensified existing social differentiation to exploit all Africans—chiefs and peasants, men and women—although peasants were adversely affected more than chiefs, and women were more exploited than men. Peasants were not merely helpless victims without control over their lives and destinies, however, but active agents whose economic choices and options had an impact on the structural constraints which they faced. While coping with labor bottlenecks, men and women established cooperative work arrangements. In the face of oppression and exploitation, and despite the colonial state's efforts to control even their aspirations, peasants kept their cultural autonomy. Peasants disrupted the place of cotton in the agricultural cycles. They retook their cotton. They used associations of all sorts, especially religious associations, and appropriated Christian-inspired teaching to resist exploitation by cotton companies. All their efforts to avoid exploitation illustrate that history and society are created by constant and purposeful individual actions that, notwithstanding their intentions, are in turn affected by history and society.

Notes
Selected Bibliography
Index

Notes

Citations of archival materials use the following abbreviations for the archives:

A.A., Brussels   Archives Africaines du Ministère des Affaires
                        Étrangères
Agri   Agriculture
A.I., Brussels   Affaire Indigène
AIMO, Brussels   Affaire Indigène et Main-d'Oeuvre
A.R.H.Z., Kisangani   Archives Régionales du Haut-Zaire, Kisangani
A.R.S., Lubumbashi   Archives Régionales du Shaba, Lubumbashi
ARSOM   Academie Royale des Sciences d'Outre-Mer
D.P.   Divers problèmes
F.P.   Force Publique
IRCB   Institut Royal Colonial Belge

Introduction

1. H. Bernstein, "African Peasantries: A Theoretical Framework," *Journal of Peasant Studies* 6 (1979): 420–43.

2. S. Amin, *Le développement inégal*(Paris: Editions de minuit, 1973); W. Rodney, *How Europe Underdeveloped Africa* (London: Bogle-l'Ouverture Publications, 1972); C. Leys, *Underdevelopment in Kenya* (London: Heinemann, 1975).

3. N. Palmer and N. Parsons, eds., *The Roots of Rural Poverty in Central and Southern Africa* (London: Heinemann, 1977); B. Freund, *The Making of Contemporary Africa* (Bloomington: Indiana University Press, 1984).

4. J. S. Hogendorn, "The Vent-for-Surplus Model and African Cash Agriculture to 1914," *Savanna* 5 (1976): 5. While proponents of vent-for-surplus, development theory, and the African initiative school argue that peasants accepted cash crop production because it benefited them, underdevelopment theorists and Marxists disagree. They correctly demonstrate that cash crop production brought oppression and exploitation and point out a variety of mechanisms whereby wealth was transferred from the periphery to the core of the capitalist economy. The market, as an exogenous force, had a bearing on crop choice, but

endogenous forces determined the actual implementation and the organization of labor. See A. Isaacman, "Peasants and Rural Social Protest in Africa," *African Studies Review* 33, no. 2 (September 1990): 16, and "Peasants, Social Protest and Africanists," *Journal of Social History* 22 (1989):763, n5.

5. L. Vail and L. White, "'Tawani, Machambero!: Forced Cotton and Rice Growing in the Zambezi," *Journal of African History* 19, no. 29 (1979)9: 239–63; A. Isaacman et al., "Cotton Is the Mother of Poverty: Peasant Resistance to Forced Cotton Production in Mozambique, 1938–1961," *International Journal of African Historical Studies* 13 (1980): 580–615; A. Isaacman, "Chiefs, Rural Differentiation and Peasant Protest: The Mozambican Forced Cotton Regime, 1938–1961," *African Economic History* 14 (1985):15–57.

6. M. Klein, *Peasants in Africa* (Beverly Hills: Sage, 1983); J. Suret-Canal, *French Colonialism in Tropical Africa, 1900–1945*, trans. Till Gotteiner (London and New York: [1964] C. Hurst, 1971); U. Sturzinger, "The Introduction of Cotton Cultivation in Chad: The Role of the Administrator, 1920–1936," *African Economic History* 19 (1983): 213–24; E. De Dampire, "Coton noir, café blanc," *Cahier d'études africaines* 2 (1960):128–47; E. Mandala, *Work and Control in a Peasant Economy* (Madison: University of Wisconsin Press, 1990); see also E. Mandala, "Commodity Production, Subsistence and the State in Colonial Africa: Peasant Cotton Agriculture in the Lower Tchiri (Shiri) Valley of Malawi, 1907–1935" (ms).

7. Isaacman, "Peasants and Rural Social Protest," 17.

8. F. Mulambu, "Introduction à l'étude du rôle des paysans dans les changements politiques," *Cahiers économiques et sociaux* 8 (1970): 435–50; Sikitele Gize, "Les racines de la révolte pende de 1931," *Etudes d'histoire africaine* 3 (1973): 99–153; M. Lovens, "La révolte de Masisi-Lubutu (Congo belge Janvier-Mai, 1944)" *Cahiers du CEDAF*, nos. 3–4 (1975): 4–136.

9. B. Rau, *From Feast to Famine* (London: Zed Books, 1991), 2.

10. Isaacman, "Chiefs, Rural Differentiation and Peasant Protest," 29; E. Mandala, "Capitalism, Ecology and Society: The Lower Tchire (Shire) Valley of Malawi, 1860–1960" (unpublished Ph. D. diss., University of Minnesota, 1983); V. Joan, "Colonial Chiefs and the Making of Class: A Case Study from Teso, Eastern Uganda," *Africa* 47, no. 2 (1977): 149; R. Howard, "Formation and Stratification of the Peasantry in Colonial Ghana," *Journal of Peasant Studies* 8, no. 1 (1980): 72.

11. R. Anstey, *King Leopold's Legacy* (London, New York, Ibadan: Oxford University Press, 1966), 56; G. Van der Kerken, *Les sociétés bantoues du Congo belge* (Brussels: Etablissements Emile Bruyant, 1920), 246; files of the Department of the Interior in A.R.H.Z., Kisangani include many cases of chiefs convicted for misappropriation of funds from peasants. Of the many reasons advanced to explain the situation, the insufficiency of resources of the chiefs figured prominently. See P. Geschiere, "Chiefs and Colonial Rule in Cameroon: Inventing Chieftaincy, French and British Style," *Africa* 63, no. 2 (1993):151–75.

12. P. Abrams, *Historical Sociology* (Ithaca: Cornell University Press, 1982), xiii.

13. S. Popkin, *The Rational Peasant: The Political Economy of Rural Society in Vietnam* (Los Angeles: University of California Press, 1979).

14. J. Scott, *The Moral Economy of the Peasant: Rebellion and Subsistence in Southeast Asia,* (New Haven: Yale University Press, 1976).

Chapter 1. The Organization of Production: The Cotton Labor Process

1. B. Jewsiewicki, "Rural Society and the Belgian Colonial Economy," in D. Birmingham and P. M. Martin, eds., *History of Central Africa,* 2 vols. (London and New York: Longman, 1983), 2:96–98; E. Leplae, "Comment les Bantous du Congo belge s'achèminent vers le paysannat," *Bulletin agricole du Congo belge* 20, no. 4 (1931): 574; J. P. Peemans, *Diffusion du progrès et convergence des prix: Congo belge, 1900–1960* (Paris and Louvain: Nauwelaerts, 1970). The decree of July 1, 1885, established the right of the state to dispose of all lands that were not effectively occupied by the Africans. The Administration thus gained the right to exploit or grant rights of exploitation over all uncultivated lands. By this decree, the state granted to different fractions of capital a legal device to take over all these lands. By a broad interpretation of the decree, Africans could be forbidden to undertake any activity outside production for subsistence.

2. Agri (369) 1/2, A.A., Brussels; A.R.H.Z., Kisangani, "Rapport économique du District du Haut-Uele," 1924; A. Bertrand, *Le problème de la main-d'oeuvre au Congo* (Brussels: Ministère des Colonies, 1933); J. Vansina, *Paths in the Rainforests,* (Madison: University of Wisconsin Press, 1990); E. Leplae, "La situation économique du Congo en 1935–1936," *Bulletin de l'institut de recherches économiques et sociales* (1937); Bilusa Baila, "Histoire de population des Uele" (Ph. D. diss., Université Libre de Bruxelles, 1993); P. Ryckmans, "Démographie congolaise," *Africa* 6, no. 3 (1933): 241–58; E. Leplae, "L'agriculture coloniale dans la discussion du budget du Congo belge pour 1914," *Revue générale agronomique* (1914): 17.

3. R. Anstey, *King Leopold's Legacy,* (London, New York, Ibadan: Oxford University Press, 1966), 61. These *cultures obligatoires et éducatives* were meant to teach the Africans civilization.

4. For instance, in 1941, the percentage of mineral exports had reached 72 percent, dropped down to 57 percent in 1945, and to 50 percent in 1950. See E. H. J. Stoffels, "Les grandes étapes de l'agriculture au Congo belge," *Bulletin agricole du Congo belge* 42, no. 2 (1951): 850; A. Bakonzi, "The Gold Mines of Kilo-Moto in Northeast Zaire, 1905–1960" (Ph. D. diss., University of Wisconsin, Madison); Chechu Dyilo, "Le recrutement de la main-d'oeuvre à Kilo-Moto, 1905–1958" (M.A. thesis, UNAZA, Lubumbashi, 1981), 42–43.

5. B. Jewsiewicki, "Rural Society," 2: 100–101; E. Leplae, "Faut-il en Afrique centrale repousser le salariat et les plantations européennes?" *Bulletin agricole du Congo belge* 20, no. 4 (1931): 570–74.

6. C. Coquery-Vidrovitch, *Afrique noire: Permanences et ruptures* (Paris: Payot, 1985), 154; A. T. Nzula et al. *Forced Labour in Colonial Africa* (London: Zed Press, 1979).

7. U. Blommaert, "Introduction du coton chez l'indigène au Congo belge," *Bulletin agricole du Congo belge* 21, no. 3 (1930): 805, and "La culture du coton au Congo belge," *Agriculture et élevage* 2 (1930): 19–22.

8. "Action du gouvernement dans le développement du coton," 7, A.R.H.Z., Kisangani.

9. J. Ruelle, "Introduction du coton au Congo belge: Motivations économique et financière" (M.A. thesis, Université Catholique de Louvain, 1985), 95.

10. E. Leplae, "La culture du coton," *Bulletin agricole du Congo belge* 7, nos. 1–2 (1917): 24–25.

11. *Rapport annuel sur l'administration du Congo belge*, 1920, 60.

12. J. Bivot, "La politique des transports et production cotonnière au Congo belge," *Bulletin du Comité Cotonnier Congolais* 13 (1939): 27, and "La culture du coton au Congo belge. Son organisation, la politique cotonnière, les transports et le réseau routier," *Bulletin du Comité Cotonnier Congolais* 1 (1936): 4–6.

13. E. Fisher, "The Growing of Cotton at Kitobola (Lower Congo) for the Season 1913–1914," *Bulletin agricole du Congo belge*, 5, no. 3 (1914).

14. A. De Meulemeester, "L'agriculture dans la Province Orientale du Congo belge en 1920," *Bulletin agricole du Congo belge* 12, no. 4 (1921): 644; J. P. Peemans, *Diffusion du progrès*; R. Palmer and N. Parsons, eds., *The Roots of Rural Poverty in Central and Southern Africa*, (Berkeley and Los Angeles: University of California Press, 1977).

15. "D (778), papiers Bertrand, dossier d'Europe. 'Culture de coton'," 5–6, A.A., Brussels.

16. Vansina, *Paths in the Rainforests*, 239.

17. "Le coton au Congo belge," *Bulletin agricole du Congo belge* 32, no. 3 (1941): 393.

18. A De Bauw, "Un groupement professionnel colonial: Le Comité Cotonnier Congolais," *Bulletin de la société belge d'études et d'expansion* 136 (1947): 413; "Agri: I.G.A.F. A.A., Brussels"; "Le coton au Congo belge," 393; A. Landeghem, "La Compagnie Cotonnière Congolaise," *Bulletin agricole du Congo belge* 21, no. 3 (1930): 820; A. Brixhe, *Le coton au Congo belge*, 3rd ed. (Brussels: Ministère des Colonies, 1958), 16.

19. "Note relative à la question cotonnière au Maniema," Kibombo, April 20, 1934, Agri (382) 33, A.A., Brussels.

20. A. De Bauw, ed., *Le coton au Congo belge* (Brussels: Cotonco, 1948), 43; A. Landeghem, "1921–1936: Quinze années de culture cotonnière au Congo belge," *Bulletin du Comité Cotonnier Congolais*, 4 (1936): 3; "Monographie du coton congolais," *Bulletin du Comité Cotonnier Congolais* 6 (1937): 57.

21. *Bulletin du Comité Cotonnier Congolais* 1 (1958): 14–23; L. Banneux, "Quelques données économiques sur le coton au Congo belge," *Bulletin d'information de l'INEAC*, série technique, 22 (1938): 22; E. Leplae, "Histoire et développement des cultures obligatoires," *Congo* 1, no. 5 (1933): 718.

22. Cotonco, "Rapport no. 5," 6, A.R.H.Z., Kisangani.

23. *Bulletin de la chambre du commerce et de l'industrie du Katanga* 54 (1946): 10; "Agri (373)," A.A., Brussels.

24. B. Jewsiewicki, "Rural Society," 113.

25. "Agri (373)," A.A., Brussels.

26. *Bulletin de la banque du Congo belge et du Ruanda-Urundi* 9 (1958): 249.

27. "Agri (378) 17," A.A., Brussels; Chechu Dyilo, "Le recrutement," 43;

B. Jewsiewicki, "Le colonat agricole européen au Congo belge, 1910–1960: Questions politiques et économiques," *Journal of African History* 20, no. 4 (1979) 559–71.

28. Chechu Dyilo, "Le recrutement," 42 and passim.

29. "Dossier Z 265, no. 459H/Agri/Coton/F," A.R.H.Z., Kisangani.

30. "Propagande cotonnière," n. d., 5 A.R.H.Z., Kisangani; "Agri (382) 33. Note relative à la question cotonnière au Maniema," Kibombo, April 20, 1934, A.A., Brussels.

31. F. Sparano, "Rapport annuel sur la culture et le commerce du coton dans les districts des Uele," 1930, A.R.H.Z., Kisangani.

32. Yogolelo Tambwe ya Kasimba, "Mission de recrutement des travailleurs de l'U.M.H.K. au Kivu-Maniema (1926–1928)" (M.A. thesis, UNAZA, Lubumbashi, 1973), 105.

33. *Bulletin du comité cotonnier congolais* 8 (1938): 14; C. Perrings, "Good Lawyers but Poor Workers: Recruited Angolan Labour in the Copper Mines of Katanga, 1917–1921," *Journal of African History* 18, no. 2 (1977): 237–59; Muteba Kabemba, "Le recrutement de la main-d'oeuvre dans le district du Lomami à destination du Haut Katanga industriel (1912–1933)" (M.A. thesis, UNAZA, Lubumbashi, 1973).

34. "D (778), Papiers Bertrand, dossier d'Afrique: Note," 2; "D (778), Papiers Bertrand, dossier d'Europe: project," 3–4; "Agri (369): 'A. Rubbens G. G.'" A.A., Brussels. Colocoton paid chiefs 10 francs per ton of seed cotton.

35. "Agri (378) 17. G. G. au Ministère." Léopoldville, May 18, 1937, A.A., Brussels; "Rapport Landeghem," 1926 A.R.H.Z., Kisangani; Van Geem, *Etude comparative des législations cotonnières en Afrique équatoriale* (Brussels: Comité Cotonnier Congolais, 1934); E. Leplae, "La culture du coton en plantations et par motoculture," *Congo* 1 (1924): 285; E. Leplae, "Comment les indigènes du Congo belge sont arrivés à produire 20.000 tonnes de coton-fibres," *Coton et culture cotonnière* 9, (1935): 3; E. Leplae, "Faut-il en Afrique centrale repousser le salariat et les plantations?" 570–74.

36. "Dossier Z 265," A.R.H.Z., Kisangani.

37. Ibid.

38. Lesage, "Voyage d'inspection en Territoire de Kabinda," September 24, 1943, A.R.H.Z., Kisangani.

39. "Rapport annuel de l'agriculture," District de Sankuru, 1928, A.A., Brussels.

40. G. Malengreau, "Les lotissements agricoles au Congo," *Bulletin agricole du Congo belge* 43 (1952): 208; A. Bertrand, *Le problème*, 33; "Rapport annuel sur l'agriculture," District de l'Uele-Nepoko, 1930, A.R.H.Z., Kisangani.

41. "Dossier Z 265 L/T," A.R.H.Z., Kisangani.

42. "Rapport annuel sur l'agriculture," District de Maniema, 1930, A.R.H.Z., Kisangani.

43. Interview with Mugaza wa Beya, Lubumbashi, August 16, 1986.

44. Interview with Mugaza wa Beya, Lubumbashi, August 16, 1986; Free translation: "A plot of cotton must be as beautiful as a flower garden"; "Rapport annuel sur l'agriculture," District de Maniema, 1930, A.R.H.Z., Kisangani.

45. E. Leplae, "Histoire et développement des cultures obligatoires de coton et de riz au Congo belge de 1917 à 1933," *Congo* 1, no. 5 (1933): 713, 705; F. Sparano, "Vade-mecum pour le personnel s'intéressant à la culture de coton dans les districts des Uele," *Bulletin agricole du Congo belge* 20, no. 1 (1929): 90–117; U. Blommaert "Introduction du coton chez l'indigène du Congo belge," *Bulletin agricole du Congo belge* 21, no. 3 (1930): 810–11.

46. E. Dejong, "Le coton dans l'Uele," *Bulletin agricole du Congo belge* 18, no. 4 (1927): 482.

47. *Conseil de Province d'Elisabethville*, 1945, ii, 95.

48. H. De la Haye, "Rapport annuel 1926–1927, ferme de Bangadi," March 31, 1927, A.R.H.Z., Kisangani. In state stations workers worked from 8 to 12 A.M. and from 2 to 5 P.M., and picked from 18 to 22 kilograms a day; Interview with Lwamba Bilonda, Lubumbashi, August 13, 1986.

49. *Bulletin du Comité Cotonnier Congolais* 13 (1939): 59; "Rapport annuel sur la culture et le commerce du coton, 1937–1938," District du Congo-Ubangi, A.R.H.Z., Kisangani. See "Aux planteurs du coton," annexe II.

50. "Agri (128) 109," A.A., Brussels; *Etudes sur le marché de certains produits congolais* (1952): 70.

51. E. Mandala, *Work and Control in a Peasant Economy*, (Madison: University of Wisconsin Press, 1990). The author documented that peasants endured similar treatments in Malawi.

52. M. Merlier, *Le Congo de la colonisation belge à l'indépendance* (Paris: Maspero, 1962), 82.

53. Bertrand, *Le problème*, 33.

54. Lioudet, "Note annexe au rapport d'inspection Fisher 1923," Buta, May 16, 1923. A.R.H.Z., Kisangani.

55. Blommeart, "Introduction du coton," 810–12; F. Sparano, "Vade-Mecum," 97; E. Leplae, "Histoire et développement des cultures obligatoires," 705.

56. *Conseil de Province d'Elisabethville*, 1944, 115.

57. Compagnie de Lubilashi, "Rapport sur la campagne cotonnière 1938–1939." Lisamba, 1939, A.A., Brussels; *Conseil de Province d'Elisabethville*, 1937, 14.

58. *Conseil de Province d'Elisabethville*, 1944, 65, 67, 77; *Conseil de Province d'Elisabethville*, 1945, ii, 95; interview with Katende, Lubumbashi, 1988; interview with Mugaza wa Beya, Lubumbashi, 1988.

59. Interview with Katayi, Lubumbashi, August 24, 1986.

60. "Rapport d'inspection de Territoire de Dungu," 1936, 4, A.R.H.Z., Kisangani.

61. *Encyclopédie du Congo belge*, vol. 1 (Brussels: Editions Bieleveld, 1951), 490.

62. Interview with Mbuyi, Lubumbashi, June, 1986.

63. L. De Koster, "Le malaise des milieux ruraux au Congo belge," *Revue générale belge* 3 (1948): 464.

64. *Conseil de Province d'Elisabethville*, 1944, 65.

65. Interview with Mozua, Kisangani, January 27, 1989.

66. V. Drachousoff, *Essai sur l'agriculture indigène au Bas-Congo*, (Brussels: 1947), 34.

67. Interview with Lwaka Mukandja, Lubumbashi, August, 1986; interview with Mugaza wa Beya, Lubumbashi, August 16, 1986.

68. Interview with Mugaza wa Beya and Lwamba Bilonda, Lubumbashi, August 16, 1986.

69. "Le coton au Congo belge," *Bulletin agricole du Congo belge,* 32, no. 3 (1941): 398, 403–5, ff. The Bambesa station, founded in 1919, selected cotton and conducted experiments for the whole area north to the Equator. Its task was to assure cross-fertilization of the Triumph variety and to provide peasants with improved seeds. Connected to the Bambesa research station were a substation, Tukpo in the Uele savanna, and experimental centers at Gemena, Bosodula, and Boketa in the Ubangi district, and at Bengamisa in the Stanleyville district.

70. There were variations in the application of this plant rotation. In some communities, eleusine rotated with sesame; in others, administrators forced peasants to rotate manioc with groundnuts and sweet potatoes; in other communities, eleusine followed sorghum.

71. M. Lassance, *Modes et coutumes alimentaires des Congolais en milieu rural* (Brussels: ARSOM, 1959); *Bulletin agricole du Congo belge* 40, no. 2 (1949): 227–70 and 40, no. 3 (1949): 473–552; Lenelle and Parent, "Malnutrition in Katanga," *Annales belges de Médecine tropicale* 42, no. 2 (1951); Tihon, "Malnutrition in Maniema," *Bulletin agricole du Congo belge* 42 (1951): 829–68.

72. "D (778): Papiers Bertrand," A.A., Brussels.

73. *Conseil de Province d'Elisabethville,* 1944, 65.

74. Dupont, "Rapport d'inspection," Territoire de Dungu, 1953, 21, A.R.H.Z., Kisangani.

75. "Rapport d'inspection du Territoire d'Ango," 1958 A.R.H.Z., Kisangani.

76. Q. Lumpungu, "Difficultés du paysannat cotonnier dans le Tanganyika" (M.A. thesis, Université de Rennes, 1968), and "Culture cotonnière et société rurale dans le nord du Katanga. Production, commercialisation, et perspective d'avenir," (Thèse de troisième cycle, Université de Rennes, 1970); M. Willaert, "Les coopératives indigènes au Congo belge," *Bulletin agricole du Congo belge* 43 special issue (1952): 85–123; O. Tulippe, "Les paysannats indigènes du Kasai," *Bulletin social belge et géographique* (1955): 58; P. Staner, "Les paysannats indigènes du Congo belge et du Ruanda-Urundi," *Bulletin agricole du Congo belge et du Ruanda-Urundi* 46 (1955); G. E. Sladden, "Evolution possible du paysannat indigène au Congo belge," *Bulletin agricole du Congo belge* 43, special issue (1952): 7–27, 135–57; A. De Fauconval et al., "Les paysannats en territoire de Mwene-Ditu," *Bulletin agricole du Congo belge* 48, no. 3 (1957): 541–57; A. De Fouconval and H. Van Beek, "Les paysannats en territoire de Gandajika, District de Kabinda, Province du Kasai" *Bulletin agricole du Congo belge* 49, no. 1 (1958): 23–45; J. Collier, "Les paysannats du nord-Sankuru (Territoire de Lodja et de Katako-Kombe)," *Bulletin agricole du Congo belge* 50, no. 3 (1959): 570–641; J. Clément, "Etude relative au paysannat indigène," *Bulletin agricole du Congo belge* 43, special issue (1952); R. Chambon and M. Leruth, "Paysannat et colonat dans le district du Tanganyika-Moero," *Bulletin agricole du Congo belge* 48, no. 2 (1957): 279–315; A. Brixhe, "Les lotissements agricoles du nord-Sankuru," *Lovania* 7 (1945): 93–133.

77. A. Brixhe, *Le coton au congo belge*, 80.

78. C. Leontovitch, "La culture du coton dans le district du Congo-Ubangi," *Bulletin agricole du Congo belge* 28 (1937): 35.

79. De Fauconval and Van Beek, "Les paysannats du territoire de Gandajika, 23.

80. *Conseil de Province du Katanga*, 1944, 116.

81. B. Jewsiewicki, "Rural Society," 120.

82. *Conseil de Province d'Elisabethville*, 1944, 65, 67, 77.

83. *Conseil de Province du Katanga*, 1945, ii, 1.

Chapter 2. Forced Cotton Production and Social Control

1. Vail and White, "'Tawani, Machambero,' 239–63; A. Isaacman, "Cotton Is the Mother of Poverty, 580–615; A. Isaacman, "Chiefs, Rural Differentiation and Peasant Protest," 15–57; W. Rodney, *How Europe Underdeveloped Africa*.

2. B. Lincoln, *Discourse and the Construction of Society* (Oxford, New York: Oxford University Press, 1989), 4.

3. "Dossier F.P. (2450), no. 163," A.A., Brussels; "Rapport politique," District de l'Ubangi, 1928, A.A., Brussels. This report was written during a long period of insurrection in Ubangi, which was the subject of the report.

4. "Dossier Z 265, Organisation de la propagande agricole no. 51/1545/Prop," Stanleyville April 16, 1951, A.R.H.Z., Kisangani; for the ratio of population administered to one member of *service territorial*, see R. Anstey, *King Leopold's Legacy* (London, New York, Ibadan: Oxford University Press, 1966), 80.

5. *Conseil de Province du Katanga*, vol. 2, 1945, 34.

6. Interview with Itambo Yakoma, Kisangani, July 11, 1989.

7. *Conseil de Province Orientale*, 1944, 9.

8. *Rapport annuel sur l'administration du Congo belge*, 1945–1946, 9. Rituals and politico-religious movements were to be replaced by newspapers and public libraries, radio propaganda, and films in order to keep peasants from subversive ideas.

9. "Rapport de fin de campagne," District de Sankuru, 1928, A.A., Brussels.

10. *Rapport annuel sur l'administration du Congo belge*, 1952, 25.

11. "Propagande cotonnière," 1939, 21, A.R.H.Z., Kisangani.

12. In 1928, for example, the *Fiche de contrôle* was already used in Sankuru district to control Tetela cotton producers; Comité des Tom Coton, "Note de la Délégation belge sur les moyens employés au Congo belge et Ruanda-Urundi en vue d'y augmenter la production du coton," A.A., Brussels, n. d., [1957]; M. Merlier, *Le Congo de la colonisation belge à l'indépendance* (Paris: Maspero, 1962), 102; A. De Bauw, ed., *Trente années de culture cotonnière au Congo belge* (Brussels: Cotonco, 1948), 59.

13. F. Grevisse, *La grande pitié des juridictions indigènes* (Brussels: IRCB, 1949), 65; to punish the offenders, the administrators referred to the May 2, 1910, decree which imposed sanctions on Africans who refused to work on public projects; *Bulletin administratif*, 1918, 736–37.

14. Interview with Sumba Ndandwe, Lubumbashi, August 23, 1986.

15. "Dossier Z 265: no. 72 Agri, 17, Janvier, 1944," A.R.H.Z, Kisangani.
16. "Rapport annuel du Territoire des Mangbetu," AIMO, 1951, 25, A.R.H.Z., Kisangani.
17. *L'informateur*, December 23, 1936, (Brussels).
18. "Rubbens G. G," April 24, 1937, A.A., Brussels.
19. "Rapport annuel de l'agriculture," Uele-Nepoko, 1928, 2–3; 1929, 3; 1930, 2, A.R.H.Z., Kisangani. E. Leplae, "Résultats obtenus au Congo belge par les cultures obligatoires alimentaires et industrielles," *Zaire* 1 (1947): 121.
20. "Dossier Z 265, Lettre no 2977," Léopoldville, March 5, 1945, A.R.H.Z, Kisangani; "Rapport annuel du Territoire de Bambesa," 1958, 25, A.R.H.Z., Kisangani. *Rapport annuel sur l'administration du Congo belge*, 1922, 58; *Rapport annuel sur l'administration du Congo belge*, 1947, 189; *Rapport annuel sur l'administration du Congo belge*, 1957, 237.
21. "Rapport d'inspection," Territoire de Dungu, 1952, 24, A.R.H.Z., Kisangani.
22. "Rapport d'inspection," Territoire de Dungu, 1934, 5, A.R.H.Z., Kisangani.
23. "Rapport d'inspection," Territoire de Dungu, 1952, 24, A.R.H.Z., Kisangani.
24. Interview with Gangala Kidumu, Kisangani, September 11, 1989.
25. Interview with Kakwa, Kisangani, February 27, 1989. "Red lips" is a nickname for a white man; *Matala-tala*, "glasses," is a metaphor for a severe colonial official who checked everything as if he had four eyes.
26. "Propagande cotonnière," 1939, 21, A.R.H.Z., Kisangani.
27. Interview with Katayi, Lubumbashi, August 24, 1986.
28. Interview with Lwaka Mukandja, Lubumbashi, August 14, 1986; interview with Mugaza wa Beya and Lwamba Bilonda, Lubumbashi, August 16, 1986; interview with Tshibanda Nduba, Lubumbashi, August, 1986.
29. F. Sparano, "Culture et commerce du coton," *Bulletin agricole du Congo belge* 22, no. 3 (1931): 414; "Agri (374)," A.A., Brussels.
30. Interview with Katayi, Lubumbashi, August 24, 1986.
31. *Conseil de Province Orientale*, 1955, question no. 3: "Rapport de Commission," 12.
32. Those who planted late were generally sentenced to 3–30 days in prison. See "Rapport d'inspection," Territoire d'Ango, 1946; "Rapport d'inspection," Territoire de Dungu, 1952, 2; 1945, 8; "Rapport d'inspection," Territoire de Bambili, 1931, 24; "Rapport d'inspection," Territoire de Dungu, 1940, 7, all in A.R.H.Z., Kisangani.
33. Interview with Kosi Genge, Kisangani, July 26, 1989.
34. "Rapport d'inspection," Territoire de Dungu, 1933, A.R.H.Z., Kisangani.
35. Interview with Mugaza wa Beya, Lubumbashi, August 16, 1986.
36. Ibid.
37. "Rapport d'inspection," Territoire de Buta, 1946, 58, A.R.H.Z., Kisangani.
38. "Rapport d'inspection," Territoire de Bambili, 1931, 28, A.R.H.Z., Kisangani, especially the section on C. I. Asigala; interview with Lwaka Mukandja, Lubumbashi, August 14, 1986.
39. Interview with Gangala, Kisangani, September, 1989.

40. "Dossier Z 265, no. 297"; "Rapport d'inspection," Territoire d' Ango, 1948, 6; "Rapport d'inspection," Territoire de Bambili, 1931, 28; "Rapport d'inspection," Territoire de Bambesa, 1958, 25, all in A.R.H.Z., Kisangani.

41. "Dossier Z 265. Lettre 2473/Aff/Ind., Noirot," Buta, le 9/11/1932; "Rapport d'inspection," Territoire de Buta, 1946, 55, especially the section on the Bayew-Bokwama court. Both in A.R.H.Z., Kisangani.

42. "Dossier Z. 265. Lettre no 1198/AO/B5," Irumu, October 10, 1939, A.R.H.Z., Kisangani.

43. "Rapport d'inspection," Territoire de Dungu, 1945, 15, A.R.H.Z., Kisangani.

44. Interview with Lufundja Mbayo, Lubumbashi, September 2, 1986.

45. "D (778) Papiers Bertrand, B: Dossier d'Europe," A.A., Brussels.

46. "Rapport d'inspection judiciaire," Territoire de Niangara, 1949, 6; "Rapport d'inspection," Territoire de Bambili, 1931, 24, in A.R.H.Z., Kisangani.

47. "Rapport d'inspection," Territoire de Buta, 1946, 58; "Rapport d'inspection," Territoire de Buta, 1954, 58, in A.R.H.Z., Kisangani.

48. J. P. Peemans, *Diffusion du progrès et convergence des prix* (Paris-Louvain: Naawelaerts, 1973); C. Young, *Politics in the Congo* (Kinshasa, 1966).

49. "Dossier A. I. (1403) 3, "A.A., Brussels; interview with Koya, Kisangani, March 1, 1989; E. Leplae, "Les cultures obligatoires," 462; A. Landeghem, "La compagnie cotonnière congolaise," *Bulletin agricole du Congo belge* 21, no. 3 (1930): 821. In 1892, tax in kind was used as a means of coercing people to gather wild rubber and ivory; in 1910, the state imposed tax in cash to compel people to produce cash crops.

50. V. Drachousoff, *Essai sur l'agriculture indigène au Bas-Congo* (Brussels: 1947), 32–33; also "Le développement de l'agriculture autochtone congolaise," *Bulletin de la banque du Congo et du Ruanda-Urandi* (August 1959).

51. Leplae, "Histoire et développement des cultures obligatoires," no. 5, 730.

52. Interview with Katayi, Lubumbashi, August 1986.

53. M. Querton, "Rapport trimestriel," Lusambo, July 16, 1926, A.R.H.Z., Kisangani.

54. "Dossier Z 265, R. Bougard, 'Procès-Verbal d'enquête préliminaire à la détermination des cultures à imposer pour la campagne agricole 1958,'" District du Haut-Uele, Territoire de Wamba, A.R.H.Z., Kisangani.

55. A. Landeghem, "Les cultures de coton et le développpement économique des régions cotonnières," *Congo* (1927): 88; A. Landeghem, who first insisted on the use of force, changed his position.

56. *Congo*, 1, no. 1 (1933): 748; E. Leplae, "Comment les indigènes," 187.

57. A. Landeghem, "1921–1936," 3; "Monographie du coton congolais," 57; De Bauw, ed., *Trente années de culture cotonnière*, 43; Brixhe, *Le coton au Congo belge*, 17; Banneux, "Quelques données," 25.

58. Orientale Province, "Rapport annuel sur la culture et le commerce du coton, 1927–1928," A.R.H.Z., Kisangani.

59. "Note de la délégation belge sur les moyens employés au Congo belge et au Ruanda-Urundi en vue d'y augmenter la production du coton," n. d., [1957], 7–8, A.A., Brussels.

60. E. Devroey, *Le réseau routier au Congo belge et au Ruanda-Urundi* (Brussels: IRCB, 1939), 77–87; L. Yaskold, "Rapport annuel sur la campagne cotonnière 1937–1938," Stanleyville, May 7, 1938, A.R.H.Z., Kisangani.

61. Sparano, "Vade-mecum," 103; De Meulemeester, "Culture cotonnière à Mahagi," Mahagi, May 9, 1919, A.R.H.Z., Kisangani; "Dossier A.I. (1403) 3," A.A., Brussels. In contrast to Belgian economic policy, the Portuguese government in Angola used tax rebates extensively to promote cotton cultivation. See also *Bulletin du Comité Cotonnier Congolais*, 2 (1936): 17.

62. Kidumu, Kisangani, October 2, 1989.

63. Interview with Kwata, Kisangani, January 19, 1989.

64. "Agri (374). Note pour Monsieur le Directeur Général Leplae, "May 17, 1932, A.A., Brussels.

65. Interview with Tshibanda Nduba Musaka, Lubumbashi, August, 1986.

66. "Agri (369) 1/4, no 1045/R," A.A., Brussels; *Conseil de Province d'Elisabethville*, 1935, 106.

67. Interview with Jete, Kisangani, July 26, 1989.

68. E. Leplae, "Histoire et développement des cultures obligatoires," 749; *Rapport annuel sur l'administration du Congo belge*, 1933, 103. In Kasai, peasants received salt and tools. See "Analyse de la campagne cotonnière 1935–1936, région sud," 9, A.R.H.Z., Kisangani.

69. Orientale Province, "Rapport annuel sur la culture et le commerce du coton, 1927–1928." A.R.H.Z., Kisangani.

70. Interview with M'Boliaka, Kisangani, July, 1989.

71. F. Grevisse, *La grande pitié*, 54.

72. E. Leplae, "Les cultures obligatoires," 458.

73. "Rapport annuel sur l'agriculture," District du Maniema, 1928, 4, A.R.H.Z., Kisangani.

74. "Dossier Z 265, no. 29001, 1957," A.R.H.Z., Kisangani.

75. *Bulletin du Comité Cotonnier Congolais* 13 (1939): 41–43.

76. Ibid.

77. M. Gluckmann, *Rituals of Rebellion* (Manchester: Manchester University Press, 1952), 25, and *Order and Rebellion in Tribal Africa* (New York: Free Press of Glencoe, 1963); H. Kupper, "A Royal Ritual in a Changing Political Context," *Cahiers d'études africaines* 12 (1972): 593–615.

78. Source of play: A. Ravet, *Bulletin du comité cotonnier congolais* 7 (1937): 72–73. "L'exposition agricole de Buta (Uele) 4 et 5 Novembre 1939" *Bulletin du Comité Cotonnier Congolais* 6 (1940), 3–5.

79. A. Ravet, "La fête de coton," *Bulletin du Comité Cotonnier Congolais* 10 (1938): 56.

80. Ibid., 55–56.

81. *Bulletin du Comité Cotonnier Congolais* 21 (1948): 11.

82. "Rapport annuel sur l'agriculture," District de Maniema, 1931, 2, A.R.H.Z., Kisangani.

83. *Rapport annuel sur l'administration du Congo belge*, 1945–46, 9. See also Banneux, "Quelques données," 20.

84. In "Propagande cotonnière," 1939, 28, A.R.H.Z., Kisangani, officers em-

phasized the use of films, humanitarian works, and collaboration with schools. Interview with Ujanga, Kisangani, September 10, 1989; Interview with Lwaka Mukandja, Lubumbashi, August 14, 1986; "Rapport annuel sur la culture et le commerce du coton, modèle C," District du Congo-Ubangi, 1938. A.R.H.Z., Kisangani.

85. Interview with Katayi, Lubumbashi, August 24, 1986; E. Leplae, "Comment les indigènes," 186.

86. Interview with Mugaza wa Beya, Lubumbashi, August 16, 1986.

87. Interview with Katayi, Lubumbashi, August 24, 1986.

88. "Agri (374) A.I." A.A., Brussels. This occurred at the depth (1932–1933) of the depression.

89. Interview with Gezo, Kisangani, September 16, 1989; see also "Dossier Papiers Bertrand D (788)," A.A., Brussels.

90. "Dossier Z 265," 1957, A.R.H.Z., Kisangani.

91. "Dossier Z 498," A.R.H.Z., Kisangani.

92. Nkulu Kalala, "Les réactions africaines aux impositions des cultures: Cas du Territoire de Kamina, 1938–1959," (M.A. thesis, Université de Lubumbashi, 1983).

93. "Dossier Z 265, Goffin aux A.T.," October 19, 1957, A.R.H.Z., Kisangani.

Chapter 3. Sharing the Social Product: Peasants and the Market

1. Vermeesh, "Rapport sur l'agriculture," Kabinda, June 30, 1920.

2. J. Berger, *Pig Earth*, (New York: Pantheon, 1979), 204–5.

3. C. Van Onselen, *Chibaro* (Johannesburg: Ravan Press, 1976); O. Likaka, "Rural Protest: The Mbole Against the Belgian Rule, 1893–1955," *International Journal of African Historical Studies* 27, no. 3 (1994).

4. Comité Cotonnier Congolais, "Notes sur l'achat du coton au Congo belge," 1941 A.A., Brussels.

5. Ibid.

6. A. Ravet, "Organisation de la culture du coton au Congo belge," *Bulletin du comité cotonnier congolais*, 5 (1936): 3.

7. *Rapport annuel sur l'administration du Congo belge*, 1917, 97–98.

8. "La culture du coton," *Mouvement géographique*, no. 45, coll. 551.

9. The legislation was modeled after the 1911 contract with the Huileries du Congo belge.

10. Banneux, "Quelques données," 4; De Bauw, ed., *Trente années de culture cotonnière*, 37; Landeghem, "La Compagnie Cotonnière Congolaise," 820; P. Joye and R. Lewin, *Les trusts au Congo* (Brussels: Société populaire d'éditions, 1961), 74. These banks included la Société Générale de Belgique, la Banque de Bruxelles, la Banque d' Outre-Mer, la Banque Josse Allard, La Banque Lambert, la banque Philipson, and la Banque Ngelmanckers, which together owned 50 percent of the shares. Industries included all the powerful companies: la Société Commerciale et Minière du Congo, la Société Anonyme Bunge, la Compagnie du Congo pour le Commerce et l'Industrie, one group of industrialists of Verviers

and another of Flandria, which together owned 25 percent of shares. Public subscribers and the state held 15 percent and 10 percent respectively.

11. "Comité Cotonnier Congolais. Sa composition, son programme d'action," *Bulletin du Comité Cotonnier Congolais* 1 (1936): 3; De Bauw, "Un groupement professionnel colonial," 414; "Documentation sur le coton au Congo belge," n. d., 25, 37, A.R.H.Z., Kisangani. Brixhe, *Le coton au Congo belge*, 16.

12. Nkala Wodjim Tantur, "L'agriculture commerciale dans le district de Lulua, 1920–1940," (M.A. thesis, UNAZA, 1974), 58. The sellers also cheated whenever they could as a countermeasure.

13. "Rapport d'inspection," Territoire de Dungu, 1947, 2, A.R.H.Z., Kisangani.

14. Interview with Lwaka Mukandja, Lubumbashi, August 14, 1986.

15. A. Moeller, "Modifications proposées au projet de décret régissant la culture et le commerce du coton," A.R.H.Z., Kisangani.

16. E. Fisher, "Rapport voyage cotonnier: Bas et Haut Uele," May 20, 1992, A.R.H.Z., Kisangani.

17. "Dossier ZIII, A. Moeller, "Modifications proposées au projet de décret régissant la culture et le commerce du coton," A.R.H.Z., Kisangani.

18. "Agri (369) 1/2." A.A., Brussels; "Rapport économique," District du Haut-Uele, 1924, A.R.H.Z., Kisangani.

19. "Dossier A.I. (1414) 6"; "Agri (374); A.I. 17: 'Impôt indigène'"; "Procès-verbal de la 34ème Réunion du Comité Cotonnier Congolais," April 30, 1934, 3, all in A.A., Brussels; Cotonco, "Rapport 1930."

20. E. Leplae, "Résultats," 135, "Agri, le coton, 1937"; "Agri (369) 1/2. Leplae au Ministère des colonies, Brussels, November 28, 1929," both in A.A., Brussels.

21. "Dossier AIMO. Landeghem, c.d.d. au Vice-Gouverneur de la Province Orientale," Buta, le 20 Décembre, 1920, A.R.H.Z., Kisangani.

22. *Rapport annuel sur l'administration du Congo belge*, 1921.

23. *Rapport annuel sur l'administration du Congo belge*, 1923.

24. Quoted in M. Merlier, *Le Congo*; Joye and Lewin, *Les trusts au Congo*; G. Malengreau, "Les lotissements agricoles au Congo belge," *Bulletin agricole du Congo belge* 43, special issue (1952): 209; A. Brenez, "La question cotonnière au Lomami," *Bulletin agricole du Congo belge* 22, no. 2 (1931): 166; "Monographie du coton congolais," 58.

25. Orientale Province, "Rapport annuel sur la culture et le commerce du coton, 1972–1928," A.R.H.Z., Kisangani.

26. Joye and Lewine, *Les trusts au Congo*.

27. "Agri (374)," A.A., Brussels; Leplae, "Comment les indigènes," 184.

28. "Dossier D (778), Papiers Bertrand"; "Agri (369) 1/2," in A.A., Brussels; "Rapport économique" District du Haut-Uele, 1924, A.A., Brussels; Merlier, *Le Congo*, 83; Kasendwe Kibonge, "Les cultures obligatoires dans le district du Tanganyika (1935–1950)" (M.A. thesis, UNAZA, Lubumbashi, 1981), 53; E. Leplae, "Transformation de l'agriculture indigène du Congo belge par les cultures obligatoires," *Technique agricole internationale* 6, no. 2 (1936): 100.

29. P. T. Bauer, *Dissent on Development* (London: Weidenfeld and Nicholson, 1971), 41.

30. "Agri (369) 1/2. 'Leplae au Secrétaire de la troisième Direction, no. 436,'" Brussels, November 4, 1929, A.A., Brussels.

31. Joye and Lewine, *Les trusts au Congo,* 81–82.

32. *Bulletin de la chambre du commerce et de l'industrie du Katanga,* 54 (1946): 11; "Dossier A.1 (1414) 6. Commission Cotonnière," March, 1937, A.A., Brussels.

33. Banneux, "Quelques données," 12–13; *Bulletin du Comité Cotonnier Congolais* 1 (1936): 8; 5 (1937): 21; 6 (1937): 54; Depi, "La caisse de réserve cotonnière," 63.

34. *Bulletin de la chamber du commerce et de l'industrie du Katanga* 54 (1946): 11; Depi, "La caisse de réserve cotonnière," 63; Agri (386) no. 120, A.A., Brussels.

35. Depi, "La caisse de réserve cotonnière," 63; P. Nauwelaert, "Le Cogerco, garantie pour le planteur," *Bulletin du Comité Cotonnier Congolais,* 2 (1958): 3; De Bauw, ed., *Trente années de culture cotonnière,* 60–61.

36. L. Jaskold, "Rapport annuel sur la campagne cotonnière, 1937–1938," Stanleyville, May 7, 1938.

37. "Rapport annuel sur l'agriculture," District du Tanganyika, 1938, 31, A.R.H.Z., Kisangani.

38. *Bulletin du Comité Cotonnier Congolais* 9 (1938): 35; see also De Bauw, ed., *Trente années de culture cotonnière,* 40; Depi, "La caisse de réserve cotonnière," 63.

39. "Agri (378). Coton, GI. Note pour Mr. le Gouverneur-Général." A.A., Brussels.

40. "Agri (378) 19," A.A., Brussels.

41. "Agri (378) 19, Coton GI. P. Ryckmans au Ministère des colonies," July 9, 1936, A.A., Brussels.

42. Banneux, "Quelques données," 14.

43. Depi, "La caisse de réserve cotonnière," 65.

44. *Conseil de Province Orientale,* 1946, 18.

45. "D.P.," April 15, 1937, A.R.H.Z., Kisangani.

46. "Agri (378)/Coton/H," September 7, 1939, A.A., Brussels.

47. "Documentation sur le coton au Congo belge," n.d., 28, A.R.H.Z., Kisangani.

48. "D.P.," July 15, 1937, A.R.H.Z., Kisangani. Landeghem, "La Compagnie Cotonnière Congolaise," 820; De Bauw, ed., *Trente années de culture cotonnière,* 20.

49. Merlier, *Le Congo,* Landeghem, "La Compagnie Cotonnière Congolaise," 825; see also A. Landeghem, "La question du coton au Congo belge," *Bulletin de la société belge d'études et d'expansion* 61 (1927): 255–61, and "Quelques particularités de l'activité cotonnière au Congo belge," *Bulletin du Comité Cotonnier Congolais* 8 (1938): 1–3; A.L., "Panorama sur le coton," February 22, 1942, A.R.H.Z., Kisangani. The Cotonco group included Cotonepo, Socobom, and Cotanga.

50. Ibid., 8; Landeghem, 825; *Echo de la Bourse,* A.A., Brussels, n.d. In 1940, for example, Compagnie Cotonnière Equatoriale Française (Cotonfran) and Compagnie du Haut-Oubangui (Cotoubangui) had capital of 11 million and 6.3 million French francs, of which Cotonco held 30 percent and 27 percent. Of a total of 10 million escudos of the *Compagnie Générale des Cotons de l'Angola (Cotonang),* Cotonco alone had 50 percent.

51. "Agri (386) 120, G.G. P. Ryckmans à Landeghem," Léopoldville, January 31, 1940, A.A., Brussels; "D.P," July 15, 1937, A.R.H.Z., Kisangani; Cotonco, "Rapport du Conseil d'Administration et du Collège des Commissaires," July 8, 1946, 7, A.A., Brussels.

52. *Bulletin du Comité Cotonnier Congolais* 18 (1947): 64; 1, no. 17 (1947): 40; Cotonco, "Rapport d'Administration et du Collège des Commissaires," July 8, 1946, 7, A.A., Brussels.

53. Brixhe, *Le coton au Congo belge*, 119.

54. Ministère des Colonies, *L'agriculture au Congo belge* (Brussels: Ministère des Colonies, 1954), 118.

55. Comité Cotonnier Congolais, Memorandum pour le ministre de colonies, November 17, 1950, A.R.H.Z., Kisangani.

56. "Memorandum complémentaire à Mr. le G.G. sur la situation des sociétés cotonnières opérant dans les zones libres des régions du Sud," A.R.H.Z., Kisangani.

57. Depi, "La caisse de réserve cotonnière," 65.

58. A. Boulanger, "Evolution économique d'un milieu rural congolais en district de Kabinda," *Bulletin du CEPSI* 5 (1957): 142.

59. Interview with Lwamba Bilonda, Lubumbashi, August 13, 1986.

60. M. Merlier, *Le Congo*, 100; "Rubbens au G. G.," July 15, 1957, A.R.H.Z., Kisangani; see *Journal des tribunaux d'outre-mer* (1950): 24; 74 (1956): 128; 98 (1958): 128.

Chapter 4. Cotton and Social Inequality

1. Isaacman, "Chiefs, Rural Differentiation and Peasant Protest," 29.

2. E. Mandala, "Capitalism, Ecology and Society: The Lower Tchire (Shire) Valley of Malawi, 1860–1960," (Ph.D. diss., University of Minnesota, 1983); also *Work and Control in a Peasant Economy* (Madison: University of Wisconsin Press, 1990).

3. Joan Vincent, "Colonial Chiefs and the Making of Class: A Case Study from Teso, Eastern Uganda," *Africa* 47, no. 2 (1977): 149. P. Nayenga, "Commercial Cotton Growing in Busoga District, Uganda, 1905–1923," *African Economic History* 10 (1981): 175–95.

4. Rhoda Howard, "Formation and Stratification of the Peasantry in Colonial Ghana," *Journal of Peasant Studies* 8, no. 1 (1980): 72.

5. R. Anstey, *King Leopold's Legacy*, 56; G. Van der Kerken, *Les sociétés bantoues du Congo belge* (Brussels: Etablissements Emile Bruylant, 1920), 274–76; "Dossiers chefferies," A.R.H.Z., Kisangani. These files are replete with examples of chiefs convicted for misappropriation of funds from peasants. Of the many reasons advanced to explain the situation, the inadequacy of resources figured prominently.

6. *Conseil de Province d'Elisabethville*, 1945, iii, annexe 2, 36; Rodney, *How Europe Underdeveloped Africa;* Isaacman et al., "Cotton Is the Mother of Poverty."

7. Orientale Province, "Rapport annuel sur la culture et le commerce du coton, 1927–1928," 1928 A.R.H.Z., Kisangani.

8. "Rapport annuel de l'agriculture," District de Lulua, 1932, 19, A.R.H.Z., Kisangani.

9. "Dossiers Z 265," A.R.H.Z., Kisangani.

10. Mandala, *Work and Control;* Howard, "Formation and Stratification of the Peasantry," 72; Isaacman, "Peasants and Rural Social Protest," 120; A. Isaacman, *The Tradition of Resistance in Mozambique: Anti-Colonial Activity in the Zambezi Valley, 1850–1921* (Berkeley: University of California Press, 1976); P. Nayenga, "Chiefs and the 'Land Question' in Busoga District, Uganda, 1895–1936," *International Journal of African Historical Studies* 12, no. 2 (1979): 183–209.

11. Vincent, "Colonial Chiefs," 149.

12. The Azande chiefs used the labor of the *Apalanga* (young) for military purposes as well as for production.

13. Interview with Katayi, Lubumbashi, August 24, 1986.

14. E. Fisher, "Rapport voyage d'inspection de Lonkala, Lusambo, Tshibala, Kabinda, Tshofa, Maniema et retour," Lusambo, July 6, 1920, A.A., Brussels.

15. E. Fisher, "Rapport voyage cotonnier Bas et Haut-Uele," Bambili, May 20, 1922, A.A., Brussels.

16. Blommaert "Introduction du coton," 812; also "La culture du coton."

17. Interview with Katayi, Lubumbashi, August 24, 1986.

18. Interview with Itambo, Kisangani, 1989.

19. C. Leontovitch, "Rapport saison cotonnière, 1937–1938," District du Congo-Ubangi, Libenge, July 2, 1938, A.R.H.Z., Kisangani; "Agri (369) 1/4 no 1045/R"; Comité Cotonnier Congolais, "Note sur l'achat du coton au congo belge," 1941, A.A., Brussels; "Dossier D(778) Papiers Bertrand," A.A., Brussels.

20. Sparano, "Culture et commerce du coton," 414.

21. *Expansion coloniale,* April 5, 1936; "Dossier D(778) Papiers Bertrand," A.A., Brussels.

22. "Dossier A.I. (1403) 3," A.A., Brussels; Landeghem, "La Compagnie Cotonnière Congolaise," 821; M. Waelkens, "Situation de l'industrie cotonnière dans la colonie," *Agriculture et levage au Congo* 89 (1930): 115.

23. A. Sohier, "La grande pitié des juridictions indigènes," *Journal des tribunaux d'outre-mer* 21 (1952): 29.

24. When the state suppressed production premiums to chiefs during the Great Depression, they allied with peasants to protest the fall of producer prices. When they received handsome gifts from cotton companies, they were eager to support cotton production, although the prices were falling. See R. Anstey, *King Leopold's Legacy,* 48, 67.

25. Lesage, "Voyage d'inspection en territoire de Kabinda," Kabinda, September 24, 1943.

26. "Dossier Z 265, no. 2460/ADB5," Kasongo, November 10, 1932; "Rapport d'inspection," Territoire de Dungu, 1945, 9; "Rapport d'inspection, tribunal des Mangbetu," 1937; Lesage, "Voyage d'inspection du territoire de Kabinda"; "Rapport d'inspection," Dungu, 1945, 8; "Rapport d'inspection," Buta, 1954, 43; "Rapport d'inspection," Niangara, 1952, 36, all in A.R.H.Z., Kisangani.

27. "Rapport d'inspection," Territoire de Dungu, 1947, 17; "Rapport d'inspection," Territoire d'Ango, 1938; "Rapport d'inspection," 1946; "Rapport

d'inspection," Niangara, 1952, 36; "Rapport d'inspection," Territoire de Dungu, 1952, 24, all in A.R.H.Z., Kisangani.

28. Drachousoff, "Le développement de l'agriculture," 33; see also *Bulletin agricole du Congo belge* 38 (1947): 471–582, 783–880.

29. "Agri (129)" A.A., Brussels.

30. "Rapport d'inspection," Territoire de Niangara, 1945, 2; "Rapport annuel de l'agriculture," Kibali-Ituri, 1929, 17, A.R.H.Z., Kisangani.

31. "Rapport annuel AIMO," Territoire des Mangbetu, 1951, 24, A.R.H.Z., Kisangani.

32. Malengreau, "Les lotissements agricoles," 208.

33. "Rapport annuel AIMO," Territoire des Mangbetu, 1951, 24, A.R.H.Z., Kisangani.

34. "Rapport annuel de l'agriculture," District du Uele-Itimbiri, 1930, 14, A.R.H.Z., Kisangani.

35. V. Drachousoff, "L'avenir de l'agriculture indigène au Congo belge," *Revue d'agronomie coloniale* 6 (1946): 14.

36. Bertrand, *Le problème de la de la main-d'oeuvre*, 140 and passim.

37. Lesage, "Voyage d'inspection en Territoire de Kabinda."

38. "Rapport annuel AIMO," Province d'Elisabethville, 1941, 38, A.R.S., Lubumbishi.

39. "Rapport d'inspection," Territoire de Rungu, 1947, 6, A.R.H.Z., Kisangani.

40. L. De Koster, "Le malaise des milieux ruraux au Congo," *Revue générale belge* 33 (1948): 463; interview with Ujanga, Kisangani, 1990; "Agri (374), Rubbens au G. G." 22. 4. 1937, A.A., Brussels; "Rapport d'inspection," Territoire de Buta, 1954, 43, A.R.H.Z., Kisangani.

41. "Congo: enquêtes démographiques," tables 17, 19, 23, in B. Fetter, *Colonial Rule and Regional Imbalance in Central Africa* (Boulder, CO: Westview Press, 1983), 173.

42. *Essor colonial et maritime*, no. 41, October 24, 1937.

43. H. Baumann, "The Division of Work according to Sex in African Hoe Culture," *Africa* 1, no. 3 (1928):308–14. Most studies suffered from generalization, ignoring that, ethnically, Africa stands for a "huge forest with many trees." It may be easy to see the forest, but it is extremely difficult to count the trees. Moreover, as a social product, the division of labor changed as the material basis of the society changed.

44. J. Vansina, *Introduction à l'éthnographie du Congo* (Kinshasa: Editions Universitaires du Congo, 1965), 30, 43, 106, 135–36, 164, 216; M. Miracle, *Agriculture in the Congo Basin* (Madison, Milwaukee, and London: University of Wisconsin Press, 1967).

45. The figures in the table represent days per year for men, women, and children.

46. Drachousoff, "L'avenir de l'agriculture indigène," 14.

47. Lesage, "Voyage d'inspection en Territoire de Kabinda."

48. Conseil de Province du Katanga, 1944, 115.

49. "Dossier Z 265," A.R.H.Z., Kisangani.

50. Interview with Ujanga, Kisangani, August, 1989.
51. Interview with Katayi, Lubumbashi, August 24, 1986; interview with Ujanga, Kisangani, September, 1989; "Dossier sur les jurisdictions indigènes," A.R.H.Z., Kisangani; Interview with Katayi, Lubumbashi, August 24, 1986.
52. *Bulletin de la banque du Congo* 2 (1947): 26.
53. *Etudes sur le marché de certains produits congolais* (1938): 51.
54. "Agri (369) 1/4, no. 1045/R," A.A., Brussels; *Conseil de Province d'Elisabethville*, 1935, 106; "Campagne cotonnière 1935–1936, région sud," 9, A.R.S., Lubumbashi.
55. Letter written by Sister Françoise-Marie in *Bulletin du Comité Cotonnier Congolais* 15 (1939): 77.
56. *Essor colonial et maritime*, no. 41, October 24, 1937.
57. "Rapport annuel," Territoire de Mangbetu, 1951, A.R.H.Z., Kisangani.
58. Interview with Tshibanda Nduba Musaka, Lubumbashi, August, 1986.
59. E. Leplae, "Notes sur le relèvement de l'agriculture du Congo," *Bulletin agricole du Congo belge* 23, no. 1 (1932): 132.
60. Interview with Lwamba Bilonda, Lubumbashi, August 13, 1986.
61. Interview with Tuale, Lubumbashi July 17, 1988.

Chapter 5. The Infrapolitics of the Cotton Cultivators

1. T. O. Ranger, ed., *Emerging Themes of African History* (Nairobi: East African Publishing House, 1968), and "Connections Between 'Primary Resistance' Movements and Modern Mass Nationalism in East and Central Africa," *Journal of African History* 9, no. 3 (1968): 437–53, 631–41; D. Crummey, ed., *Banditry, Rebellion and Social Protest in Africa* (London: Heinemann, 1986); Isaacman, *The Tradition of Resistance;* California Press, 1976); Sikitele Gize, "Les racines de la révolte pende de 1931," *Etudes d'histoire africaine* 5(1973): 99–153.
2. J. Scott, *Domination and the Art of Resistance* (New Haven: Yale University Press, 1990), xiii, 198.
3. "Propagande cotonnière," n. d., 9, A.R.H.Z., Kisangani.
4. E. Dejong, "Le coton dans l'Uele," *Bulletin agricole du Congo belge* 18, no. 4 (1927): 453.
5. A. De Meulemeester, "L'agriculture dans la Province Orientale du Congo belge en 1920," *Bulletin agricole du Congo belge* 12, no. 4 (1921): 646–47.
6. A. Brenez, "La culture du cotonnier au Lomami," *Bulletin agricole du Congo belge* 19, no. 1 (1928): 105.
7. F. Sparano, "Rapport sur la campagne cotonnière, 1924–1925," Bondo, May 10, 1925.
8. "Rapport d'inspection," Territoire de Buta, 1946, 17, A.R.H.Z., Kisangani.
9. Leplae, "Comment les indigènes," 179.
10. J. Blassingame, *The Slave Community: Plantation Life in the Antebellum South* (New York: Oxford University Press, 1972).
11. *Rapport annuel sur l'administration du Congo*, 1934, 9, 1938, 9, 1955, 78; *Conseil de Province de l'Equateur*, 1955.

12. After 1933, flight to the forests and bush offered shelter only to those peasants located near international borders, backwater regions, and where the density of administrative interaction remained poor.

13. Bryant T. Shaw, "Force Publique: Force Unique. The Military in the Belgian Congo, 1914–1939" (Ph.D. dissertation, University of Wisconsin, Madison), map 79, 134–42.

14. "Dossier F.P. (2459) no. 237," A.A., Brussels; "Rapport agricole. Première partie," 1937, 52, A.R.H.Z., Kisangani.

15. "Dossier F.P. (2459), no. 237," A.A., Brussels; *Rapport annuel sur l'administration du Congo belge,* 1936, 54.

16. Interview with Losa, Kisangani, October 11, 1989.

17. *Rapport annuel sur l'administration du Congo,* 1955, 78, 1934, 9; the Kalui group in Kamina struggled in this way. They deserted the village by crossing the River Kalui, a branch of Lovoi River, to hide in the bushes, see Nkulu Kalala, "Les réactions africaines," 87.

18. Interview with Dabet Ngandali, Minneapolis, January 16, 1990.

19. "Rapport d'inspection," Territoire de Dungu, 1953, 21, A.R.H.Z., Kisangani; *Rapport annuel sur l'administration du Congo belge,* 1955, 66, 1938, 9, 1957, 72, 1958, 72.

20. *Rapport annuel sur l'administration du Congo belge,* 1955, 68.

21. P. Nayenga, "Commercial Cotton Growing in Busoga District, Uganda, 1905–1923," *African Economic History* 10 (1981).

22. *Cotton Trade Journal,* January 13, 1940.

23. "Rapport d'inspection" Territoire de Dungu, 1948, A.R.H.Z., Kisangani.

24. "Rapport d'inspection," Territoire de Dungu, 1943, 6, A.R.H.Z., Kisangani. Colonial officials indicated that because the economic situation was better in the Belgian Congo, the indigenous people were returning by the thousands.

25. Conseil de Province d'Elisabethville, 1945, iii, annexe 2, 36.

26. *Bulletin du CEPSI* 2 (1946–47): 8–20; *Bulletin du Comité Cotonnier Congolais* 17 (1946): 59.

27. *Essor Colonial et Maritime* no. 41, October 24, 1937.

28. Letter by Sister Françoise-Marie, quoted in *Bulletin du Comité Cotonnier Congolais,* 15 (1939): 77.

29. *Conseil de Province d'Elisabethville,* 1949, 11.

30. Nkala Wodjim Tantur, "Agriculture commerciale," 77.

31. *Bulletin Comité Cotonnier Congolais* 17 (1946) 1: 38.

32. *Conseil de Province Orientale,* 1958, 1–3, 12; Ernest, "L'activité du Seneloka," *Bulletin du Comité Cotonnier Congolais* 17 (1946): 25; "Rapport annuel AIMO," Territoire des Mangbetu, 1955, 49, A.R.H.Z., Kisangani.

33. *Bulletin du Comité Cotonnier Congolais* 17 (1947): 39, 17 (1946): 15.

34. *Rapport annuel sur l'administration du Congo belge,* 1945–46, 10.

35. *Conseil de Province d'Elisabethville,* 1944, 62; "Rapport d'inspection," Territoire de Dungu, 1947, 9, A.R.H.Z., Kisangani; *Rapport annuel sur l'administration du Congo belge,* 1943, 6.

36. Amrhyn, "Rapport du mois de mars et avril 1920 sur la culture du coton chez l'indigène au Territoire de Mahagi (Ituri)," A.R.H.Z., Kisangani.

37. Stocker, "Rapport sur la campagne cotonnière 1923–1924," Niangara, April 30, 1924; Leplae, "Résultats," 115–140; "Culture du coton dans l'Uele," A.R.H.Z., Kisangani; J. Vansina, personal notes. His source is Mikwepy Anaclet's mother and the information applies to the Mweka area before c. 1950.

38. *Bulletin agricole du Congo belge* 21 (1930): 808. It was also the "laziness" of the agronomists which was at fault. They wanted fields near the roads where they could go and see the producers by car.

39. C. Leontovitch, "La culture de coton dans le district du Congo-Ubangi," *Bulletin agricole du Congo belge* 28, no. 1 (1937): 37.

40. M. Querton, "Rapport sur la propagande cotonnière dans le district de Sankuru," *Bulletin agricole du Congo belge* 16, no. 2 (1925): 348.

41. A. De Meulemeester, "L'agriculture dans la Province Orientale du Congo belge," *Bulletin agricole du Congo belge* 7, no. 4 (1921): 646–47; M. Querton, "Rapport sur la propagande," 348–50.

42. Letter by Sister Françoise-Marie quoted in *Bulletin du Comité Cotonnier Congolais* 15 (1939): 77; Nkulu Kalala, "Les réactions africaines," 86; Sparano, "Rapport sur la campagne cotonnière 1924–1925"; Blommaert, "La culture du coton," 86; Pres, "Avis et considrations sur l'état de l'agriculture du district pendant le premier semestre, 1926," Lusambo, April 14, 1926, A.A., Brussels.

43. Stocker, "Rapport sur la campagne cotonnière, 1923–1924."

44. F. Sparano, "Rapport annuel sur la culture et le commerce du coton dans les districts des Uele," August 26, 1930.

45. "Dossier Z 265," A.R.H.Z., Kisangani. The maximum penalties for women were 7 days in prison, 15 francs in fines, and 12 lashes.

46. Bertrand, *Le problème*, 140.

47. "Rapport d'inspection," Territoire de Buta, 1946, 17, A.R.H.Z., Kisangani; F. Sparano, "Rapport sur la situation des plantations indigènes de coton," September 1, 1923; "Rapport sur la culture du coton au District du Bas-Uele durant le mois d' Octobre et Novembre 1921," Buta, December 19, 1921; Mascart, "Rapport officiel de l'activité du service agricole de la compagnie cotonnière congolaise dans les Uele 1931–1932," 208. Mascart's estimates are based on a sample of three chiefdoms: Moma, Kalepaie, Zukumbwa; Sohier, "La grande pitié," 29; E. Fisher, "Rapport voyage cotonnier Bas et Haut-Uele," Bambili, May 20, 1922; "Rapport du mois de mars et avril sur la culture du coton chez l'indigène au Territoire de Mahagi"; Coperus, "Rapport de la fin campagne cotonnière, 1927–1928," 1928, all the preceding in A.R.H.Z., Kisangani; "Agri (382) 33, Récolte cotonnière de 1940." A.A., Brussels.

48. Camara Laye, *The Dark Child*, trans. James Kirkup and Ernest Jones (New York: Farrar, Straus, and Giroux, 1985), 53.

49. J. Scott, *Weapons of the Weak: Everyday Forms of Peasant Resistance* (New Haven: Yale University Press, 1985).

50. "Rapport annuel," Territoire des Mangbetu, 1953, 25, A.R.H.Z., Kisangani.

51. "Dossier D (778), Papiers Bertrand, Dossier d' Afrique," A.A., Brussels.

52. "Rapport d'inspection," Territoire de Dungu, 1946, 5, A.R.H.Z., Kisangani.

53. Interview with Itambo, Kisangani, July 11, 1989.

54. Kasendwe Kibonge, "Les cultures obligatoires."

55. "Dossier D (778), Papiers Bertrand, Dossier d'Europe," A.A., Brussels.

56. Sparano, "Vade-mecum," 113; Blommaert, "Introduction du coton," 818.

57. "Agri (369) 1/4. Stanleyville, télégramme no 3, relatif aux achats de coton," A.A., Brussels.

58. "Analyse de la campagne cotonnière, 1935–1936. Conclusions, régions sud," 9, A.R.H.Z., Kisangani."

59. In 1927, for example, stones mixed with cotton caused a fire in Titule gins. Referring to this incident, the minister of colonies pointed out to the governor-general that agents had bought humid cotton without unpacking it, and this not only caused fire but also allowed peasants to sell cotton mixed with stones. See "Dossier D (778). Papiers Bertrand, Dossier d'Europe," A.A., Brussels.

60. *Rapport annuel sur l'administration du Congo belge*, 1933, 185.

61. Interview with Mboli Ndoko, Kisangani, September 21, 1989.

62. "Rapport d'inspection," Territoire de Dungu, 1934, 17, A.R.H.Z., Kisangani.

63. "Rapport d'inspection," Territoire de Dungu, 1947, 4, A.R.H.Z., Kisangani.

64. "Rapport d'inspection," Territoire d'Ango, 1949, 12–13, A.R.H.Z., Kisangani.

65. "Rapport d'inspection." Territoire d'Ango, 1949, 12–13, A.R.H.Z., Kisangani. The former husband was also convicted and ordered to pay 50 francs in fines and to spend 21 days in prison. "Rapport d'inspection," Territoire de Poko, 1951, 34, A.R.H.Z., Kisangani.

66. "Rapport d'inspection," Territoire d'Ango, 1949, 12–13, A.R.H.Z., Kisangani.

67. "Rapport d'inspection," Territoire d'Ango, 1949, 9, 11, A.R.H.Z., Kisangani.

68. "Rapport AIMO," 1957, 27, A.R.H.Z., Kisangani.

69. Interview with Mboli Ndoko, Kisangani, February 24, 1989.

70. "Rapport d'inspection," Territoire d'Ango, 1949, chefferie Gindo; "Rapport annuel AIMO," Territoire de Rungu, 1953, 4, 1955, 3; "Rapport d'inspection," Territoire d'Ango, 1948; "Dossier Z III, circonscriptions indigènes: tribunaux des chefferies indigènes," all in A.R.H.Z., Kisangani.

71. "Rapport d'inspection," Territoire de Buta, 1946, 31, 22, A.R.H.Z., Kisangani.

72. As we can see, the rebellion of married women also involved men (brothers and fathers) on their side, which explains why the all-male Native Tribunals could rule in their favor.

73. "Rapport d'inspection," Territoire de Buta, 1954, 43, A.R.H.Z., Kisangani.

74. Interview with M' Boliaka, Kisangani, March 12, 1989. Many verdicts show that husbands who used excessive beatings were sentenced to prison. In other cases, where wives lost teeth, eyes, or were wounded, the in-law intervened and retaliated violently; interview with Sumba, Lubumbashi, 1986.

75. "Dossier Z 265;" "Rapport d'inspection," Territoire de Buta, 1958, 14;

"Rapport d'inspection," Territoire de Poko, 1951, 34; "Rapport d'inspection," Territoire d'Ango," 1949, 12, 13, all in A.R.H.Z., Kisangani. Repudiations were not effective in controlling women, because the latter could and did claim part of cotton-generated money.

76. "Dossier Z 265," A.R.H.Z., Kisangani.

77. "Rapport d'inspection," Territoire de Buta, 1957, 14; "Rapport d'inspection," Territoire de Buta, 1946, A.R.H.Z., Kisangani.

78. J. Delumeau, *Injures et blasphèmes* (Paris: Imago, 1989); C. P. Flynn, *Insult and Society* (Port Washington, NY:, Kennikat Press, 1977), 71, 112. Using cross-cultural materials, Flynn has shown that, among their many functions, insults are a powerful mechanism of social control.

79. Interview with Yanga Yanga, Kisangani, February 11, 1989.

80. Kasendwe Kibonge, "Les cultures obligatoires," interview with Katayi, Lubumbashi, 1986; Guilmin, "La polygamie dans l'Equateur," *Zaire* no. 1 (1947): 1001–23. Guilmin does not directly link polygyny to cotton.

81. Leplae, "Notes sur le relèvement de l'agriculture," 1.

82. Interview with Katayi, Lubumbashi, August 1986.

83. Bertrand, *Le problème*.

84. *Conseil de Province Orientale*, 1956, 31. Territorial administrators described these conflicts in a variety of ways: loosening of traditional moral standards, increasing individualism, emancipation of the youths, and disaffection toward ancestral works.

85. "Dossier A.I (1397)," A.A., Brussels; "Rapport politique du 2ème semestre 1926," District du Lomami, 1926, A.R.H.Z., Kisangani.

86. Vansina, *Paths in the Rainforests*, 246. Secret societies existed in many cultures before the colonial conquest. When state agents everywhere outlawed public divining, poison ordeals, many healing rituals, and human sacrifices at funerals, new healing and witch-finding cults sprang up to defend social and somatic harmony.

87. *Conseil de Province Orientale*, 1956, 28.

88. "Dossier A.I. (1397)," A. Verbeken, "La sorcelerie chez les noirs africains," December 29, 1935, A.A., Brussels.

89. "Rapport d'inspection," Territoire d'Ango, 1947, A.R.H.Z., Kisangani.

90. Healing practices were expressions and means of resistance against colonial exploitation. They also were fields of internal struggle and represented, at least partly, social mechanisms for the redistribution of power, wealth, and prestige. However, they were not always protests against the existing structures of power and social relations, as demonstrated by the case of Bapaenge, who charged fees while his wife left agricultural work to women who were treated by her husband.

91. *Conseil de Province Orientale*, 1956, 28. The budget for 1957 proposed the creation of about twenty schools as a anti-Kitawala movement measure; K. Fields, *Revival and Rebellion in Colonial Central Africa* (Princeton: Yale University Press, 1985).

92. *Conseil de Province d'Elisabethville*, 1945, 1–2, 21; B. Lincoln, "Notes to-

ward a Theory of Religion and Revolution," in B. Lincoln, ed., *Religion, Rebellion, Revolution* (New York: St Martin's Press, 1985), 276.

93. *Rapport annuel sur l'administration du Congo belge,* 1939–44, 9.

94. Interview with Soni, Lubumbashi, August 11, 1986.

95. *Conseil de Province d'Elisabethville,* 1938, 14–15.

96. *Rapport annuel sur l'administration du Congo belge,* 1938, 9.

97. *Rapport annuel sur l'administration du Congo belge,* 1945–46, 9, 13; 1938, 9; 1950, 88; 1951, 77.

98. *Conseil de Province Orientale,* 1945, 16; 1956, 41; *Conseil de Province de l'Equateur,* 1954, 5.

99. N. Hunt, "Domesticity and Colonialism in Belgian Africa: Usumbura's Foyer Social, 1946–1960," *Signs* 15, no. 3 (1990): 447–74; "L'avant-projet de budget pour 1958," 3, in *Conseil de Province Orientale,* 1957.

100. M. Turnbull, *The Lonely African* (New York: 1962), 162–79; H. Van Geluwe, *Les Babali et les peuplades apparentés* (Tervuren: 1960); Joset, *Les sociétés secrètes des hommes-léopards en Afrique centrale* (Paris: 1955).

101. "Rapport politique du 2ème trimestre," District de l'Ubangi, 1926, A.R.H.Z., Kisangani.

102. "Rapport d'inspection," Territoire de Bambili (Bambesa), 1931, 20, A.R.H.Z., Kisangani.

103. "Rapport d'inspection," Territoire de Niangara, 1952, 36, A.R.H.Z., Kisangani.

104. "Rapport d'inspection," Territoire de Dungu, 1940, 7; "Rapport d'inspection," Territoire de Bambili, 1931, 21; "Rapport d'inspection," Territoire d'Ango, 1946, all in A.R.H.Z., Kisangani.

105. Interview with Sumba Ndandwe, Lubumbashi, August 23, 1986.

106. "Rapport d'inspection," Territoire de Dungu, 1945, 91; "Rapport d'inspection du tribunal de chefferie des Mangbetu Mavaazanga," 1937, in A.R.H.Z., Kisangani.

107. "Rapport d'inspection," Territoire d'Ango, 1938; Lesage, "Voyage d'inspection en Territoire de Kabinda," in A.R.H.Z., Kisangani.

108. Isaacman, "Peasants and Rural Social Protest," 3.

109. Rhoda Howard, "Differential Class Participation in an African Protest Movement: The Ghana Cocoa Boycott of 1936–38," *Canadian Journal of African Studies* 10, no. 3 (1976):469–80; J. L. Amselle, "La conscience paysanne: La révolte de Ouolosse-bougou (Juin 1968, Mali)," *Canadian Journal of African Studies* 12, no. 3 (1978): 339–55.

110. A. T. Nzula et al., *Forced Labor in Colonial Africa.*

111. Blassingame, *The Slave Community;* E. R. Price, ed., *Maroon Societies: Rebel Slave Communities in the Americas* (New York: Anchor Press, 1972).

112. A. Isaacman, "Coercion, Paternalism and the Labor Process: The Mozambican Cotton Regime, 1938–61," *Journal of Southern African Studies* 18 (1992): 487 ff.; O. Likaka, "Forced Cotton Production and the Colonial Work Ethic in Zaire," *Canadian Journal of African Studies* (forthcoming); Lincoln, *Discourse and the Construction of Society.*

113. *Rapport annuel sur l'administration du Congo belge,* 1945–46, 9; *Conseil de Province du Katanga,* 1944, 22, 78.

114. *Conseil de Province Orientale,* 1958, 1–3, 12. Cotton growers used 155 tons of "superphosphate triple." Tractors were available on a rental basis. These changes were at an experimental stage.

Conclusion

1. Tosh, "The Cash-Crop Revolution in Tropical Africa: An Agricultural Reappraisal," *African Affairs* 79, no. 314 (1980): 81.

Selected Bibliography

Archival Materials

Archives Africaines du Ministère des Affaires Étrangères, Brussels

Agri (369) Correspondance générale, 1925–1927.
Agri (129) Correspondance générale, 1931–1936.
Agri (128) Divers.
Agri (370) Coton dans l'Uele, 1919–1929.
Agri (371) Rapport campagne cotonière, 1927–1931.
Agri (372) Usines à coton, 1919–1922.
Agri (372) La crise cotonière de 1930, 1930–1931.
Agri (373) Ordonance 144/bis, 1933–1936: Correspondance, divers.
Agri (373) Arrêtés, divers, 1934–1956.
Agri (373) Allocations pour le coton, 1940–1046.
Agri (373) Comptoir de Ventes des cotons du Congo, 1954.
Agri (376) ICAC (Comité Consultatif International du Coton).
Agri (375) ICAC.
Agri (374) Documentation: Correspondance, études, divers, 1924–1954.
Agri (371) Campagne cotonnière.
Agri (377) Rapports, 1932–1939; 1946; 1949.
Agri (378) Politique cotonnière, 1934–1951.
Agri (378) Propagande cotonnière, 1939.
Agri (378) Prix des cotons congolais, 1935–1945.
Agri (374) Coton: Documentation, nos. 13–15.
Agri (379) Zones cotonnières, 1939–1945.
Agri Surtaxe cotonnière 1939–1945.
Agri (379) Divers: Questions parlementaires.
Agri (38–) Sociétés cotonnières.
Agri (380) Compagnie Cotonnière Congolaise, Cotonco, 1925–1949.
Agri (380) Correspondance générale, rapports, études, divers.
Agri (381–387) and Agri (128) Statistiques trimestrielles, 1951–1960.

Agri (375) Documents. Rapports des réunions plénières, 1946–1954.
Agri (376) Documents. Rapports des réunions plénières.
Agri (133) Covenco, 1950–1961.
Agri (385) Tableaux, situation des ventes.
Agri (386) Ventes coton Ruzizi-Kivu; ventes et livraison des cotons.
Agri (386) Comité Cotonnier Congolais.
Agri (378) Commission cotonnière du Minicol.
Agri (381), nos. 29–31.
Agri (377) Coton 110 ICAC. Commission permanente.
A. I. (1403) Divers.
A. I. (1414) Correspondances diverses, 1928–1940.
A. I. (1415) Sanctions à charge des Travailleurs.
A. I. (1415) Transplantation collective de la main-d'oeuvre indigène.
D (66) Papiers Muteba.
D (778) Papiers Bertrand.
Dossier F. P. (2450), Dossier F. P. (2459).
D (778) Papiers Bertrand.

Archives Régionales du Haut-Zaire, Kisangani

Rapports d'inspection

Besteau. "Rapport sur la campagne cotonnière, 1927–1928."
Cotonco. "Rapport 1930."
De la Haye, H. "Rapport annuel 1926–1927, ferme de Bangadi." March 31, 1927.
Ermens, P. "Rapport fin campagne cotonnière, 1937–1938." Léopoldville, October 7, 1938.
Goffin, A. "Rapport d'inspection." Territoire de Niangara, 1952, 1955.
Heyse, T. "Notes sur la production du coton au Congo belge." January 1, 1941.
Leontovitch, C. "Rapport sur la campagne cotonnière 1927–1928." District de l'Ubangi.
Lesage, "Voyage d'inspection en Territoire de Kabinda." September 24, 1943.
Sparano, F. "Rapport sur la campagne cotonnière 1924–1925." Bondo, May 10, 1925.
Stocker, "Rapport sur la campagne cotonnière 1923–1924." Niangara, April 23, 1924.
Vaessen, H. "Rapport d'inspection." Territoire de Niangara, 1952.
Van Velde, J. J. "Rapport d'inspection." Territoire d' Ango, 1949.
Vermeesh, "Rapport sur l'agriculture." Kabinda, June 30, 1920.
Wauters, J. L. "Rapport d'inspection." Territoire de Niangara, 1956.

Conseil de Province d'Elisabethville, 1937, 1944.
Conseil de Province du Katanga, 1945.
Conseil de Province Orientale, 1944, 1946, 1955, 1956.
Conseil de Province de l'Equateur, 1955.
"Rapports annuel AIMO." Territoire de Niangara, 1950, 1955, 1957.
"Rapport annuel AIMO." Territoire d'Ango, 1950–56, 1959.

"Rapport annuel A. I.," 1959.
"Rapport annuel sur la situation de l'agriculture." District de l'Uele, 1931, 1933.
"Rapport annuel sur l'agriculture." District de Tanganyika, 1930, 1931.
"Rapport annuel sur l'agriculture." District de Lulua, 1930, 1931.
"Rapport annuel sur l'agriculture." District de Maniema, 1928, 1929, 1930, 1932.
"Rapport d'inspection." Territoire de Dungu, 1929, 1933, 1934, 1935, 1936, 1940, 1942, 1943, 1944, 1947.
"Rapports d'inspection." Territoire d'Ango, 1934–1958.
"Rapport d'inspection." Territoire de Poko, 1936, 1951.
"Rapport d'inspection." Territoire de Bambili, 1931, 1957; Territoire de Bambesa, 1958.
"Rapport d'inspection." Territoire de Buta, 1946, 1949, 1952, 1954, 1957, 1959.
"Rapport sur la culture et le commerce du coton." District de Lomami.
"D.P.": Divers Problèmes.

Dossiers Z: Travaux d'ordre économique et éducatif

Z 4, 08, 41, 111, 261, 262, 265, 265.5, 424, 426, 427, 498, 655, 707, 721–304.

Published Materials

Colonial Journals

Agriculture et élevage au Congo belge (1920–30).
Bulletin agricole du Congo belge (1910–60).
Bulletin de la banque du Congo belge et du Ruanda-Urundi (1936–56).
Bulletin du Comité Cotonnier Congolais (1936–58).
Bulletin d'information de l'INEAC, série technique (1938–57).
Bulletin de l'institut agronomique et des stations des recherches de Gembleaux (1932–55).
Coton et culture cotonnière (1920–35).
Etudes sur le marché de certains produits congolais (1939–60).
Journal des tribunaux d'outre-mer.
Lovania (1945–47).
Mouvement géographique (1917–28).
Revue d'agronomie coloniale (Bukavu).
Revue de la société belge d'études et d'expansion (1927–47).
Technique agricole internationale.
Trade Journal.

Articles and Books

Anonymous

"Agriculture au Congo belge en 1938." *Bulletin agricole du Congo belge* 30, no. 4 (1939): 536–56.
"Compagnie Cotonnière Congolaise." *Congo* 1, no. 1 (1924): 100–101.
"La culture cotonnière au Congo belge. Son organisation. La politique cotonnière. Les transports et réseau routier." *Bulletin du comité cotonnier congolais* 27, no. 1 (1936): 4–6.

"La culture du coton." *Mouvement géographique* no. 17, April 25, 1920, coll. 222.

"L'agriculture au Congo belge en 1936 d'après les rapports provinciaux." *Bulletin agricole du Congo belge* 28, no. 2 (1937): 251–66.

"L'agriculture au Congo belge en 1937 d'après les rapports provinciaux." *Bulletin agricole du Congo belge* 29, no. 3 (1938): 431–50.

"L'agriculture au Congo belge en 1935 d'après les rapports provinciaux." *Bulletin agricole du Congo* 27, no. 4 (1936): 507–47.

"Le coton au Congo." *Mouvement géographique* no. 25, 1922, coll. 343.

"Monographie du coton congolais." *Bulletin du Comité Cotonnier Congolais* 28, no. 6 (1937): 48–60.

"Le coton au Congo belge." *Bulletin agricole du Congo belge* 32, no. 3 (1941): 383–453.

"Travaux de sélection de coton." *Bulletin de l'information de l'INEAC*, série technique, (1936) 5: 1–107.

Abrams, P. *Historical Sociology.* Ithaca: Cornell University Press, 1982.

Amin, S. *Le développement inégal.* Paris: Editions de Minuit, 1973.

Anstey, R. *King Leopold's Legacy.* London, New York, Ibadan: Oxford University Press, 1966.

Asiwaju, A. "Migrations as Revolt: The Example of the Ivory Coast and Upper Volta before 1945," *Journal of African History* 17 (1976): 577–94.

Austen, R. *African Economic History.* Portsmouth: Heinemann, 1987.

Bakonzi, A. "The Gold Mines of Kilo-Moto in Northeast Zaire, 1905–1960." Ph.D. diss., University of Wisconsin, Madison.

Bandy, C. *The Rise and Fall of the South African Peasantry.* Berkeley: University of California Press, 1979.

Banneux, L. "Quelques données économiques sur le coton au Congo belge." *Bulletin d'information de l'INEAC*, série technique, 22 (1938): 1–46.

Bannink, L. "La fumure minérale du cotonnier dans la zone forestière de l'Uele." *Bulletin de l'information de l'INEAC* 8, no. 3 (1951): 147–51.

Bashizi, C. "Paysannat et salariat agricole rural au Bushi (ancien territoire de Kabare, Province du Kivu), 1920–1960." Ph. D. diss., UNAZA, Lubumbashi, 1980.

Basset, T. J. "The Development of Cotton in the Nothern Ivory Coast, 1910–1965." *Journal of African History* 29, no. 1 (1988): 267–84.

Basset, T. J. "Breaking Up the Bottlenecks in Food-crop and Cotton Cultivation in Northern Côte d'Ivoire." *Africa* 58, no. 2 (1988): 147–74.

Bauer, P. T. *Dissent on Development.* London: Weidenfeld and Nicholson, 1971.

Baumann, H. "The Division of Work according to Sex in African Hoe Culture." *Africa* 1, no. 3 (1928): 308–14.

Berger, J. *Pig Earth.* New York: Pantheon, 1979.

Bernstein, H. "African Peasantries: A Theoretical Framework." *Journal of Peasant Studies* 6, 4 (1979): 420–443.

Bertrand, A. *Le problème de la main-d'oeuvre au Congo.* Brussels: Ministère des Colonies, 1933.

Bilusa Baila, "Histoire de population des Uele." Ph. D. diss., Univrsité Libre de Bruxelles, 1993.

Bivot, J. "La politique de transports et la production cotonnière au Congo belge." *Bulletin du Comité Cotonnier Congolais* 13 (1939): 27–33.

Blassingame, J. *The Slave Community: Plantation Life in the Antebellum South.* New York: Oxford University Press, 1972.

Blommaert, U. "La culture du coton au Congo belge." *Agriculture et élevage au Congo belge* 25–26 (1929): 1 (1930): 5–7. 2 (1930), 19–22 6 (1930): 84–86.

Blommaert, U. "Introduction du coton chez l'indigène au Congo belge." *Bulletin agricole du Congo belge* 21, no. 3 (1930): 805–19.

Boahen, Adu A., ed., *Unesco General History of Africa.* Abridged edition. California: James Currey, 1990.

Bonnivair, P., and Guesquiere, J. "A propos de la sélection du coton au Congo belge." *Bulletin agricole du Congo belge* 15, no. 1 (1924): 42–73.

Bonnivair, P., and Ghesquiere, J. "Réglementation de la culture, de l'achat, et du commerce du coton." *Bulletin agricole du Congo belge* 15, no. 2 (1924).

Bonnivair, P., and Ghesquiere, J. "Ferme de sélection à Bambesa." *Bulletin agricole du Congo,* 15, no. 1 (1924).

Boulanger, A. "Evolution économique d'un milieu rural en district du Kabinda." *Bulletin du CEPSI* 5 (1957).

Brédo, H. J. "La culture et le commerce du coton au Congo belge." *Bulletin agricole du Congo belge* 25, no. 2 (1934).

Brenez, A. "La question cotonnière au Lomami." *Bulletin agricole du Congo belge* 22, no. 2 (1931): 165–169.

Brenez, A. "La culture du cotonnier au Lomami." *Bulletin agricole du Congo belge* 19, no. 1 (1928): 105–12.

Brixhe, A. "Les lotissements agricoles du nord-Sankuru." *Lovania* 7 (1945): 93–133.

Brixhe, A. *Le coton au Congo belge.* 3rd ed. Brussels: Ministère des Colonies, 1958.

Calhoun, C. J. "The Radicalism of Tradition: Community Strength or Venerable Disguise and Borrowed Language?" *American Journal of Sociology* 88, no. 5 (1983): 886–914.

Chambon, R., and Alofs, M. "Le district agricole du Tanganyika." *Bulletin agricole du Congo belge* 49, no. 6 (1958): 1467–1500.

Chambon, R., and Leruth, M. "Paysannnat et colonat dans le district du Tanganyika-Moero." *Bulletin agricole du Congo belge,* 48, no. 2 (1957): 279–315.

Chechu Dyilo, "Le recrutement de la main-d'oeuvre à Kilo-Moto, 1905–1958." M.A. thesis, UNAZA, Lubumbashi, 1981.

Clément, J. "Etude relative au paysannat indigène." *Bulletin agricole du Congo belge* 43, special issue (1952): 135–157.

Clément, J. "L'agriculture dans le district du Sankuru (Réflection sur son développement)." *Bulletin agricole du Congo belge* 44, no. 2 (1953): 272–412.

Collart, E. "Transformation des produits bruts du sol pour la vente et les besoins locaux." *Bulletin agricole du Congo belge* 43, (1952): 35–44.

Collier, J. "Les paysannats du nord-Sankuru (Territoires de Lodja et Katako-Kombe)." *Bulletin agricole du Congo belge* 50, no. 3 (1959): 570–641.

Coquery-Vidrovitch, C. *Afrique noire: Permanences et ruptures.* Paris: Payot, 1985.

Corbion, "Le crédit agricole indigène au Congo belge." *Bulletin agricole du Congo belge* 43, (1952): 53–56.

Crummey, D., ed. *Banditry, Rebellion and Social Protest in Africa*. London: Heinemann, 1986.

De Bauw, A. "Comment utiliser les ressources des caisses administratives des chefferies." *Bulletin du Comité Cotonnier Congolais* 7 (1937): 69–71.

De Bauw, A. "Cotton Growing in the Belgian Congo." *The Empire Cotton-Growing Review* 14, no. 4 (1937): 277–85.

De Bauw, A. "Créons de nouveaux besoins aux indigènes." *Bulletin du comité congolais* 3 (1936).

De Bauw, A. "A groupement professionel colonial: le comité cotonnier congolais." *Bulletin de la société belge d'études et d'expansion*, 136 (1947): 413–420.

De Bauw, A., ed. *Trente années de culture cotonnière au Congo belge*. Brussels: Cotonco, 1948.

De Coene, R. "Le bananier dans la rotation en zone cotonnière nord." *Bulletin de l'information de l'INEAC* 5, no. 2 (1956): 113.

De Coene, R. "Méthodes statistiques pour l'étude des essais de rendement cotonniers à Bambesa." *Bulletin agricole du Congo belge* 39, no. 4 (1948): 803.

De Craene, A. "Considérations agricoles sur la région de Mahagi." *Lovania* 10 (1946): 68–109.

De Craene, A. "Nouvelles considérations agricoles sur la région de Mahagi." *Lovania* 12 (1947): 46–76.

De Fauconval, A., and H. Van Beek. "Les paysannats en territoire de Gandajika, District de Kabinda, Province du Kasai." *Bulletin agricole du Congo belge* 48, no. 1 (1957): 23–45.

De Fauconval, A., et al. "Les paysannats en territoire de Mwene-Ditu." *Bulletin agricole du Congo belge* 48, no. 3 (1957): 541–57.

De Gorgio, S. "Voyage agricole au district de Tanganyika-Moero." *Bulletin agricole du Congo belge* 14, no. 4 (1923): 469–534.

De Greef, M. G. "Monographie agricole de la zone orientale du Haut-Uele." *Bulletin agricole du Congo belge* 8, nos. 1–2 (1917): 120–48.

De Hemptine, J. "La politique économique et sociale du Congo belge." *Congo* 2 (1928): 579–87.

Dejong, E. "La ferme de sélection cotonnière de Bambesa, Bas-Uele." *Bulletin agricole du Congo belge* 14, no. 1 (1923): 90–97.

Dejong, E. "Le coton dans l'Uele." *Bulletin agricole du Congo belge* 18, no. 4 (1927) 4: 451–536.

De Koster, L. "Le malaise des milieux ruraux au Congo belge." *Revue générale belge* 3 (1948).

De Laveleye, "Etude sur la situation cotonnière dans la plaine de la Ruzizi." *Bulletin agricole du Congo belge* 29, no. 1 (1938): 3–26.

Delumeau, J. *Injures et blasphèmes*. Paris: Imago, 1989.

De Meulemeester, A. "L'agriculture dans la Province Orientale du Congo belge en 1920." *Bulletin agricole du Congo belge* 7, no. 4 (1921): 639–60.

Depi, G. "La caisse de réserve cotonnière." *Bulletin de la banque centrale du Congo belge et du Ruanda-Urundi* 47 (1956): 63–68.

De Plaen, G. "Délimitation des diverses régions cotonnières de la zone Nord." *Bulletin d'information de l'INEAC* 6, no. 5 (1957): 285–300.

Derkinderen, G. *Les carrières agricoles au Congo belge face à l'évolution de l'économie rurale indigène.* Brussels: Ministère des Colonies, 1955.

De Schlippe, P. "Sous-station d'essais de l'INEAC à Kurukwata." *Bulletin agricole du Congo belge* 39, no. 2 (1949): 361–408.

De Schlippe, P. *Shifting Cultivation in Africa: The Zande System of Agriculture.* London: Routledge, 1956.

Deuleessauwer, A. M., and Devos, C. *Le coton et le kapok.* Brussels: Édition Universitaire, 1962.

Devroey, E. *Le réseau routier au Congo belge et au Ruanda-Urundi.* Brussels: IRCB, 1939.

Drachousoff, V. "Le développement de l'agriculture autochtone congolaise." *Bulletin de la banque du Congo belge et du Ruanda-Urundi* (August 1959).

Drachousoff, V. *Essai sur l'agriculture indigène au Bas-Congo.* Brussels: 1947.

Dubois, G. "Politique agricole en milieux ruraux au Congo belge." *Bulletin agricole du Congo belge* 43 (1952): 17–35.

Du Bois, H. "Types d'assolement en culture extensive de la zone cotonnière du nord." *Bulletin d'information de l'INEAC,* 6, no. 4 (1957): 227–41.

Dumont, A. "Le travail obligatoire dans les colonies." *Bulletin de l'institut agronomique et des stations de la recherche de Gembleaux* 2, no. 4 (1933): 11–12.

Engels, A. "L'évolution de la culture cotonnière dans les régions du Sud." *Bulletin du Comité Cotonnier Congolais* 10 (1938): 46–48.

Engels, A. *Les problèmes de la main-d'oeuvre au Congo belge. Rapport de la commission de main-oeuvre indigène, Province du Katanga, 1930–31.* Brussels: 1931.

Ernest, L. "L'activité du Sineloka." *Bulletin du Comité Cotonnier Congolais* 17 (1946): 24–41.

Feierman, S. *Peasant Intellectuals: Anthropology and History in Northern Tanzania.* Madison: University of Wisconsin Press, 1990.

Fetter, B. *Colonial Rule and Regional Imbalance in Central Africa.* Boulder, Co: Westview Press, 1983.

Fields, K. *Revival and Rebellion in Colonial Central Africa.* Princeton: Yale University Press, 1985.

Fisher, E. "The Growing of Cotton at Kitobola (Lower Congo) for the Season 1913–1914." *Bulletin agricole du Congo belge* 5, no. 3 (1914).

Flynn, C. P. *Insult and Society.* Port Washington, NY: Kennikat Press, 1977.

Freund, B. *The Making of Contemporary Africa.* Bloomington: Indiana University Press, 1984.

Geertz, C. *Agricultural Involution.* Berkeley: University of California Press, 1963.

Geiger, S. "What's So Feminist About Women's Oral History?" *Journal of Women's History* 2, no. 1 (1990): 169–80.

Geschiere, P. "Chiefs and Colonial Rule in Cameroon: Inventing Chieftaincy, French and British Styles." *Africa* 63, no. 2 (1993): 151–75.

Ghesquiere, M. J. "Fausse anthracnose du coton provoquée par la piqure du dysdercus." *Bulletin agricole du Congo belge* 12, no. 4 (1921).

Ghesquiere, M. J. "Principales maladies du coton au Kasai et au Sankuru." *Bulletin agricole du Congo belge* 19, no. 4 (1928).

Ghilain, J. "L'organisation des transports des produits agricoles au Congo belge." *Bulletin agricole du Congo belge* 29, no. 2 (1938): 323–32.

Gluckmann, M. *Rituals of Rebellion*. Manchester: Manchester University Press, 1952.

Gluckmann, M. *Order and Rebellion in Tribal Africa*. New York: Free Press of Glencoe, 1963.

Gordio, E. "Culture Cotonnière," June 24, 1946, A. A., Brussels.

Gramisci, A. *Lettres from Prison*. New York: Harper and Row, 1973.

Grevisse, F. *La grande pitié des jurisdictions indigènes*. Brussels: IRCB, 1949.

Guilmin, "La polygamie dans l'Equateur." *Zaire* (1947) 1: 1001–23.

Guyer, J. I. "The Multiplication of Labor: Historical Method in the Study of Gender and Agricultural Change in Modern Africa." *Current Anthropology* 29, no. 2 (1988): 247–72.

Haardt, G. M., and Audouin-Dubreuil, L. "Expédition Citroen Centre-Afrique. Deuxième mission Haardt-Audouin-Dubreuil." *La géographie* 45, nos. 3–4 (1926): 121–57; 45, nos. 5–6 (1926): 295–331.

Harroy, J. L. *Afrique, terre qui meurt: La dégradation des sols africains sous l'influence de la colonisation*. Brussels: Mariel Hayes, 1944.

Henrard, J. "Rapport annuel de 1932 sur la culture et le commerce du coton dans la Province Orientale (saison 1931–1932)." *Bulletin agricole du Congo belge* 24, no. 3 (1933): 352.

Henrard, J. "Rapport annuel sur la culture et le commerce du coton dans la Provinve Orientale (Congo belge)," *Bulletin agricole du Congo belge* 24, no. 3 (1933): 352–58.

Hogendorn, J. S. "The Vent-for-Surplus Model and African Cash Agriculture to 1914." *Savanna* 5 (1976): 15–28.

Homes, M. V. "L'utilisation des engrais au Congo belge." *Bulletin agricole du Congo belge* 42, no. 2 (1952): 21–36.

Howard, R. "Formation and Stratification of the Peasantry in Colonial Ghana." *Journal of Peasant Studies* 8, no. 1 (1980): 61–80.

Hunt, N. "Domesticity and Colonialism in Belgian Africa: Usumbura's Foyer Social, 1946–1960." *Signs* 15, no. 3 (1990): 447–74.

Huybrechts, A. "Les routes et le trafique routier au Congo." *Cahiers économiques et sociaux* 5, no. 3 (1967).

Huybrechts, A. *Transports et strucutres de développement au Congo. Etude du progrès économique de 1900 à 1970*. Paris: Mouton-IRES, 1970.

Ilunga Badimbwa K. "L'impôt indigène dans la province du Katanga de 1920 à 1940." M.A. thesis, UNAZA, Lubumbashi, 1974.

Inwen Mur-Sawul, "La suppression du portage au Katanga (1925–1930)." M.A. thesis, UNAZA, Lubumbashi, 1974.

Isaacman, A. "Chiefs, Rural Differentiation and Peasant Protest: The Mozambican Forced Cotton Regime, 1838–1961." *African Economic History* 14 (1985): 15–57.

Isaacman, A. "Colonial Mozambique. An Inside View: The Life History of Raul Honwana." *Cahiers d'études africaines* 109 (1988): 59–88.

Isaacman, A. *Cotton Is the Mother of Poverty: Peasants, Work, and Rural Struggle in Colonial Mozambique, 1938–1961*. Portsmouth: Heinemann, 1996.

Isaacman, A. "Peasants and Rural Social Protest in Africa." *African Studies Review* 33, no. 2 September (1990): 1–120.

Isaacman, A. "Peasants, Social Protest and Africanists." *Journal of Social History* 22 (1989): 745–66.

Isaacman, A. *The Tradition of Resistance in Mozambique:* Anti-Colonial Activity in the Zambezi Valley, 1850–1921. Berkeley: University of California Press, 1976.

Isaacman, A., and R. Roberts, R., eds., *Cotton, Colonialism, and Social History in Sub-Saharan Africa*. Portsmouth: Heinemann, 1995.

Isaacman, A., et al. "Cotton Is the Mother of Poverty: Peasant Resistance to Forced Cotton Production in Mozambique, 1938–1961." *International Journal of African Historical Studies* 13 (1980): 580–615.

Janssens, A. *Le coton en Afrique tropicale*. Brussels: Édition Bausart, 1932.

Janssens, J. P. "La culture du coton au Kasai." *Bulletin agricole du Congo belge* 7, nos. 1–2 (1916): 131–57.

Jewsiewicki, B. "Les archives administratives zairoises de l'époque coloniale." *Annales Aequatoria* 1 (1980): 169–84.

Jewsiewicki, B. "Le colonat agricole européen au Congo belge, 1910–1960: Questiones politiques et économiques." *Journal of African History* 20, no. 4 (1979): 559–71.

Jewsiewicki, B. "La contestation sociale et naissance du prolétariat au Zaire." *Canadian Journal of African of African Studies* 10, no. 1 (1976): 45–70.

Jewsiewicki, B., ed. "Contribution to a History of Agriculture and Fishing in Central Africa." *African Economic History* no. 7 (1979): 559–72.

Jewsiewicki, B. "The Great Depression and the Making of the Colonial Economic System in the Belgian Congo." *African Economic History* no. 4 (1977): 153–176.

Jewsiewicki, B. "Histoire de l'agriculture dans l'ancienne province du Katanga." *Likundoli* série B, 3, no. 3 (1973): 55–113.

Jewsiewicki, B. "Histoire économique d'une ville coloniale, Kisangani, 1877–1960." *Les Cahiers du CEDAF,* 5.

Jewsiewicki, B. "Notes sur l'histoire socio-économique du Congo, 1880–1960." *Etudes d'histoire africaine,* 3 (1972): 209–42.

Joset, P. E. *Les sociétés secrètes des hommes-léopards en Afrique*. Paris: 1955.

Joye, P., and Lewin, R. *Les trusts au Congo*. Brussels: Société belge d'Éditions, 1961.

Jurion, F. "Quelques considérations sur l'orientation de la sélection cotonnière au Congo belge." *Bulletin agricole du Congo belge* 22, no. 4 (1941): 677–96.

Kanku Mukengeshi, "Les réseaux d'achat de coton dans le nord-Katanga." Unilu: M.A. thesis, 1985.

Kasendwe Kibonge, "Les cultures obligatoires dans le district de Tanganyika (1935–1950)." M.A. thesis, UNAZA, Lubumbashi, 1981.

Kiwanguna Mpenza-Seley, "Evolution de quelques cultures commerciales au Kasai, 1945–1959 (Caoutchouc, coton, huile de palme, maïs et riz)." I.S.P., Senior paper, Mbuji-Mayi, 1975.

Klein, M. *Peasants in Africa*. ed., Beverly Hills: Sage, 1983.

Knaff, E. "Note sur la propagande agricole. Etude de son intensification." *Bulletin agricole du Congo belge* 41, no. 3 (1950): 731.

Landeghem, A. "1921–1936: Quinze années de culture cotonnière au Congo belge." *Bulletin du Comité Cotonnier Congolais* 4 (1936): 3–4.

Landeghem, A. "La Compagnie Cotonnière Congolaise." *Bulletin agricole du Congo belge* 21, no. 3 (1930): 820–29.

Landeghem, A. "Le coton. Son transport, son conditionnement." *Congo* 2 (1925): 797–807.

Landeghem, A. "La culture du coton et le problème des transports au Congo belge." *Bulletin de la société belge d'études et d'expansion* 86 (1932): 270–73.

Landeghem, A. "Les cultures de coton et le développement économique des régions cotonnières." *Agriculture et élevage au Congo belge* 8 (1927): 85–89.

Landeghem, A. "De l'influence des cultures du coton par les indigènes sur le développement économique des régions cotonnières." *Congo* 2 (1927): 298–303.

Landeghem, A. "Quelques particularités de l'activité cotonnière au Congo belge." *Bulletin agricole du Congo belge* 8 (1938): 1–3.

Landeghem, A. "La question du coton au Congo belge." *Bulletin de la société belge d'études et d'expansion* 61 (1927): 255–61.

Landeghem, A. "Utilisation des éléphants comme moyens de transport dans l'Uele." *Congo* 1 (1923): 759–66; 2 (1923): 91–98.

Lassance, M. *Modes et coutumes alimentaires des Congolais en milieu rural.* Brussels: ARSOM, 1959.

Laye, Camara. *The Dark Child.* Translated by James Kirkup and Ernest Jones. New York: Farrar, Straus, and Giroux, 1985.

Leconte, M. "Recherches sur le cotonnier dans les régions de la savanne de l'Uele." *Bulletin d'information de l'INEAC*, série technique, 20 (1938): 2–33.

Lee, R. *The !Kung San. Men, Women, and Work in a Foraging Society.* New York: Cambridge University Press, 1977.

Leloup, G. *Arbitrage des achats et des ventes de coton.* Liège: Univrsité de Liège, 1932.

Lemborelle, A. "L'agriculture indigène dans l'Ubangi." *Bulletin agricole du Congo belge* 24, no. 1 (1933): 44–68.

Leontovitch, C. "L'agriculture indigène dans l'Ubangi." *Bulletin agricole du Congo belge* 24, no.1 (1933): 44–68.

Leontovitch, C. "Le coton dans la rotation dans le territoire de Banzyville (Ubangi)." *Bulletin agricole du Congo belge* 20, (1929): 148–54.

Leontovitch, C. "La culture du coton dans le district du Congo-Ubangi." *Bulletin agricole du Congo belge* 28 (1937): 35–68.

Leontovitch, C. "Notes au sujet de la culture du coton dans le Congo-Ubangi." *Bulletin agricole du Congo belge* (1940): 126–43.

Leplae E. "L'agriculture au Congo belge en 1930." *Bulletin agricole du Congo belge* 21, no.4 (1930): 1007–28.

Leplae, E. "L'agriculture coloniale dans la discussion du budget du Congo belge pour 1914." *Revue générale agronomique* (1914).

Leplae, E. "La bataille du coton au Congo belge." *Bulletin du Comité Cotonnier Congolais* 3 (1936): 3–10.

Leplae, E. "Comment les Bantous du Congo belge s'achèminent vers le paysannat." *Bulletin agricole du Congo belge* 22, no. 4 (1931): 574–80.

Leplae, E. "Comment les indigènes du Congo belge sont arrivés à produire annuellement 20.000 tonnes de coton-fibre." *Coton et culture cotonnière* 9, no. 3 (1935): 169–92.

Leplae, E. "Le coton: culture et utilisation." *Congo* 2 (1925): 129–39.

Leplae, E. "La culture du coton." *Bulletin agricole du Congo belge* 7, nos. 1–2 (1917): 24–39.

Leplae, E. "La culture du coton à la station de Gandajika." *Agriculture et élevage* 12 (1932).

Leplae, E. "La culture du coton au Congo belge, 1915–1919." *Bulletin agricole du Congo belge* 11, nos. 1–2 (1920): 80–106.

Leplae, E. "La culture du coton au Congo belge en 1916–1917." *Bulletin agricole du Congo belge* 8, nos. 1–4 (1918): 29–35.

Leplae, E. "Les cultures obligatoires dans les pays d'agriculture arriérée." *Bulletin agricole du Congo belge* 20, no. 4 (1929): 449–77.

Leplae, E. "Faut-il en Afrique centrale repousser le salariat et les plantations européennes?" *Bulletin agricole du Congo belge* 22, no. 4 (1931): 570–74.

Leplae, E. "Histoire et développement des cultures obligatoires de coton et de riz au Congo belge de 1917 à 1933." *Congo* 1, no. 5 (1933): 645–753.

Leplae, E. "Importance de l'agriculture au Congo belge." *Bulletin agricole du Congo belge* 5, no. 1 (1914): 3–20.

Leplae, E. "Notes sur le relèvement de l'agriculture du Congo belge." *Bulletin agricole du Congo belge* 23, no. 1 (1932).

Leplae, E. "Peut-on cultiver le coton au Congo belge?" *Bulletin agricole du Congo belge* 5, no. 3 (1914): 25–29.

Leplae, E. "Pour un nouveau progrès agricole des indigènes: L'emploi obligatoire des graines de coton pour la fertilisation des terres." *Bulletin des séances de l'IRCB* 7, no. 2 (1936): 266–95.

Leplae, E. "Progrès récents de la culture de coton au Congo belge." *Coton et culture cotonnière* 3, no. 1 (1928): 1–7.

Leplae, E. "A propos des maladies du coton dans l'Uele." *Agriculture et élevage* 15 (1932): 169–171.

Leplae, E. "Résultants économiques et éducatifs de la culture obligatiore du coton." *Bulletin agricole du Congo belge* 23, no. 1 (1932): 127–32.

Leplae, E. "Résultats obtenus au Congo belge par les cultures obligatories alimentaires et industrielles." *Zaire* 1 (1947): 115–140.

Leplae, E. "Rôle du service de l'agriculture au Congo belge." *Bulletin agricole du Congo belge* 1, no. 2 (1910).

Leplae, E. "Transformation de l'agriculture indigène du Congo belge par les cultures obligatoires." *Technique agricole internationale* 6, no. 2 (1936): 93–116.

Leplae, E. "Le ver rose du coton dans la région du lac Kivu." *Bulletin agricole du Congo belge* 19 (1928): 262–76.

Leys, C. *Underdevelopment in Kenya*. London: Heinemann, 1975.

Likaka, O. "Forced Cotton Cultivation and Social Control in the Belgian Congo," in A. Isaacman and R. Roberts, eds., *Cotton, Colonialism, and Social Hisrory in Sub-Saharan Africa*. Portsmouth: Heinemann, 1995, 200–220.

Likaka, O. "Rural Protest: The Mbole Against the Belgian Rule, 1893–1955." *International Journal of African Historical Studies* 27, no. 3 (1994): 589–617.

Lincoln, B. *Discourse and the Contruction of Society.* Oxford, New York: Oxford University Press, 1989.

Lincoln, B. "Notes toward a Theory of Religion and Revolution," in B. Lincoln, ed., *Religion, Rebellion, Revolution.* New York: Saint Martin's Press, 1985.

Lovens, M. "La révolte de Masisi-Lubutu (Congo belge, Janvier–Mai, 1944)," *Cahiers du CEDAF* nos. 3–4 (1974): 4–136.

Lugard, W. J. "De l'accession des noirs à la propriété foncière individuelle du code civil." *Zaire* 1, no. 4 (1947): 339–433.

Lugard, W. J. "Insectes nuisibles au cotonnier." *Agriculture et élevage* 9 (1931).

Lugard, W. J. "Rapport sur un essai de culture de coton à Nyangwe." *Bulletin agricole du Congo belge* 7, nos. 1–2 (1915): 60–63.

Lumpungu, Q. "Culture cotonnière et société rurale dans le nord du Katanga. Production, commercialisation et perspective d'avenir." Thèse de troisième cycle, Université de Rennes, 1970.

Lumpungu, Q. "Difficultés du paysannat cotonnier dans le Tanganyika." M.A. thesis, Université de Rennes, 1968.

Lwamba Bilonda, "Histoire du mouvement ouvrier au Congo belge (1914–1960): Cas de la Province du Katanga." Ph.D. diss., Université de Lubumbashi, 1985.

Malengreau, G. "Les lotissements agricoles au Congo belge." *Bulletin agricole du Congo belge* 43, special issue (1952).

Mandala, E. "We Toiled for the White Man in Our Own Garden: The Conflict Between Cotton and Food in Colonial Malawi," in A. Isaacman and R. Roberts, eds., *Cotton, Colonialism, and Social History in Sub-Saharan Africa.* Portsmouth: Heinemann, 1995, 285–305.

Mandala, E. *Work and Control in a Peasant Economy: A History of the Lower Tchiri Valley in Malawi, 1859–1960.* Madison: University of Wisconsin Press, 1990.

Mauss, M. *The Gift.* Translated from the French by W. D. Halls. New York: W. W. Norton, 1990.

Merlier, M. *Le Congo de la colonisation belge à l'indépendance.* Paris: Maspero, 1962.

Miracle, M. P. *Agriculture in the Congo Basin: Tradition and Change in African Rural Economies.* Madison, Milwaukee, and London: University of Wisconsin Press, 1967.

Moeller, A. "Contribution à l'histoire du coton congolais." *Bulletin agricole du Congo belge* 5 (1937): 20–22.

Monti, J. R. "Agriculture congolaise." *Bulletin agricole du Congo belge* 45, no. 4 (1954): 887–957.

Mulambu, F. "Introduction à l'étude du rôle des paysans dans les changements politiques." *Cahiers économiques et sociaux* 8 (1970): 435–50.

Mulambu, F. "Cultures obligatoires et colonisation dans l'ex-Congo belge." *Cahiers du CEDAF* nos. 6–7 (1974): 7–99.

Muteba Kabemba, "Le recrutement de la main-d'oeuvre dans le district de Lomami à destination du Haut Katanga industriel (1912–1933)." M.A. thesis, UNAZA, Lubumbashi, 1973.

Nauwelaert, P. "Le Cogerco, garantie pour le planteur." *Bulletin du Comité Cotonnier Congolais* 2 (1958).

Nayenga, P. "Commercial Cotton Growing in Busoga District, Uganda, 1905–1923." *African Economic History* 10 (1981): 175–95.

Nelson, S. *Colonialism in the Congo Basin, 1880–1940.* Athens: Ohio University Press, 1994.

Netting, R., Stone, M. P., and Stone, G. D. "Kaffir Cash-Cropping: Choice and Change in Indigenous Agricultural Development." *Human Ecology* 17, no. 3 (1989): 299–319.

Nkala Wodjim Tantur, "L'agriculture commerciale dans le district de Lulua, 1920–1940." M.A. thesis, UNAZA, Lubumbashi, 1974.

Nkulu Kalala, "Les réactions africaines aux impositions des cultures: Cas du Territoire de Kamina, 1938–1959." M. A. thesis, Université de Lubumbashi, 1983.

Nolf, A., and Pilette, M. "L'égrenage et emballage du coton au Congo belge." *Bulletin agricole du Congo belge* 22, no. 4 (1931): 459–67.

Nzula, A. T., et al. *Forced Labour in Colonial Africa.* London: Zed Press, 1979.

Offerman, P. "Le gibier dans l'économie rurale de la colonie." *Bulletin agricole du Congo belge* 43 (1952): 57–62.

Palmer, N., and Parsons, N., eds. *The Roots of Rural Poverty in Central and Southern Africa.* Berkeley and Los Angeles: University of California Press, 1977.

Peemans, J. P. *Diffusion du progrès et convergence des prix: Congo belge, 1900–1960.* Paris-Louvain: Nauwelaerts, 1970.

Perrings, C. "Good Lawyers but Poor Workers: Recruited Angolan Labour in the Copper Mines of Katanga, 1917–1921." *Journal of African History* 18 (1977) 2: 237–59.

Pitcher, M. A. "Sowing the Seeds of Failure: Early Portuguese Cotton Cultivation in Angola and Mozambique, 1820–1926," *Journal of Southern African Studies* 17, no. 1 (1991): 41–70.

Pittery, R. "Quelques données sur l'expérimentation cotonnière." *Bulletin de l'information de l'INEAC,* série technique, 8 (1936): 1–61.

Popkin, S. The Rational Peasant: The Political Economy of Rural Society in Vietnam. Los Angeles: University of California Press, 1979.

Querton, M. "Rapport sur la propagande cotonnière dans le district de Sankuru." *Bulletin agricole du Congo* 16, no. 2 (1925): 347–52.

Ranger, T. O. *Emerging Themes of African History.* Nairobi: East African Publishing House, 1968.

Rau, B. *From Feast to Famine: Official Cures and Grassroots Remedies to Africa's Food Crisis.* London: Zed Books, 1991.

Ravet, A. "La culture du coton dans l'Uganda." *Bulletin du Comité Cotonnier Congolais* 3 (1936): 13–15.

Ravet, A. "L'exposition agricole de Buta." *Bulletin du Comité Cotonnier Congolais* 16 (1940): 3–4.

Ravet, A. "La fête du coton." *Bulletin du Comité Cotonnier Congolais* 10 (1938): 55–56.

Ravet, A. "Organisation de la culture cotonnière au Congo." *Bulletin agricole du Congo belge* 27 (1936): 3–9.

Rivière, C. *Classes et stratifications sociales en Africa. Le cas guinéen.* Paris: Puf, 1978.

Rodney, W. *How Europe Underdeveloped Africa.* London: Bogle-l'Ouverture Publications, 1972.

Ruelle, J. "Introduction du coton au Congo belge: Motivations économique et financière." M.A. thesis, Université Catholique de Louvain, 1985.

Ryckmans, P. "Démographie congolaise." *Africa* 6, no. 3 (1933): 241–58.

Schoolmeesters, J. "Plan de culture du domaine Balibati (Haut-Ituri)." *Bulletin agricole du Congo belge* 40, nos. 3–4 (1949): 2268–78.

Scott, J. *Domination and the Art of Resistance.* New Haven: Yale University Press, 1990.

Scott, J. *The Moral Economy of the Peasants: Rebellion and Subsistence in Southeast Asia.* New Haven: Yale University Press, 1976.

Scott, J. *Weapons of the Weak: Everyday Forms of Peasant Resistance.* New Haven: Yale University Press, 1985.

Sennit, R. S. "Treatment and Quality of Cotton in the Belgian Congo." *Empire Cotton-Growing Review* (1947).

Shaw, B. T. "Force Publique: Force Unique. The Military in the Belgian Congo, 1914–1939." Ph. D. diss., University of Wisconsin, Madison.

Shouteden, "Le pink bollworm au Congo." *Agriculture et élevage* 1 (1928): 1–2.

Soyer, D. "Les caractéristiques du cotonnier au Lomami." *Bulletin de l'information de l'INEAC,* série technique, 16 (1937).

Soyer, A. "La grande richesse des juridictions indigènes." *Journal des tribunaux d'outre-mer* 21 (1952).

Sparano, F. "Culture et commerce du coton." *Bulletin agricole du Congo belge* 22, no. 3 (1931): 386–415.

Sparano, F. "Vade-Mecum pour le personnel s'intéressant à la culture et au commerce du coton dans les districts des Uele." *Bulletin agricole du Congo belge* 22, no. 1 (1929): 90–117.

Staner, P. "La désinfection des grains de coton." *Bulletin agricole du Congo bege* 21, no. 3 (1930): 830–32.

Staner, P. "Les maladies du cotonnier dans l'Uele." *Bulletin agricole du Congo belge* 20, no. 2 (1929): 213–27.

Staner, P. "Les paysannats indigènes du Congo belge et du Ruanda-Urundi." *Bulletin agricole du Congo belge* 46 (1955).

Staner, P. "Le port et la pathologie du cotonnier. Influence des facteurs météorologiques." *Bulletin de l'information de l'INEAC,* série technique, 9, no. 1 (1936): 1–32.

Stoffels, E. H. J. "Les grandes étapes de l'agriculture au Congo belge." *Bulletin agricole du Congo belge* 42, no. 2 (1951): 831–54.

Sunseri, T. "Peasants and the Struggle for Labor in Cotton Regimes of the Rufiji Basin, Tanzania (1885–1918)," in A. Isaacman and R. Roberts, eds., *Cotton, Colonialism, and Social History in Sub-Saharan Africa.* Portsmouth: Heinemann, 1995, 180–99.

Sunseri, T. "Slave Ransoming in German East Africa, 1885–1922." *International Journal of African Historical Studies* 23, no. 3 (1993): 481–512.

Sunseri, T. "A Social History of Cotton Production in German East Africa, 1884–1914." Ph.D. diss., University of Minnesota, 1992.

Thiry, N. "Note sur la conduite d'un paysannat." *Bulletin agricole du Congo belge* 43 (1952) special issue: 243–62.

Tihon, "Malnutrition in Maniema." *Bulletin agricole du Congo belge* 42 (1951): 829–68.

Tshibangu Kabet, "L'impact socio-économique de la grande crise économique des années 1929–1935 sur l'ancien Haut-Katanga industriel." Ph. D. diss., UNAZA, 1980.

Tulippe, O. "Les paysannats indigènes du Kasai." *Bulletin social belge et géographique* (1955).

Turnbull, M. *The Lonely African.* New York: Simon and Schuster 1962.

Vail, V., and White, L. "'Tawani, Machambero': Forced Cotton and Rice Growing in the Zambezi." *Journal of African History* 19, no. 29 (1979): 239–63.

Van der Kerken, G. *Les sociétés bantoues du Congo belge.* Brussels: Etablissements Emile Bruylant, 1920.

Van Geem, *Etude comparative des législations cotonnières en Afrique équatorile.* Brussels: Comité Cotonnier Congolais, 1934.

Van Geluwe, H. *Les Babali et les peuplades apparentés.* Tervuren, 1960.

Van Onselen, C. *Chibaro.* Johannesburg: Ravan Press, 1976.

Vansina, J. *Introduction à l'éthnographie du Congo.* Kinshasa: Editions Universitaires du Congo, 1966.

Vansina, J. *Paths in the Rainforests: Toward a History of Political Tradition in Equatorial Africa.* Madison: University of Wisconsin Press, 1990.

Vincent, J. "Colonial Chiefs and the Making of Class: A Case Study From Teso, Eastern Uganda." *Africa* 47, no. 2 (1977): 140–59.

Waelkens, M. "Situation de l'industrie cotonnière dans la colonie." *Agriculture et élevage au Congo* 8 (1930): 130–33; 9 (1930): 113–16.

Willaert, M. "Les coopératives indigènes au Congo belge." *Bulletin agricole du Congo belge* 43 special issue (1952): 85–123.

Zwejsen, R. "Synthèse des problèmes d'établissement du paysannat en chefferie Alur Pandoro." *Bulletin agricole du Congo belge* 51, no. 3 (1960): 683–738.

List of Interviews

Avochi, Kisangani. March, 1989.
Akombe, Kisangani. September, 1989.
Asumani, Kindu. April, 1986.
Asi Loosa, Kisangani. July, 1989.
Bili, Kisangani. August, 1989.
Bobwande, Lubumbashi. July, 1986.
Boloko, Kisangani. April, 1989.
Bondo, Kisangani. May, 1989.
Bwise, Kisangani. June, 1989.
Bombe, Kisangani. June, 1989.
Bula Nusi, Kisangani. April, 1989.

Denda, Kisangani. June, 1989.
Dombo, Kisangani. March, 1989.
Elila, Kisangani. February, 1989.
Esano, Kisangani. February, 1989.
Inyandja, Kisangani. July, 1989.
Itambo, Kisangani. March, 1989.
Kabwe, Likasi. September, 1989.
Kambo Yeka, Lubumbashi. August, 1986.
Kanampung, Likasi. February, 1989.
Kasala, Lubumbashi. June, 1989.
Kashi, Lubumbashi. September, 1988.
Katayi, Lubumbashi. August, 1986.
Katumbo, Lubumbashi. July, 1986.
Kidumu, Kisangani. July, 1989.
Kumbo, Kindu. September, 1989.
Lufundja Mbayo, Lubumbashi. August, 1986.
Lufwa, Lubumbashi. January, 1989.
Lwaka Mukandja, Lubumbashi. August, 1986.
Lwamba Bilonda, Lubumbashi. August, 1986.
Mbala, Lubumbashi. October, 1989.
Mbombo, Lubumbashi. September, 1988.
Mosolo, Kisangani. February, 1989.
Mugaza wa Beya, Lubumbashi. August, 1986.
Mugaza wa Beya and Lwamba Bilonda, Lubumbashi. August, 1986.
Mumba, Lubumbashi. March, 1988.
Ngandali Dabet, Minneapolis. July, 1990.
Ngongo, Kindu. July, 1988.
Ngoyi Bukonda, Minneapolis. March, 1990.
Ngoyi Mukulu, Likasi. October, 1988.
Ntumba, Likasi. October, 1988.
Tshibanda Nduba Musaka, Lubumbashi. August, 1986.
Tshishiku, Lubumbashi. October, 1989.
Ujanga, Kisangani. July, August, September 1989.
Umba, Lubumbashi. April, 1988.
Sua, Kisangani. May, 1989.
Sumba Ndandwe, Lubumbashi. July, 1986.
Vura, Kisangani. March, 1989.

Index